WITHOUT PARADE

WITHOUT PARADE

The Life and Work of Donald Hankey,
'A Student in Arms'

James Kissane

The Book Guild Ltd
Sussex, England

First published in Great Britain in 2003 by
The Book Guild Ltd
25 High Street
Lewes, East Sussex
BN7 2LU

Typesetting in Garamond by
Acorn Bookwork, Salisbury, Wiltshire

Printed in Great Britain by
Antony Rowe Ltd, Chippenham, Wiltshire

A catalogue record for this book is available from
The British Library.

ISBN 1 85776 703 9

It was the worries of all these wet millions in mud-brown that worried him. They could die, they could be massacred, by the quarter million, in shambles. But that they should be massacred without jauntiness, without confidence, with depressed brows: without parade ...

Ford Madox Ford, *No More Parades*

Contents

Acknowledgements

I am grateful to the following institutions and their staffs for making available to me material on which this work is based, for unfailing courtesy and many acts of kindness large and small: the Borough Local Studies Library; the British Newspaper Library (Colindale); the General Register Office; the Grinnell College Library; the Massachusetts Historical Society; the Public Record Office (Kew); the University of Georgia Library.

I also wish to express thanks to the following publishers and others for granting me the permissions here indicated: HarperCollins Publishers for permission to quote from Volume I of *Hankey, Man of Secrets*, © 1970 by Stephen Roskill; The Massachusetts Historical Society for permission to quote from a letter by J. St. Loe Strachey in the Ellery Sedgwick papers in the Society's possession; Oxford University Press for permission to quote material from *The Great War and Modern Memory*, 1975 by Paul Fussell; Penguin Putnam Inc. for permission to quote a passage from *Gravity's Rainbow*, by Thomas Pynchon; extracts from *A War Imagined*, by Samuel Hynes, published 1990 by The Bodley Head, used by permission of The Random House Group Limited; The Stansfeld Oxford and Bermondsey Club for permission to reproduce the pencil drawing of Donald Hankey in the Club's possession.

Every effort has been made to contact copyright holders for material used in this book. The publishers or the author will be pleased to hear from any copyright holders they have been unable to trace.

Prologue: Death of a Hero

Private A. Crudgington, an officers' servant in the First Battalion of the Royal Warwickshire Regiment, pours a small measure from each of the officers' water bottles into his own canteen. Then he wraps a strip of rag around a stub of candle to make a small fire. Thrusting his bayonet deep into the side of the trench, Private Crudgington hangs his canteen onto the protruding hilt of that weapon and puts his fire under the canteen. Before long tea will be ready for the officers of the company, and soon after that God knows what will start happening.

It is 1:30 in the afternoon of Thursday, 12 October 1916. The weather is dull but dry. Since the night before last the Royal Warwickshires have been in this attack trench near Le Transloy on the Somme. The great offensive that began so disastrously in July had been renewed and repulsed through the autumn; the daylight attack planned for 2:00 this afternoon is one more attempt to push the front at least a few kilometres forward before offensive operations are suspended for the winter. Earlier in the day, Pte Crudgington, who is a cook for the officers' mess, had been ordered by Lieutenant Donald Hankey to stay in the trench during the attack and look after the officers' packs. Lt Hankey, a gentle and rather enigmatic presence in the company, seems to Pte Crudgington almost more like a chum than an officer, and he had therefore made bold to ask the subaltern if one of the 'old men'—Pte Allen, for instance—could take his place minding the packs so that he might go over the top with the other boys. Hankey spoke to Captain Walters, and then gave Crudgington permission to join in the assault.

Before Pte Crudgington can serve out the tea Lt Beamish had ordered him to prepare, some clay from the side of the trench falls into the water heating in his canteen. So much precious water could not be wasted, so Pte Crudgington goes ahead with the tea and sugar; but it does seem a pity to offer a muddy drink like that to gentlemen, some of whom would never drink again.

'Never mind, soldier,' Lt Hankey tells him. 'It looks like milk in the tea.'

Minutes later the regiment charges out of its trench and meets heavy fire from the Germans. Pte Crudgington's account of this action tells how his fellow soldiers began to fall around him, how the survivors were ordered to stop and then to advance again, how the French on their right and the Irish on their left began to retreat, how he and the others were ordered to dig in then dig towards one another to form a trench. He tells of trying to get help for a wounded officer who died before stretcher bearers could get to him; he remembers seeing Lt D. Hankey wave his men forward and seeing them follow him into the barrage and the rifle and machine gun fire. But when Pte Crudgington next saw Lt Hankey, he lay dead along with three of the battalion's other officers, and Crudgington was asked by Lt Beamish to help another soldier dig a pit and lay Hankey and his brother officers in it.

Pte Crudgington's account of Donald Hankey's last day was furnished to his first biographer twelve years after the event. It shows the particularity of a conscientious witness, but there are also signs of a conscious furthering of a legend in the making. When ex-Private Crudgington wrote what that biographer, Kenneth Budd, calls 'this graphic description and beautiful tribute,' he knew that Lt Hankey was the celebrated author of *A Student in Arms*. He may, in fact, have had some idea of Hankey's newly-acquired status as a writer even before his death in battle. It is not clear whether Crudgington was himself a first-hand source or merely appropriated to his narrative the words Donald Hankey is reported to have spoken to his platoon as they waited for the signal to charge on that fatal afternoon—words, whether or not Hankey actually uttered them, which naturally became part of the heroic story: *If you are wounded, 'Blighty'; if killed, the Resurrection!*[1]

The value of Pte Crudgington's testimony lies, in any case, not so much in its relationship to the factual truth as in what it shows of the impression Donald Hankey made on at least one member of the 'other ranks' and what is thereby suggested about the quality and impact of his personality.

> If I was an artist [Crudgington wrote] I would draw a picture of D. Hankey leading his men in that charge, as it is in my mind, where it will always be fresh as the day it happened. I would not give it the title, 'An Officer Leading His Men,' but 'A Man Leading His Comrades.'
>
> (Budd, p. 146)[2]

Pte A. Crudgington goes on to reveal that his own son was named Donald in honour of Lt Hankey, and to say that 'if he is only a quarter as good as D. Hankey, I will be proud of him.' The private's letter indulges in a survivor's natural

---

[1] Donald Hankey's sister Hilda also reports these words—on the testimony, as she says, of one of her brother's men (Hankey, Donald (1917) *A Student in Arms, Second Series* (henceforth *ASIA, II*), (p. 31). New York: E. P. Dutton & Co.).

[2] Budd, K. (1931) *The Story of Donald Hankey*, p. 46. London: Student Christian Movement Press.

fears that people are beginning to forget the sacrifice and the horrors of war. But he attributes 'great foresight' to the officer whose humanity and bravery he remembers: 'I think that if D. Hankey were alive he would be a great advocate for peace throughout the world' (Budd, p. 146).

Donald Hankey's life is hard to separate from legend. Those who knew him—even members of his family and close friends—write of him as if they were not confident of having understood him, much less of being able to portray him adequately to others. His biographer's characterization of Hankey as 'a modern saint' (Budd, p. v) is not a measured summing up but an acknowledgment that his subject has largely eluded him. There was always about Hankey, along with much charm, an element of strangeness, of the distant or inexplicable or undisclosed. But then he himself trafficked in legends, compounding even as he tried to unriddle or clarify them. He wrote a small book that sought to get behind the veil of dogma and orthodox tradition obscuring the human truth of Jesus. His most celebrated essay, written as a memorial to an officer under whom Hankey served, created for thousands of readers the idealized, unmistakably Christ-like figure of 'The Beloved Captain'. Hankey puzzled—excessively, he often admitted—about his own identity; and the two books that brought him legendary if relatively brief fame as 'A Student in Arms' do not tell us much about the 'student' that might help solve the puzzle.

The first of these volumes consisted of essays that had begun to appear anonymously at the end of 1915, mostly in the *Spectator*. The book was published the following April and by the end of 1916 had already gone through eight printings and was being widely read throughout the empire and in the United States. Lieutenant Hankey's death in battle was announced in the editions appearing posthumously; sales of his book grew the more rapidly. A 'Second

4

Series' of *A Student in Arms* followed in 1917; this was a more miscellaneous collection, containing a variety of writings about the war, some of them hitherto unpublished, including a one-act play, a series of 'imaginary conversations', and also fragmentary reminiscences from the author's earlier life.

Donald Hankey's cousin, Dorothy Gurner, speaking of this favourite relative from her own standpoint, described him as 'the most beautiful thing that ever happened'. (*ASIA II*, p. 32). Her feelings would have been earnestly seconded by many readers of *A Student in Arms*, lacking Miss Gurner's personal knowledge of its author but grateful for the sympathetic first-hand picture it gave of the men in Britain's embattled 'citizens' army'. Gratitude, and some degree of reassurance, also attached to Donald Hankey's thoughtful and unpretentious meditations on what young Englishmen brought to the strangeness of military life and the ordeal of trench warfare from their experience at home, and on what the war experience in turn might make of these men as part of a future society.

Hankey made his impact upon British readers as the war entered particularly anxious and disheartening days, days that brought shortages and Zeppelin raids at home, tragic failure in Gallipoli, the armies of France being fed into the abattoir that was Verdun, at sea not a Nelson-like triumph but the costly stand-off near Jutland and Lord Kitchener drowned on his way to Russia, the appalling first of July on the Somme that produced not the promised break-through but casualty lists longer than the worst fears could have imagined. His writings about untested English soldiers in a desperate war touched a peculiarly responsive chord in a susceptible public. Or many different chords perhaps.

Here was a man who spoke with no claim to constituted authority or settled wisdom but only as a *student*. A few of Hankey's friends who read these essays while they were

5

appearing anonymously in the *Spectator* immediately recognized him as their author; but the public at large knew nothing of this student—of his having been a commissioned officer well before the war, of his then having attended Oxford and clergy school, of his work as a farm hand in the Australian bush and as a manager of a boys' club in a London slum, or of his enlistment as a private soldier in August 1914. Nevertheless, they responded to his curiously detached self-assurance and the inclusive concern for his fellow soldiers that set him apart from the other, noisier, voices they were hearing.

Examining these essays in our time, listening to their old-fashioned tone of decency and idealism, fair-mindedness and modesty, reticent piety and pious reticence, it is possible to mistake them as run-of-the-mill expressions—relatively tolerable but hardly remarkable—of patriotic uplift. Modern readers will bring to such work as Donald Hankey's all that more recent, more shattering depictions of violent conflict have taught us. Such readers are likely also to have absorbed the invaluable lessons of war as it was seen 'from below' and passed on by other soldiers who became more jaded and disillusioned about the war they survived and Hankey did not.

If Hankey's work is thereby dismissed or altogether neglected, we deprive ourselves of a richly illuminating text. The two volumes of *A Student in Arms* are, in fact, a challenge to the polarized conception of public sentiment in Britain during the 1914–18 war—an *either/or* conception that opposes patriotic zeal fed by righteous condemnation of the atrocious Hun, on the one hand, and utter moral repudiation of war as stupid or insane, on the other. The dream of a stirring and decisive cavalry charge contrasted with an unending nightmare of suffering in the trenches; rousing speeches and swarming recruiting lines juxtaposed with boat-trains chugging into Victoria Station packed with victims of shell shock, men blinded and disfigured by mustard gas, amputees; Rupert Brooke's gallant 'forever England' contradicted by Wilfred Owen's exposure of 'the old lie: *dulce et decorum est pro patria mori.*'

Donald Hankey's war writing eludes these polarities; it does not, taken in sum, fit tidily into either opposing category. His aim was not to glorify war nor to condemn it, not to reveal its peculiar horrors or gloss them over with tales of courage. The contemporary welcome that greeted *A Student in Arms* (referred to in the citations from it that follow as *ASIA*) leaves considerable room for a more adequate judgement of its meaning and its merits, but that acclaim itself figures among the ways in which Hankey's work—and the life of the 'Student' who wrote it—adds to the picture of the British experience in The Great War.

1

A Fragment of Autobiography (1884–1903)

At the height of his fame Donald Hankey was thought by many to hold a secure and distinctive place among those young Englishmen whose deaths in the 1914–18 war cut short lives of particular promise. He was included in a book memorializing some twenty-five such men considered worthy to be praised as *The New Elizabethans*. A small lane in south London, near Kipling Street, was renamed 'Hankey Place' in his honour. His biographer found it possible to describe him as 'a modern saint'.

It was as a writer that Hankey attained that degree of eminence. His essays on the experience of a citizens' army at war had first appeared anonymously as contributed by 'A Student in Arms,' and once Donald Hankey was known to be their author his name and 'The Student' were interchangeable to the public. However, the character of what he wrote and then his own death in battle resulted in Hankey's personality and the drama of his life becoming in time more valued than those writings themselves. The interest Hankey commanded as a writer inevitably faded when the crisis itself ended and as the work of others, who described the war more graphically and reacted more bitterly to its atrocious human cost, began to crowd in. Then the appeal of his life also lessened, as it was bound to do. Surfeited with heroic sacrifice, disillusioned and distracted into flighty self-indulgence, England could hardly remain fascinated by this 'Student in Arms'. Though Donald

Hankey continued to be well-remembered by those who knew him personally and probably by many who had read his essays first in the *Spectator* and then collected in volumes as the war's ordeal ground on, by the time a biography appeared in 1931 his brief renown had already passed.

Near the end of his life Hankey described himself as a 'theological journalist' (*Letters*, p. 428).[1] Writing, in fact, had long been an important part of his life, at least from the time he left the military academy and found himself serving in the colonial outpost of Mauritius. His earliest published letters are from that period; he had just turned twenty and was facing a strange new experience with little confidence and not much sense of purpose. He began trying his hand at fiction,[2] but it was in letters, mostly to his sister Hilda, that he found a means of taking hold of his experience, describing his impressions, sorting out his thoughts, and discovering the kind of person he was and might want to become.

The letters collected and published in 1921 remain the major source of information and insight concerning him. Throughout this study I have drawn extensively upon these letters. They often convey a vivid sense of their author's personality, and to an uncommon degree they tell his own story. The letters to Hilda are by no means the only revealing ones, but they are particularly marked by Hankey's talent for writing as if he were thinking out loud—seldom profoundly, but coherently, unpretentiously, candidly. He also wrote autobiographical fragments about

---

[1] Miller, E. (1921) *Letters of 'A Student in Arms'* (*Donald Hankey*). London: Andrew Melrose, Ltd.
[2] But according to Hilda (*ASIA, II*, p. 6), Donald 'started to write [stories] at the age of six.' The stories and novels he attempted while serving in Mauritius, and the novel he began in the early months of 1916, have not survived.

his early life—home and school—which are included in the second, posthumous volume of *A Student in Arms*. Among his other writings there are passages of additional biographical value. Donald Hankey did not see his personal life as a particularly compelling subject for his pen—naturally modest, he nevertheless warned himself frequently against excessive preoccupation with 'self'—but in fact it is from Hankey the writer that emerges most of what can be known and surmised of Donald Hankey the man. Striving to be selfless, he created through what he wrote an image of himself that is not the least of his achievements as a writer.

In the 'Fragment of Autobiography' published with *A Student in Arms, Second Series* Donald Hankey acknowledges the custom of biographers to build their work on a foundation of vital statistics and an abundance of circumstantial detail. 'I suppose,' he remarks, 'that is all that they can learn' (*ASIA, II*, p. 199). But his sketch of those early years aims at more: 'a picture', as he pointedly calls it, of the home which formed his nature and set it on the course it followed (*ASIA, II*, pp. 199-200). Nonetheless, the factual stock-in-trade of biography may be assembled from Donald's writing with the addition of what his sister Hilda provides by way of supplement.[3]

Donald William Alers Hankey was born at Brighton on 27 October 1884. He was, as he puts it, 'an afterthought'—by seven years the youngest of six children surviving infancy who were born to Robert Alers Hankey (1838-1906) and Helen Bakewell (1845-1900). Robert, after being educated at Rugby School and Cambridge, had been sent to South Australia for his health. There he became a successful

---

[3]Volume I of the biography of Donald's important brother Maurice by Stephen Roskill (*Hankey: Man of Secrets* [London: HarperCollins 1970]) is also a source of family history.

11

sheep farmer, married Miss Bakewell of Adelaide in 1865, and eventually returned to England broken in health but with a fair measure of intellectual vigour. Donald's childhood home was 1 Chesham Place in that attractive town on the Channel coast, which the Hankeys had chosen probably for a climate and an absence of urban bustle agreeable to the father's physical frailty and somewhat reclusive habits. Donald characterized the Hankeys' domestic life as rather typical of an upper-middle-class late Victorian family established in a 'high, respectable, ugly and rather inconvenient' house in a comfortable seaside town. 'We hadn't many friends, we didn't entertain much, we had dinner in the middle of the day, and supper in the evening' (*ASIA, II*, p. 201). Donald describes the Hankeys as 'singularly self-sufficing'; they did many things together as a family, including regular holidays in the south of France. In these surroundings Robert Hankey assumed the not unfamiliar role of a Victorian patriarch, more retiring than autocratic, living, not idly but self-indulgently, more detached from than encircled by a large family, leaving nearly all of the day-to-day decisions and responsibilities to a resourceful and seemingly uncomplaining wife. He took most of his meals by himself and spent much of his time reading philosophy and popular theology.

Donald's mother, known in the family as 'Ma', must have been a person of substantial ability and good sense, shouldering capably the burdens her husband chose not to shoulder and retaining sufficient spirit and good humour to enjoy her six children. They in turn looked upon 'Ma' as a friend and companion. Donald has much to say about only two of his siblings: Hugh, the eldest, and Hilda, the younger of his two sisters. The others were 'G' (Gertrude), 'Tommy' (Clement), and 'B' (for 'Baby'—that was Maurice, who would eventually become the 1st Baron Hankey). Hugh was Ma's favourite and Hilda's shining hero. Their worship of the 'great and glorious' Hugh, who filled much of the emotional space in the family circle unclaimed by the father, rubbed off on Donald. During his increasingly infrequent visits home from Rugby, then Sandhurst, Hugh 'stood for all that is wholesome, strenuous, out of doors' in Donald's life. 'Without him,' Donald surmised, perhaps thinking of his father's example, 'I should have been a mere sedentary' (*ASIA, II*, p. 208). Little Donald himself was a sweet, not very robust child with a radiant smile and a particularly arresting look out of his eyes, one of which was entirely blue and the other predominantly brown. He did not mind that three elder brothers, with Hugh in the lead, undertook to direct his boyhood along properly 'hearty' lines aimed to correct a suspected lack of manliness. That meant 'great tramps over the downs', which Donald loved, and plenty of cricket. Hugh was an ardent boxer and gymnast, pursuits for which Donald accordingly feigned enthusiasm. What better suited the child's fanciful and often dreamy moods were intervals spent conducting imperial mock battles with toy soldiers from every corner of the earth. A fitting enough pastime, it would seem, for the future Student in Arms.

The example of his brothers was not all in the direction of rugged high spirits; Tommy, as Clement was known to the family, apparently had some of the father's reflective nature, which made him in Donald's memory 'a curiously solitary youth ... who played the 'cello with great perseverance and considerable success' (*ASIA, II*, p. 206). Clement also gave young Donald lessons on that instrument 'with clockwork regularity', as Hilda puts it (*ASIA, II*, p. 5). At some point Donald developed a serious interest and some talent in painting; the humorous pen and ink sketches that illustrate his letters show a fluent gift for caricature.

Nothing very extraordinary emerges from Hankey's autobiographical 'pictures', but they give a deft glimpse of childhood. Long hours passed pleasantly in the nursery at the top of the house, with Ma, an adored presence, constantly in and out and Pa's appearances ('A small thin man with gentle grey eyes' [*ASIA, II*, p. 203]) notable only by their infrequency. ' "Ma" was everything,' Donald emphasizes. It is more than a conventional sentiment, as he at least partially understands: 'The only woman who has ever had my whole love, my whole trust and has made my heart ache with the desire to show my love' (*ASIA, II*, p. 203).

As the autobiographer assesses his childhood for early signs and portents, he naturally enough lingers over memories of churchgoing. These are marked by the fact that all members of the family suited themselves as to which service to attend (mostly, of course, within the Anglican communion). These places of worship and reasons for choosing them ranged from the high to low church, even to revival meetings on the beach, and from good music or interesting sermons to anti-papist sentiments. Donald's own preference seems prophetic of his later experience:

Ma and I go to All Souls', because it is the nearest poor church, and Ma finds it easier to worship where there are no pew rents, and the seats are uncushioned, and there are few rich people. I am ever loyal to Ma.

(*ASIA, II*, p. 209)

Then for the evening service Mr Hankey would venture abroad to St. Paul's at the far end of town, often taking his youngest son with him. Walking home with his father through some of Brighton's dingier streets, Donald remembers talks about Australia, solemn discussions of theology, and 'of the past and the future' (*ASIA, II*, p. 210).

Until he was fourteen Donald Hankey was a day student

at a Brighton school kept by a Mr Wathen, one of the Hankeys' neighbours, and the father of Ronnie, the one childhood companion Donald recalls from outside the family. Then in the autumn of 1899 he was sent to Rugby School. From the family's point of view it was the natural choice; Donald's room at the school was the same one each of his three older brothers had occupied.

Presumably it was the father, Robert Hankey, who chose Rugby for all his sons. After all, it had been his own school, and no doubt he was proud of its tradition. Perhaps his was a more genteel form of those sentiments spoken by Tom Brown's father in that idyll of life at Rugby, *Tom Brown's School Days*.[4] 'I don't care a straw for Greek particles, or the digamma, no more does his mother,' declares the forthright Squire Brown concerning his boy's education. 'If he'll only turn out a brave, helpful, truth-telling Englishman, and a gentleman, and a Christian, that's all I want' (*Tom Brown's School Days*, p. 64). Indeed it is hard to imagine that the Hankeys were unacquainted with Hughes's popular novel, which had appeared in 1853 (when Donald's father was twenty years old) or with Dean Stanley's famous *Life and Correspondence of Thomas Arnold* (1844). Rugby in the years since Dr Arnold's headmastership had become not only a favourite school with the upper-middle-class generally, but particularly the frequent choice for boys going on to military careers. No one could think of Rugby—and certainly no student could pass through its halls—without a strong sense of the Arnoldian tradition of character-building and the ideal of service. That particular emphasis Thomas Hughes's book places on the Rugby experience is one of which the elder Hankey must have approved: school as the place one comes to

---

[4]Hughes, T. (1910) *Tom Brown's School Days*. Everyman's Library.

understand life as essentially a battle against the forces of evil and to acquire the strength of character to fight the good fight:

> After all, what would life be without fighting, I should like to know? [Hughes's narrator interposes] From the cradle to the grave, fighting, rightly understood, is the business, the real highest, honestest business of every son of man.
>
> (*Tom Brown's School Days*, p. 251)

That a reclusive and meditative man like Donald Hankey's father should have subscribed to such an aggressive view of life may seem incongruous, but the fact remains that after Rugby his sons continued their training at Sandhurst or Woolwich Military Academies or at the Royal Naval College at Greenwich. In Donald's case at least, it was other, less military aspects of Dr Arnold's legacy at the school that suited his nature; and if it did not particularly ready him for Woolwich Academy, it eventually served him well in his years at Oxford.

'Never did a boy enter Rugby with better chances,' Hankey asserts. 'The memory of my three brothers still lived in the house' (*ASIA, II*, p. 217). They had been prefects (or 'sixths', in the jargon of that school) and had all distinguished themselves in games. Donald's friend Ronnie and another boy from the day school in Brighton also entered Rugby with him. 'But though I loved Rugby and was happy there,' Hankey remembers, 'I can't say I was a success.' Those things that counted—friends, prowess at rugger or cricket, prefectural leadership—eluded him; yet Hankey does not reproach himself for having failed to make more of Rugby. He got into the sixth early and left when he was only sixteen, 'and it is between 16 and 18 that the full enjoyment of school life comes and boys reap the harvest they have sown' (*ASIA, II*, pp. 218–19). Other events during those years hit him much harder than any sense of disappointment at school.

The first of these was the death of his oldest brother, Hugh, 'shot in a glorious but futile charge at Paardeberg' in the South African war. The news reached Donald at Rugby in the spring of 1900, and he describes receiving it with numb detachment:

> I can't realize it. I am an object of interest, of envy almost, to the whole school. The flag is half-mast because my brother is dead. Every one is kind, touched. I put on an air as of a martyr.
>
> (*ASIA, II*, p. 210)

He thinks of another brother, Maurice, now a young officer in the Royal Marines, who is with the fleet in the Mediterranean, far from the comfort of his family. But it is his mother who suffers the greatest shock—along with Hilda, of course, but his sister has youth and resilience. Donald receives a heartbroken letter from Ma. If he goes home to her 'we shall make each other worse,' so he is sent 'to Uncle Jack's and shoot rabbits.' 'There is a huge piece taken out of Ma's life. . . . Pa, also, has lost much, but he is a philosopher.' Ma sends her daughters away 'for a long change'; upon their return 'something about Ma frightens them' (*ASIA, II*, p. 211). Evidently having suffered a stroke, Mrs Hankey with Donald in attendance goes without her husband for a summer holiday in Wales. 'Ma forgets things. She is more loving than ever, but her memory is going.' Back in Brighton, the mother takes to her bed. Donald recalls coming home from a long early morning tramp with an armload of heather he has gathered on the Downs.

> I find my uncle and cousins getting into a cab. Some one says, 'How lovely! Are these for me?' I grip them

in despair. They are for Ma. 'Quite right,' says some one. A day or two later my heather was placed, still blooming, on Ma's grave.

(ASIA, II, p. 212)

After his mother's death Donald seems to have been hurried through Rugby; in the autumn of 1901, when he was not yet seventeen, he was sent to the Royal Military Academy at Woolwich. There he spent what his autobiographical fragment on 'School' calls 'the two most miserable years of my life' (*ASIA, II*, p. 220). Hankey had already felt a vague inclination to become a clergyman, but his father advised him that even if he was serious about a career in the church, military training and service would provide the most suitable preparation for such a life (*ASIA, II*, p. 225).

But Donald remembers 'the Shop'—as Woolwich Academy was known to those who went through it—as a dreadful place. Its tone and its curriculum were so alien to his temperament as to make the Shop indeed the least likely of choices a sensible parent would make for such a boy. 'My first experience,' he recalls, 'was unfortunate.' At the initial interview with the Adjutant, young Hankey was asked what games he could play. When he answered modestly that he had little skill in any, the officer—'a keen sportsman and a bit of a tartar'—forthwith pronounced the young cadet 'a good-for-nothing' and terminated the interview (*ASIA, II*, p. 221).

Donald Hankey's misery at Woolwich was not the result of any active ill-treatment, but he was entirely out of his element in a place whose stern but superficial discipline combined with essential moral neglect. The barrack-like living quarters struck Donald as 'pretty barbaric' (*ASIA, II*, p. 226) in their drab contrast to his snug little study at Rugby with its diamond-paned window, wallpaper of one's own choosing, baize curtains, eggshell blue cupboards, and

'bim ledge' for photos and keepsakes. Still more oppres-
sive, life among the cadets at the Shop seemed dominated
by that most predictable of adolescent fascinations:

> As far as I remember, the one eternal topic of con-
> versation and subject of 'wit' was the sexual relation.
> ... Consequently the place was continually circulated
> with filthy books, pictures, stories, etc.
>
> (*ASIA, II*, p. 222)

Although realizing that the other boys had themselves
'never been taught sensibly anything' about sex, Donald
emphasizes his own extreme innocence and lack of
curiosity on that subject. He surmises that he had been
'recently the more disposed to purity through the death of
my mother,' and at all events let 'the poisonous stream
flow continually by me, shrinking from its stench, and
finding more and more relief in my own company.' He
then adds a touch of wry objectivity that is often a saving
grace of Donald Hankey the autobiographer and letter
writer, and even of the Student in Arms: 'I must have been
a very unpleasant person at that time' (*ASIA, II*, p. 222).

Yet he did make one friend—Fleming, without whom 'my
life at the Shop would have been intolerable' (*ASIA, II*, p.
223)—and he does recall participating in a few boyish rags
he admits were 'jolly' (*ASIA, II*, p. 231). He discovered an
antipathy not only to sexual coarseness but also to those
other cadets who formed the 'Bible circle', or so-called 'Pi
Squad'. Though 'seeking relief from my uncongenial
surroundings in religion and theology,' Hankey claims to
have been 'always peculiarly sensitive about priggishness in
those who professed themselves to be religious openly'
(*ASIA, II*, p. 225). But he does not suppose his own
religious understanding at that period to have gone very
deep, nourished as it was 'mainly [by] fairly regular atten-

19

dance at Matins and Communion.' However, 'I emphatically declined to believe in hell' (*ASIA, II*, p. 226).

Few of the academic subjects at the Shop appealed to Hankey; his failure to pass an 'electricity exam.' kept him there for an extra term. He did take a dabbler's interest in military history, in part at least because of Hugh's small but poignant place in it, and managed to write a prize essay on the Boer War that was printed in the Academy magazine. Repelled by his surroundings and uninspired by his studies, Donald sought the comforts of reading 'good novels'—from childhood he was steeped in Dickens and George Eliot; the Brontës, Scott, Jane Austen, Thackeray, and Walter Besant are also mentioned, and particularly the work of A. C. Benson. Weekends spent at home, though lacking now his mother's presence, are remembered as his happiest times. No doubt the fact that he was at last becoming better acquainted with his father, who stimulated his son's 'theological bent', contributed to this pleasure. Donald recalls one memorable non-domestic outing made possible when his brother Maurice, by then assigned to the Admiralty, made his London flat available to him and Fleming for a weekend on the town. Neither boy knew London, but they made of it what seemed to them a proper adventure:

> We dined at Frascati's—a place of splendour in our eyes— and went to His Majesty's to see Beerbohm Tree in Ulysses. When it came to Hades, we held each other's hands!
>
> (*ASIA, II*, p. 233)

Indeed, it is clear that from boyhood there was a degree of adventurousness in Hankey, an appetite for new experience—as long as the outcome was not likely to be *too* unpleasant. For joined to this appreciation for life's romance was his instinct for good food and drink, for

20

handsome surroundings and well-made clothes. Yet he was honest in claiming that 'my heart has never been wholly in this world' (*ASIA, II*, p. 215). These somewhat competing tendencies are complicated by the tension between his sense of class and the strong contempt for social distinctions that became increasingly characteristic of Hankey. His account of that London spree with Fleming continues into Sunday and attendance at St. Peter's, Vere Street, where the boys' impatience and disgust at the delay in the service while privileged pew holders arrived took them then to a dissenting chapel in Audley Street, 'a most queer little place':

> It was full of monuments to the dependents of peers, in which the peers figured very largely and the dependents fared humbly—the epitome of flunkeydom. Among these tablets one was inscribed—'To John Wilkes, Friend of Liberty.' Truly refreshing!
>
> (*ASIA, II*, p. 233)

Uncongenial though it was for young Hankey, his time at the Shop cannot simply be put down as a step in the wrong direction, a waste of precious years in a short life. It was the beginning of his experience with things military that would help him as a soldier and a writer in wartime. More than that, though it left him far short of true confidence and ripe self-knowledge, it taught him much about himself and, one might say, put him more at ease in his own company. Another year at Rugby and from there straight on to Oxford would have readied his capacities for a more conventional career, or even for great success, but he may thereby have cut a fairly ordinary figure and, the chances are, a rather smug one. Hazarding some conclusions of his own, Hankey writes that he sometimes thought of himself as 'unconsciously a bit of a hero at Woolwich, standing out for purity and religion in an atmosphere of filth and blasphemy.' But having conjured up this tempting image, a compensation for everything unpleasant in the experience, Hankey rejects it: 'I have come to the conclusion ... that there is nothing in this' (*ASIA, II*, p. 234). He does not soften his judgement upon the Academy as 'singularly pernicious'. 'But as to my heroism,' he adds, 'I am reluctantly compelled to be sceptical' (*ASIA, II*, p. 235). As far as he was concerned, it is the claim to heroism that is the real temptation, not the appeal of conventional wickedness.

> It required no self-control to prevent myself from slipping into blasphemy and filth. On the contrary, in order to do so I should have had to violate my strongest instincts.
>
> (*ASIA, II*, p. 235)

Having seen this far into himself, Hankey ventures yet further—towards a revealing conclusion:

> To say the truth, I have never felt the sway of passions to anything like the same extent as most men seem to. I have never cared for the society of women for its sexual attraction. Consequently all my women friends have been just the same to me as my men friends.
>
> (*ASIA, II*, p. 236)

Hankey wrote this fragment of autobiography in 1916 while he was a soldier at the front, attempting a summing up, perhaps a coming to terms, in the face of possible death. The balance of candour with reserve is striking; whatever their aim at the time, these words seem calmly, carefully meditated. Whether they are disingenuous or innocently forthright it is difficult to say. But they are redolent of a bygone era unused to much parading of the psyche's secrets, or even to the suspicion that such secrets might exist:

I don't boast of this [he concludes], I only state the fact. I am not proud of it because I know that some passion is necessary to make heroes and even saints.

(*ASIA, II*, p. 236)

2

Life and Letters (1903–1906)

Not yet nineteen years old, Donald had finished with the
Royal Military Academy at Woolwich and received his
commission in 1903. He then joined the Royal Garrison
Artillery at Sheerness, out at the mouth of the Thames,
where he waited three months for a vacancy to open in
the gunnery school at Shoeburyness. This was a dull period
for him, and the rest of the time he spent before sailing to
Mauritius and taking up a subaltern's duties there proved
hardly more satisfying.

Actual military life as an officer and a gentleman, Donald
was discovering, appealed to little in his deeper nature; but
he could enter into the swim of it more easily than at
Woolwich. After all, the forms and manners of such a life
had been embodied for him, and in some sense been legiti-
mized, through his three older brothers. Youngest siblings
learn to be outwardly pliant, and Donald, who never
lacked charm and had what people of his class might call
'good breeding', could play his role in a passable way. He
could be merry with the other subalterns of the mess, no
stranger to good wine, taking whisky-and-soda, and holding
his liquor much better than most. He could join easily at
the snooker table and even at cards. His objections to
gambling were only 'conventional'; a game of 'slippery
Sam' did not disgust him as did filthy language (Budd,
pp.16-17). There is a clubbable, particularly fun-loving side
to Donald Hankey that shows again and again in his letters,

even under unpromising conditions and in unlikely circumstances.

Hankey's published letters take up when he sails to Mauritius[1] at the age of twenty and continue until a few days before his death at the age of thirty-two. Editing these letters shortly after the end of the War, Edward Miller took for granted the popular interest in the 'Student in Arms', but he claimed for Hankey's letters the inherent value of 'enduring literature' (*Letters*, p. 7). In a period like our own, when we hear it soberly proposed that texts appearing on tee shirts and beermats are no less 'inherently valuable' than Baudelaire's poems, such a claim may seem as pointless as it is old-fashioned and naive. But when he made it, Hankey's editor was registering a not-unwarranted sense that the letters have a rare appeal, much of it irrespective of the reputation of their author. If Edward Miller, M.A. exaggerated their power to attract future

---

[1]Some 500 miles east of Madagascar, Mauritius has the distinction of being the place where the dodo was first discovered, by Portuguese sailors who visited it in the 16th century. Later the Dutch occupied it in 1598 and named it in honour of Prince Maurice of Nassau. In the 18th century it was settled by the French, who called it île de France. Slaves were brought from Africa to work in sugarcane plantations. In 1810, during the Napoleonic War, it was captured by the British who restored its Dutch name. With the abolition of slavery in 1835, indentured labourers were introduced from India. Until the opening of the Suez Canal in 1869 made possible more direct travel between England and India, Mauritius was a British outpost of major practical and strategic importance on the route around the Cape of Good Hope. It remained sufficiently so for Maurice Hankey, then a captain in the Royal Marines and attached to the Naval Intelligence Department, to have visited Mauritius while his brother was in hospital there (August 1906). Captain Hankey was a member of a committee charged with inspecting 'Advanced Bases of the Fleet' aboard the cruiser *Terrible*. Donald Hankey remarks upon (and attempted to paint) the island's considerable natural beauty, but the tropical climate of Mauritius (no doubt in combination with the lifestyle of a military garrison) made it a notoriously unhealthy place for soldiers when he served there. Excluding the British presence, about two–thirds of its population at that time were from India, about a quarter were Creole (mixed French and African background), with the remainder being Chinese and French. English was of course widely spoken, and Donald's French was certainly good enough for it to be useful to him as well.

25

generations of readers, he did not say too much in prizing these letters as 'true human documents' (*Letters*, p. 7). Even at their most ordinary there is nothing wooden or inert or characterless about them. They do satisfy the basic requirement of all published letters: they put us in lively company. At their best, the letters of Donald Hankey pulse convincingly with the thoughts and feelings of one who, if he lacks the standing of a major historical personage and the scope of ripe historical perspective, followed a course that made him a peculiarly sensitive witness to vital history—to a compelling era in the past century about which the more we know the more keenly we are torn between wanting to revisit it and wishing it had been much different from what it was.

The collected letters begin as a journal of Hankey's voyage to and arrival in Mauritius, virtually a one-sided epistolary conversation with Hilda, whose closeness to her brother enabled him to write to her almost as if he were in dialogue with himself. Apparently without other strong attachments of her own, Hilda was the confidante whose interest and understanding Donald could take for granted. They had a good many interests in common—art and literature especially—and seem in easy rapport; but there was a distance as well, and that was probably useful to their correspondence as a dimension of their mutual need. They were, as both acknowledged, each other's second best, compensating for, yet consciously unable to replace, a more intense affection: Hilda could never assuage the loss of their dead brother Hugh; Donald gave his whole heart to no one but their mother. Knowing that about each other seems to have conferred a particular trust, a strong respect, and also (one guesses from Donald's side of their correspondence) a willingness on Hilda's part to leave some of her younger brother's nature and aims only partially explained.

Up to a point, however, Donald's letters to Hilda are direct and revealing. At age twenty, at the outset of an adventure on the other side of the world, with time to read and reflect, to store up impressions and to ponder various roads into the future, it is good to have an older sister who can share one's thoughts. Hilda welcomed serious introspection as much as she appreciated lively description and a spirited ongoing report of life in a colonial outpost. For Hankey, Mauritius is clearly not the first step in a wholeheartedly chosen career but a stage of self-discovery. Before sailing, he had expressed to his father his doubts as to his fitness for military life, his leaning towards a vocation in the church. Himself a serious reader of theology, the elder Hankey would hardly oppose what was then little more than a tentative interest in that direction. But for two of his sons, at least, the military had been a sound choice, and Donald had hardly given his own exposure to that life a chance to 'take'. In any case, a few years of army service would be no bad preparation for a pastor, the father advised; Donald should first see what he made of his commission, or it of him. If it failed to bring success and satisfaction, then his father would consider sending him to Cambridge.

That is how things stood with young Hankey as this new chapter in his life—the first chapter of his published letters—begins. There is another issue besides the choice of a career that one might well expect to find adumbrated in this correspondence between a young officer making his way in strange surroundings and an older sister: the question of women acquaintances and eventual matrimony. And indeed these early letters show some traces of that topic. On the first leg of his voyage aboard 'a rotten little ship' (*Letters*, p. 16) Donald encloses in a letter to Hilda 'a picture [sketch?] of the beautiful lady who has entranced the whole ship from the Captain and the Colonel

27

downwards.' 'Another person rather interests me,' Donald continues, 'a very pretty refined-looking girl, the daughter of a quarter-master (ranker).' That parenthetic detail leads Hankey away from sentiment, towards the dismally predictable subject of *class*.

> How is it possible? The other ranker's daughter is dark (the pretty one is fair) and has the peculiar red, shiny complexion of her class, the thick fingers, and straight hair, yet they are fast friends!
>
> (*Letters*, p. 20)

Here is the prejudice and naïveté of a privileged young man; yet we also note the way Hankey's attention shifts from conventional admiration to disinterested human curiosity.

After he reached his destination and had had a month or so to size up Mauritian society, Donald reports to Hilda, in what may be mock dismay, 'I am afraid there are no lady eligibles in the island except the governor's niece, whom I have not yet met' (*Letters*, p. 30). This oblique reference to the search for a suitable mate suggests that the subject was a familiar source of banter—good-natured but at some level earnest—between brother and sister. Many years older than Donald, Hilda was herself facing spinsterhood; therefore the banter may not have been in one direction only.

Whatever Donald Hankey was seriously seeking from his posting in Mauritius, a wife was not high on the list. Women figure importantly in his life, but in ways that seem motherly, sisterly, even (in one striking instance) grandmotherly. Hilda describes their cousin, Dorothy Gurner, as 'Donald's best woman pal' (*ASIA, II*, p. 243), and Dorothy on her part thought Donald 'the most beautiful thing that has ever happened' (*ASIA, II*, p. 32). This attachment, which Hilda seems disposed to romanti-

28

cize, lasted throughout Hankey's life. But as he sailed towards Mauritius, Donald replied to a letter from Dorothy in a way that has the mark of a light-spirited but deliberate check to his cousin's admiration and a setting of bounds to their friendship:

> Thanks awfully for your letter. But don't wax senti-
> mental. ... You have taught me more than anyone
> except my mater; you remind me of her always, and in
> my library of memories the volumes about you and her
> shall be bound alike, and placed next to each other....
> (*Letters*, p. 23)

A few days earlier Donald had written similarly to Hilda, but in the broader terms of a difference he was asserting between women and men generally:

> By the way, I am afraid _____ is given to idealism. It is
> a most pernicious disease, for a woman especially,
> because she sees only one side of a man's character
> (his holiday side), while a man generally gets glimpses
> of the working side of a woman's character, if she is at
> all a good sort.
> (*Letters*, p. 21)

The subject of Donald's uneasiness here (whether unnamed by him or concealed by the editor) was almost certainly this same Australian cousin, Dorothy Gurner. It is obvious that even as he values his friendship with her he would keep it jolly and manageable. By no means is he to be mistaken for his splendid brother Hugh, especially because there is no mistaking Dorothy for his sister Hilda.

From the outset, Donald was determined to make the best of army life. 'Don't worry about me,' he wrote to his father; 'at last I am a serious soldier. ... before I touch Staff college

29

work I am going to become a real good gunner' (*Letters*, p. 40). But a sense of inadequacy was deep in him at this period of his life, and it produced a certain parallel between his view of the military and his feeling towards women:

> One thing I have grasped [he confides to Hilda]: that instead of the army being not good enough for me, it is rather I who am not good enough for the army.
>
> (*Letters*, p. 34)

Yet despite the wide-ranging self-disparagement found in the letters, one gets the impression of a young man who rather enjoys being who he is:

> I am afraid I have very little ambition. If I can get through life without doing much harm to anybody, and with luck doing a little good, it will be more than I expect!
>
> (*Letters*, p. 35)

And until ill-health overtook him during his second year in Mauritius, Hankey's service there was not on the whole unpleasant. Considering his age and inexperience, he had no great difficulty accommodating himself to the undemanding routine of a subaltern's life in that out-of-the-way post of empire. Donald made a dutiful effort at games and found himself improving in field hockey and playing better tennis than most of his brother-officers. He was appointed wine secretary to the mess and attended dances and other social functions, probably less grudgingly than he indicates to Hilda:

> No, I don't believe in being dragged into society by one's major, and I have sternly refused to be dragged any further.
>
> (*Letters*, p. 60)

There was time for 'sketching' in paint whatever caught his eye in the way of scenic beauty and local colour, for walks, for reading, for pipe-smoking solitude, for many letters, and even for some attempts to capture in fiction the life of this at times dull yet strangely appealing place. A 'moral tale' is mentioned, then 'a short *Conte Maurici-enne*':

> There are things about this island which appeal to the imagination, but it's a minor key they touch. They whisper of loneliness, and darkness of soul, of ruined lives and deep misanthropy, of ravages of fever and plague, of gaiety turned to mourning, and joyous life to devastating death.
>
> (*Letters*, p. 57)

From this somewhat Conradian impression of his surroundings Hankey then turns sharply towards 'things in the island which appeal to one's sense of humour,' and then to 'scenes ... which appeal to one's artistic eye, harmonious colouring, and wealth of ornament.' This leads, however, to an oddly dismissive conclusion:

> And yet on the whole, over one's philosophic pipe, one cannot help feeling that it is not comic enough, or beautiful enough, to justify its existence, especially when one considers all the tragedy of wasted and debased humanity that is found upon it.
>
> (*Letters*, p. 57)

What is it, one wonders, that causes Hankey to pull back, as he does in other respects and on other occasions, from the appeal this island made to his aesthetic and imaginative instincts? Why is he unwilling to put these powers of response to anything resembling a serious test? His pleasure in painting is manifest, but he represents himself to Hilda as free of illusions about that activity and content to stick with literal rendering. He generously praises his sister's artwork ('So take courage, O Hilda! and once more wield the brush when you have a chance'); but as for himself, 'I have no divine spark; I merely laboriously copy what I see, and any resemblance is due to a laboured attempt at mathematical accuracy' (*Letters*, p. 31).

Hankey clearly had an inkling of the connection between his recreational sketching with paint and brush and his general development, perhaps his destiny. A letter of 9 February (1905) offers Hilda some thoughts in a rather decided tone:

My experience is this. As long as I keep to the thing in front of me, and look at things as they come, I am all right— not self-conscious, and quite simple and direct.

But the moment I begin to think of anything not quite plain, straightforward, and material, my head swells to five times its normal size and my brain plunges into a whirl of egotistical verbosity, loses all sense of proportion, all straightforwardness, and clearness of vision, and naturally enough feeling itself ridiculous, becomes sensitive and self-conscious.

(*Letters*, p. 36)

But this, after all, is the tone of a young man not so much explaining matters to his sister as lecturing to himself, one side of his nature trying to scold the other into seeing reason: '*Resolved*, to be very matter of fact, to have no truck at all with so-called "higher things" till I have mastered a few of the low ones.'

What is it that makes this twenty-year-old, who can often be comically playful to this same sister, sound like someone's parody of a prim and pompous Victorian parent?

32

I don't think one is meant to be introspective, or anything of that sort, and I am inclined to agree that some natural hobby is a healthier direction for one's faculties of analysis, than one's 'soul' or one's 'sub-conscious self' and all the host of verbosities of which Heaven alone knows the meaning. I don't find much about introspection, or anything of that sort, in the gospels, but I do find a lot about plain practical charity . . .

(*Letters*, p. 36)

It is a relief to find Donald Hankey capable of assuming a more 'off-duty' tone with his sister and a more accepting attitude towards himself: yielding to the pleasures of his present situation and looking positively at the future. There is this letter of 9 July 1905, addressed for once not to 'Dear Hilda' or 'My Good Hilda', but to 'Dear Hilzy':

This place suits me admirably. There is very little 'Militarism', which is what gives me the hump in England. One is not compelled to go into society—by no means a wholesome recreation. There is a certain amount of sound work done. One gets to know one's men better than in England. . . .

There is no sport to speak of, and honestly I don't think I shall ever care much for shooting. . . . On the other hand, I have been educated to enjoy walks, and games, and jolly scenery, and flowers; and all these things I get in Mauritius.

But what I want is to be a parson in England. I am presumptuous enough to think that I should make a better parson than a soldier, and that it would give me a big incentive to work.

Now I work from a sense of duty, and that is much better than not working at all; but I should like to work for the love of it.

(*Letters*, pp. 53–4)

In a Christmas letter (1905) to Hilda, Donald writes as if he had persuaded himself to settle for an undistinguished— or as he would say, 'unsuccessful'—army career. Appendicitis had put him out of action for a fortnight, and 'the impressions of the last six months have been crystallizing' (*Letters*, p. 70). He still speaks of the clergy as his 'ideal life—what I would like to be able to do,' but now his conclusions about that life resemble what he had been saying of the military: 'I think, after all, I am not good enough' (*Letters*, p. 70).

The fact is, I don't think my training has suited me. I have read too miscellaneous a lot of books—in short, I fear lest my religion, though good for a layman and a help, is not deep or strong enough for a priest. It is strong enough to guide me, but not to guide others through me. I am afraid if I were a priest it might develop a false tone and become a bit forced, affected, ill-balanced. I am very sorry to give it up, but if I did not really feel that it was the honestest way, I would not write about it on this great day of all days.

(*Letters*, p. 71)

'So,' he concludes with halfhearted bonhomie, ' "Vive l'armée!" sez I, and though I do not think I am good for Staff appointments, or positions of great responsibility or trust— my capacity being but moderate—I hope to pursue a useful and honourable career, as a good gunner, a good gentlemen and a good Christian.' A concluding sentence seems an attempt to burn his bridges on the matter of a career: 'You may show this to any one you like' (*Letters*, p. 71).

But in the midst of this outpouring to Hilda, Donald includes a reason for resisting the appeal of the church that paradoxically tells more about his underlying state of mind than anything else he wrote on that Christmas day:

34

I am afraid of binding myself where I want to be free.

(Letters, p. 70)

At times Hankey can sound like a typical young sahib vacillating between varying degrees of disgust at the ways of all non-whites ('. . . they are mostly awful swine'; 'John Chinaman . . . compares most favourably with the stinking Creoles') and fascination with their exotic charm ('All these Creoles have lovely dark eyes and beautiful black hair of which they are inordinately proud' [*Letters*, p. 39]; 'I am glad I came here. The Island is so lovely, the people so exceptionally nice . . .' [*Letters*, p. 40]). None of these feelings, positive or negative, seems particularly deep-seated; if his antipathy is merely the leavings of an officers' mess, his admiration for strange people and their ways is superficial and patronizing:

> I would like to show you this place [he writes to his boyhood chum Ronnie]. I'd like to see you laugh at the quasi-European airs of the better class Creoles; or the merchants, stately and splendid, walking hand-in-hand like children!

(Letters, p. 41)

While Hankey was reacting in these contradictory but thoroughly conventional ways to various forms of local colour, he was making some important friendships. He discovered few common interests with most of his fellow subalterns, and it was easy to grow tired of them. Very few fed his intellectual curiosity or his emerging, if always limited, attraction to the unconventional. One who did so, identified in the *Letters* only as 'K', was described to Hilda as 'a curious blend of Italian and Welsh'. A reader of Latin classics 'for recreation' and 'a great lover of Italy', 'K' loaned Hankey his copy of Gibbon (about whom Donald makes several alert remarks) and impressed him by his tastes in literature and music, 'prefer[ring] Gibbon to Guy Boothby, and Mozart to Monkton, which of course is a sign that he is mad!' (*Letters*, p. 95). Donald obviously admires this man's originality even as he dismisses it as 'futile'. 'He is hopelessly unambitious and contented, treats the army as a joke, and yet having done so brilliantly at Shoebury is out of reach of censure' (*Letters*, p. 96).

These are the traits of the man Hankey, or one side of him, would himself have liked to be.

Oh, he is an odd fellow, is K., and though I regard him as the most unsound man I have met for a long time, he is rather a refreshing person!

(*Letters*, p. 96)

This admiring disapproval of 'K' turns out to be a rather complicated form of self-criticism. In him, Donald sees a glamourized self-image in the presence of whom the real Donald Hankey feels unworthy:

K. is so frightfully well read that he always leaves me utterly behind, and merely makes me feel uneducated.

(*Letters*, p. 110)

In the case of another officer, with whom Hankey formed a stronger and more consequential friendship, the attraction must have been more simply that of opposites. This was 'X', who has been identified as Orde Browne, 'extremely handsome and brilliantly clever in many ways', half Irish and half French, 'educated by Jesuits, but spent his holidays amongst atheists' (*Letters*, p. 44).

Like 'K', Browne was a scoffer, but at religion rather than at the army. Though Donald's 'natural sloth of speech' put him at a disadvantage, he did not feel out of his depth in countering the clever and specious arguments Browne put forward 'with a fearful Zest'. 'I saw they were all founded on his profound ignorance of religion.' Neither man succeeded in altering the other's convictions, but that did not impede their friendship. 'We look at things from an entirely different standpoint,' Donald writes. 'He is an extravagant fellow, but makes beautiful coffee' (*Letters*, p. 44).

Amidst the myriad petty annoyances of garrison life, Orde Browne proved to be Hankey's 'saving clause' (*Letters*, p. 51)—a good-natured, generous-hearted man. Pushed into the social swim by another brother-officer, Donald attends a fancy dress ball with Browne. 'X' accoutres himself cavalierly in red velvet, pink silk, and glass buckles as the Duke of Buckingham; Donald goes as a Puritan in sober black (*Letters*, p. 56). During Browne's absence in South Africa Hankey greatly missed his company and was grateful for it during the trials of illness in his later months of duty on the island. In fact, at a couple of points in his correspondence with his sister, Donald seems almost to be recommending his friend Browne as a person in whom Hilda too might take a special interest:

As an Irishman he is superb, and his conversation is like ... bubbling champagne. He is awfully 'good value,' as his expression has it. You would like him immensely. He is as a rule delightfully unconscious of himself, and is eminently presentable all the same.

(*Letters*, p. 69)

Hankey's other notable discovery amongst the inhabitants of Mauritius was the Anglican bishop. 'He is a brick, is the Bishop. He doesn't mind how trivial one's doubts and difficulties are, but treats them sympathetically'

37

(*Letters*, p. 85). Bishop Gregory was evidently just the kind of tie to the church Donald was capable of valuing at the time: loose enough to accommodate Hankey's intellectual restlessness in a way that did not belittle it; firm enough to represent loyalty to a faith Donald kept discovering he needed:

> It is for want of a broad-minded generous adviser like him that so many officers, trying to worry things out in their own heads, fall into those unholy Calvinistic views of salvation and damnation and nothing at all between.
>
> (*Letters*, p. 85)

While he was venturing boldly into Gibbon and also into Darwin (whose scrupulousness and sensitivity moved him strongly), Hankey continued reading works less at odds with orthodoxy. His struggle with the question of a vocation smouldered on, the choice between sticking it out in the army or putting all reservations behind him and dedicating himself to becoming a parson after all being more a matter of the mood of the moment than of a readily charted process of maturation or self-discovery. Perhaps his illness, signs of which appear from the close of the year 1905, brought matters to a head by eventually forcing him to think it all through decisively while the infection ran its course and then left him as a convalescent. In the end his spiritual and his physical ordeals collaborated in resolving the issue for young Hankey: the state of his health ruled out the option of continued military service, and he had coincidentally made a discovery that seemed to point to the church as the right path in which to seek a life's work.

In the 'Personal Explanation' that accompanied Hankey's contribution to *Faith or Fear? An Appeal to the Church of*

England,[2] a collection of religious essays by several hands published in 1916, he treats this 'discovery' as if it had been a spiritual revelation, a voice speaking with an almost scriptural authority, pointing the way to be followed. From the vantage point of some ten years after the fact, and in the midst of the war that would claim his life, Hankey dramatizes his situation in Mauritius as a crisis of faith:

> At last, when I was in a distant tropical colony, I found that I was on the brink of materialistic determinism. . . . Just as I had almost decided that the only honest thing to do was to abandon all pretence of religion, I had an experience which revealed to me once for all that it was impossible for me to deny the reality of the human soul. . . .
>
> *(Faith or Fear?* , p. 12)

It comes home to him then that man was, '*by virtue of his unique self-consciousness* . . . immeasurably greater than any purely physical organism' *(Faith or Fear?*, p. 13; emphasis added). So the very human quality Hankey had repeatedly denounced (i.e., self-consciousness, 'ego') was affirmed in that revelatory moment as the rock on which shaken belief may be built anew.

'From that day I was a theist,' Hankey writes, looking back from 1916. 'It was something, but not enough.'

> I longed for something more inspiring, and one day this sentence flashed across my mind: 'If you would know Christ, behold He is at work in His vineyard.'
>
> *(Faith or Fear?*, p. 13)

---

[2]Hankey, D. *et al.* (1916) *Faith or Fear? An Appeal to the Church of England.* London: Macmillan and Co. Ltd.

Rehabilitated 'self-consciousness' may be the grounds of abstract faith, but Hankey's most pressing struggle, despite the testimony of the rather conventionally presented conversion narrative he sketches for *Faith or Fear?* is his effort towards a line of action, a calling, a job of work, something 'of practical use'. And here it is: 'I took the vineyard to mean poorer England' (*Faith or Fear?*, p. 13).

Hankey's published letters do not claim nearly as much in the way of a transforming experience as does this belated 'Personal Explanation'. They do, however, rather more straightforwardly identify Donald's discovery of 'poorer England' with something he had been reading, with his discovery of 'a ripping book' by Arthur F. Winnington Ingram called *Work in Great Cities* (1896). The 'work' Winnington Ingram (Head of Oxford House Settlement in Bethnal Green) discusses is of course missionary social work in the urban slums. From his first encounter with it, that book seems to have energized and focused Hankey's sense of purpose. Even as he seeks to reassure Hilda that Winnington Ingram's account of such work among the poor is too honest and graphic to encourage foolish enthusiasm, he admits that the book's appeal on behalf of the poor has taken a strong grip on him:

> Don't you fret yourself, my dear! There are no illusions to the reader of W. I.! My first feeling was, 'I couldn't do it; I haven't got it in me.' My second was, 'but, by Jove, it's worth trying at all costs; and even if I couldn't rise to the East End, I might do a little in a less difficult place.'

> (*Letters*, p. 58)

He concludes that letter to Hilda (20 September 1905) with what must be taken as a teasing ambiguity:

> Well, I must stop, but if you have any thoughts that I

have illusions about parsoning, read *Work in Great Cities*, and you will see that illusions are henceforth *impossible*.

(*Letters*, p. 59)

Hilda is hereby on notice that practical realities, not illusions, will guide her brother; but at the same time Donald is telling her that the option of work among the poor is not a sentimental fantasy but an eye-opening challenge.

No single book, not even Winnington Ingram's, could remove every obstacle in Hankey's way; nor did it change him entirely or overnight. Firm resolution is hardly the note of this passage from a letter to his father dated 10 February 1906:

> I think you are quite right in advising me to stick to the gunners, though if you think I have any ambition, you are mistaken! ... I have no hankering after weighty responsibilities, no incendiary ambitions with regard to the Thames, no desire to hear my name in people's mouths. ... The side street for me! and after all there is a lot to be done in the side streets. ... I have not enough personality, character, or vitality to be 'great' as Hugh or Maurice might be.
>
> (*Letters*, pp. 74-5)

One may suspect that Donald is painting here a particularly humble picture of his prospects in the army in order ultimately to manoeuvre his father into a more approving view of civilian, most likely clerical, alternatives. In any case, three days later Donald writes again to his father begging him to 'Please cancel my remarks on ambition in last letter!' (*Letters*, p. 76). If he is trying to head off a

41

paternal lecture, he is also, on reflection, reminding himself that meaningful self-sacrifice could never be merely a line of least resistance.

Thus even as Hankey's vacillations regarding his future and his religious faith continued, the possibility of a life far from the centres of power and embracing human wretchedness had been planted in his mind. Pious sentiments about the example of Jesus crystallized in the very practical, though fearfully difficult, project of working for and with the poor in some great city. That might temper his self-consciousness; it might transform his sense of inadequacy into something like an asset; it might even—by representing what a true calling in the church could be—assuage his doubts as to his fitness for the clergy.

During his second year in Mauritius Donald suffered serious health problems. What at first seemed to be appendicitis was later described as an abscess on the liver: 'the prevalent complaint in the R. G. A. [Royal Garrison Artillery],' Hilda explains, though on what grounds is unclear (*ASIA, II*, p. 16). A 'severe operation' and prolonged convalescence resulted in his being invalided home at the end of 1906. Abdominal surgery under such conditions, especially if a ruptured appendix had been the cause of the liver infection, was a risky procedure, and Donald was fortunate to have lived through it. Serious illness stands high among those things that can concentrate the mind. Long days in military hospital at the inland station of Curepipe gave him a chance to ponder and clarify his ambitions, and at times his letters suggest that he was becoming the sort of person who might succeed in realizing them. He writes consolingly but entertainingly to his married sister Gertrude Spelman after the death of an infant son. By mid-July Donald knows he is scheduled to return to England and writes to Hilda as if Mauritius were already past-tense:

I cannot say that Mauritius is a particularly invigorating place, but I am not sorry to have been here. I have made two very good friends, both of whom have inspired not a little hero-worship. ... Even the period of ill-health was rather beneficial than otherwise. It teaches one to make allowances for people's irritation. ... I have not made use of my leisure to acquire languages or anything of that sort. All the same I believe that I am a more contented person than when I came.

(Letters, p. 106)

That belief is supported by the tone of his letters anticipating his departure and the likelihood of leaving the army. Self-disparagement remains Donald's style, but it takes on a more positive note. Accepting 'mediocrity', he tells his sister, saves him from envy and leads to a more generous admiration and encouragement of other people. 'I used to be envious,' he rather surprisingly confesses, ' and it spoilt my enjoyment, and made me rather bitter and ungenerous. ... I am ambitious in a way now, but it is not a way which will interfere with any one else' (*Letters*, p. 107). That would seem to represent greater self-assurance: an accommodation between the old impulses of self-consciousness and attraction to what he saw in others that had tended to take the form of inert hero-worship.

None of this is particularly remarkable in a young man of twenty-two, but we are watching the unfolding of a personality that in time a range of acquaintances and thousands of readers came to find luminous and compelling. His last published letter from Mauritius (to Hilda, from Curepipe, 24 September 1906) gives a premonitory view of the Donald Hankey who made so strong, albeit short-lived, an impression on the English in his day and generation. It begins unpromisingly: 'I think I should say that I do not find much use for very intellectual people as a rule'

(*Letters*, p. 110). Despite what he has written about envy, it remains apparent in what he says about 'K' in comparison to Bishop Gregory, who is equally 'well-read' yet, unlike 'K,' free of intellectual pride. Each of these men embodies qualities Donald himself longs to have; but then his thoughts take another turn; to his schoolboy friendship with Fleming (to whom he has recently written) and from that to something Donald describes as a 'rather humiliating discovery',

> namely, that the man for whom I now feel most kindness (after Fleming) is one of whom I was always rather ashamed, and whom I always pretended to despise.

As Hankey explores this 'discovery', his former shame turns upon itself:

> I am very glad I was fond of him, and very sorry I was ashamed of him, because I now know what I did not know then, that 'society' can forgive every sin but that which it is itself free from, and does not care for any virtues much except its own. .... I know, too, that the society of cadets, though physically robust and courageous, was morally cowardly and cruel, narrow and selfish.
>
> (*Letters*, p. 112–3)

Donald follows up that 'little moral story' with this question: 'How far is one justified in telling a boy, as I have often been told from the pulpit, to choose his friends on account of their virtues?' Hankey's own answer reveals his often masked, sometimes reluctant unconventionality, the unconventionality of a quiet but strangely fearless man:

> I don't think one ought to [choose friends on the basis of their approved virtues], but that one ought to be

44

guided entirely by affection and instinct, because if one looks for virtues it so often means accepting a thing of no value at society's valuation, and if one follows instinct it means very often the finding of an own mine of incalculable treasure.

(*Letters*, pp. 113–14)

If not such a mine, this letter contains at least a nugget of some value, a sign of boyhood well outgrown and a goodbye to the kind of soldiering Hankey had experienced as a colonial subaltern.

3

The Dreaming Spires and the Crucified Life
(1907–1911)

Donald Hankey had not been home from Mauritius as much
as a month when his father suddenly died. Though son and
father had become somewhat closer since the death of
Donald's mother, losing his surviving parent was not a
particularly shattering blow. Whether the loss of a father
with an active interest in theology deprived Donald of
valuable support and guidance or, on the other hand, gave
him licence to think his own religious thoughts more
freely, there is no way of knowing. Financially, at any rate,
he was now possessed of the means to follow his own
inclination when it came to choosing a career and setting
out to prepare for it.

Lieutenant Hankey did not officially resign his commission in the Royal Garrison Artillery until May of 1907, but
he assumed when he left Mauritius that his military career
was over. The way was clear, and he felt sufficiently ready
to take the first steps towards Holy Orders. At some point
Hilda had established herself in a pretty house at the end of
Eldon Road in Kensington; Donald could make that his
home while he prepared for university, and it would be his
London headquarters after he went up to Oxford to read
theology. His preparations were two-fold: study with a
crammer in the Charterhouse and involvement in the activities of Rugby House, a home mission founded in 1885 by

members of Rugby School. Described by an early historian of the settlement movement as 'distinctly religious', Rugby House provided clubs for girls and boys, sports, lectures and other cultural opportunities in a district where some of London's worst poverty and crime festered in proximity to well-to-do areas.[1] Donald was acting on the inspiration he had gained from Winnington Ingram's *Work in Great Cities*; however, in attempting with due modesty a less challenging neighbourhood than the East End, he had in fact ensured for himself a particularly difficult initiation to life in the slums. Hankey was brought up short by the experience and did not feel his four months at Rugby House had been a success. Characteristically, however, he accepted the failing as his own rather than the fault of those he had wished to help:

> The men and boys of Notting Dale who toil all day . . . make me feel so inferior that I feel I cannot enjoy luxury with self-respect again, and can only obtain happiness with self-respect by going and living amongst them, and trying to help them bear their heavy burdens which humanity to its shame has laid upon them.
>
> (*Letters*, p. 127)

First, however, Donald would go and live with other privileged youths amid the dreaming spires of Oxford University. The quoted passage (undated) was written there and may reflect an impatience with luxury—and an inclination to preach against it—that belonged more to Hankey's undergraduate years than to his brief encounter with poverty at Rugby House.

---

[1]Picht, W. (1914) *Toynbee Hall and the English Settlement Movement* (p. 230). Translated by Lilian A. Crowell. London.

Hankey was as well-suited and comfortable at Oxford as he had been a misfit at Woolwich Academy. His college, Corpus Christi, was at that time (in Donald's own words) 'distinctly religious in tone' (Budd, p. 38), but Hankey was pleased to find virtually no fussing, on the part of young dons or undergraduates, 'to "get hold of people" for their own good.' Corpus, in his view, 'was a very pleasant, sociable little college' (Budd, p.39).

The intellectual stimulation of the university was as welcome to Hankey as was his college's easy social atmosphere. 'I learnt to reconcile Genesis and the "Origin of Species", or rather to read the one without being worried by recollections of the other. ... I learnt to be intellectually a Modernist, and to find that I could be a Christian without doing violence to my intellectual honesty' ('A Personal Explanation', *Faith or Fear?*, pp. 13–14). Donald was sufficiently happy at Oxford, and in any case happiness was incidental. No doubt he would have understood Newman's idea of a university education as an end in itself and his fellow-Rugbeian Matthew Arnold's emphasis on the 'disinterestedness' which should be the aim of high culture; but Hankey's own purposes at Oxford, though ultimately unselfish, were immediate and practical. He was there not for those attainments that distinguish the gentleman, but for what would help him towards effective work in the Lord's vineyard.

And Oxford did serve that purpose, not only by making Donald more freely at home in pondering theological questions, more satisfied as to the basis of his own faith, but more confident also in his power to bring that faith to bear upon the lives of others. His particular circumstances were largely the reason for this new confidence. At Oxford as in other places he had been, Donald clearly stood apart from the generality; but there, as he himself recognized, his most obvious differences from others were all in his favour. Being a Rugbeian gave him some standing to begin with, but of much more consequence was what he jokingly mentions to Hilda as 'my great age' and also what accounts for that: his previous career in the military (*Letters*, p. 163). Donald was some four years senior to most of his Oxford classmates and he must have worn his greater experience unassumingly but with that touch of elegant aloofness that his acquaintances frequently noted. 'Like the Princes of the blood,' he writes matter-of-factly to his sister, 'I am above criticism in social matters, as long as I am here' (*Letters*, p. 164).

It is the particular value Hankey placed on this kind of freedom that makes it important. He mentions it in the context of a frank epistolary discussion he is having with Hilda about the 'fetters' he observes to be 'extraordinarily numerous' in London society (not excluding his sister's own circle)—'and by that I mean all the upper middles, as well as the uppers' (*Letters*, p. 162). It is the same at Oxford, Donald concedes, and such snobbery makes it very difficult for 'the ordinary man' to get on with 'the "best people" ' and still be friends with 'Jones'—that is, with 'a person of great originality who has a great attraction' but is not 'one of the optimates': 'You cannot know Jones and Mammon!' (*Letters*, p. 163). 'Of course,' Donald explains candidly, 'this doesn't affect me.' He is free to respond to whatever claims Jones or others ' "of the Household of the Faith" ' may have on a fellow-Christian. Donald, be it noted, is by no means blind to social distinctions; he is, rather, rejoicing in a fortunate exemption from them: 'I am able to do as I like' (*Letters*, p. 164).

Given such freedom—a condition whose unlikely and deepest sources Hankey searched for all his life—there was in the environment of Oxford considerable opportunity for Donald to exert his influence over other undergraduates in need of counsel or simply lacking a responsive friend. His letters to these younger Oxford friends are in a register rather new to Hankey: not that of the younger brother, cousin, or tractable son, nor the callow new member of the officer's mess; but more seasoned, trustworthy and sympathetic yet not fully approachable, free with encouragement and advice but careful not to bully or pry; one whose consistent but unspoken message is something like, 'Yes, I really am interested, and I think I understand.' It is obvious from the subjects Donald discusses that here is a pastor-in-the-making, but clearly of the more thoughtful, sensitive, and sensible sort. It is not quite so easy to imagine this voice, lacking as it does some of the undertones still greater self-confidence might bring, speaking with authority to lads in a Bermondsey boys' club or in a trench on the Somme.

A letter Donald writes to 'M____. C____.' towards the end of his first year at Oxford (24 April 1908) is accompanied by one of few really informative notes supplied by the editor of Hankey's *Letters*. This note offers the outline of a little drama that makes the reader wish to know more. M.'s widowed mother disclosed to Edward Miller, the editor, that before her son went to the university she felt he needed to be instructed 'about the all-important question of personal purity' and warned of 'the inevitable risks of college life' (*Letters*, p. 117n.). It seems, then, from Miller's note that at some time when Donald was visiting this fellow-student and his mother she found herself out in the garden caught in a sudden shower of rain. The editor renders this story with details that make it a kind of 'period' vignette, dated, to be sure, yet perhaps not quite beyond the reach of modern appreciation:

She was bending over a bed of sweet william, and rose to find Donald Hankey holding an umbrella over her. As they walked up to the house Donald said: 'It's all right about M. I have talked to him about all a fellow should know before he goes among fellows.' ... The old lady added: 'There was something so pure and gentle in his tone as he said this frankly and shyly that I felt as if one of the flowers had spoken to me! My heart was satisfied. I knew it was well with my boy with Donald as his friend.'

(*Letters*, p. 118n.)

Hankey's extant letters to this same 'M' offer not sex education but a bland and general recommendation of Christianity as a means of explaining 'moral facts'. These include such puzzles as why 'foolish things so often strike us as "noble"... and "right".' Hankey was probably thinking then of how his brother Hugh may have thrown away his life with needless bravery, but he uncannily steps momentarily into the shadow of his own destiny:

It is a foolish thing to die in battle for one's country, but 'dulce et decorum est pro patria mori'.

(*Letters*, p. 119)

When Hankey does discuss 'purity'— as in a letter to one of his closest Oxford friends, Bernard Hartley—he means more than the mere avoidance of schoolboy urges: it is 'knowledge of God', which is gained in the struggle against all forms of 'worldly desire' (*Letters*, p. 129). This may indicate that Hankey has found a way to regard more positively his repeatedly worrying personal qualities: an absence of intense feeling on the one hand and a lack of ambition on the other. Buddhist detachment has its appeal, he concedes to a fellow Corpus Christi undergraduate, but it may be 'translated' into Christian terms: 'the duty of man is to put aside all personal aims and ambitions, and to try and put his whole life under the influence of the divine

51

will' (*Letters*, p. 138). His friend Dugdale's questions about 'a future life' fall into the category of such 'personal aims'.

> I don't think I can quite believe in the idea of Salvation, or rather the lack of it, applying so much to the future life as to the present ... I don't believe it's much good worrying about a future life; what we are here for is to try and realize the Kingdom within ourselves.
>
> (*Letters*, pp. 136, 138-9)

But Hankey is not endorsing any form of ascetic inwardness: 'unselfish service is the best thing in the world' (*Letters*, p. 134).

Least of all does he dogmatize when corresponding with his fellow undergraduates. He stresses how vague and undefined his own ideas are; he apologizes for seeming to preach to these younger friends ('I am arguing with myself, with you as a referee as much as anything!' [*Letters*, p. 129]); he suspects he has fallen under the accusation of false piety and feels ashamed ('since a combination of pijawing and a rotten attitude in practice is about the worst thing a man can produce' [*Letters*, p. 147]). But he is full of his subject, and it is clear he feels he is on to something: that what lies at the heart of Christianity is not a system of formal belief but the character and example of Jesus. 'Christ was, if one may say so, the will of the Father expressed in terms of man' (*Letters*, p. 151).

'Jesus, as the perfect man, accepted the rule of God in His life without reserve' (*Letters*, p. 139). The Cross was not only suffering but abject shame; clearly Jesus, in the world's terms, 'was not a success'. He exemplifies for us, Hankey explained to his friend 'R', the distinction between 'the dignity of God' and what should truly shame us: 'our petty dignity on which we set so much store' (*Letters*, pp.

126, 127). Hankey's sense of this shameful worldliness led him increasingly to identify it with social standing:

> If only we could drop this class prejudice and realize our oneness with our fellow-men, we should begin to understand the universal brotherhood in Christ . . . This is the highest good.
>
> (*Letters*, p. 127)

In the same undated letter Hankey writes that since his experience of the labourers in Notting Dale has made him ashamed of enjoying luxury, his only chance of happiness lies in 'going and living amongst them'. Living by Jesus's example, for Hankey the core of Christian belief, requires him above all to shake free of the fetters of his social caste and embrace the life of the poor.

*

Exactly when Donald Hankey made his first expedition to Bermondsey and precisely how he first came to hear of Dr Stansfeld's Oxford Medical Mission south of Tower Bridge is not known; but given the direction of Hankey's religious thoughts almost from his first days at Oxford, it is hardly surprising that he found his way to one or another of the university missions, or settlements, in the urban slums. The 'OMM'—it changed its name in 1910 to the Oxford and Bermondsey Mission (the 'OBM')—was by no means the most likely such foundation for Hankey to have chosen. Someone at Rugby House in Notting Hill, at the other end of London, may have had a connection with the mission in Bermondsey. Dr. Stansfeld himself ('The Doctor' to all who knew him) made many flying visits to Oxford to challenge undergraduates to join him in 'the crucified life in Bermondsey'. Perhaps Donald met this man on one such occasion and responded positively to Stansfeld's brisk,

53

compelling, intensely practical, and indomitable personality. We do know that Hankey, when he was revisiting Mauritius on his way home from Australia in 1913, preached a sermon there on the subject of Doctor Stansfeld and the Oxford and Bermondsey Mission (*Letters*, p. 308). His most important involvement with the OBM came after 1910, when Dr Stansfeld's connection with the mission had become occasional though still meaningful. Donald would have honoured The Doctor's legacy in the OBM, would certainly have respected his legendary indifference to comfort and his religious sincerity, but he could not be counted among the most ardent of John Stansfeld's numerous disciples.[2]

The mission itself, in any case, made a strong impact upon Hankey, though its relation to his aims and purposes did not dawn on him quickly. Bermondsey as a whole, at that time an appallingly squalid and neglected sector of south London, was a challenge to everything Donald had told himself and others about wishing to merge his lot with that of the poor. A neighbourhood of docks and warehouses, leather tanneries, canneries, and breweries, whose residential streets included dismal tenements, dark and narrow alleyways, and houses lacking even the sparest amenities, Bermondsey had the highest incidence of tuberculosis of any part of greater London. Jacobs' Island, site of Fagin's lair in *Oliver Twist* and Bermondsey at its worst, remained much as Dickens had described it, despite the relatively recent appearance of the gleaming Victorian Gothic pinnacles of Tower Bridge as a dominant landmark. Writing from the trenches of World War I, Hankey confesses his early revulsion towards Bermondsey:

---

[2]Barclay Baron, *The Doctor* (London, 1952), pp. 167–71, discusses Donald Hankey in the context of John Stansfeld's notable 'disciples' in the OBM.

Once I loathed it. It chilled me as now it warms me. Its smells nauseated me, the aspect of its people sent my spirits down to zero, its streets obsessed me as in a nightmare. It aroused all my aesthetic prejudices.

('Home', *OBM Annual Report*, 1915)

But apparently even his initial encounters with Bermondsey told Hankey it held what he had found in no other place. His letters from Oxford include an undated, unaddressed fragment he probably never posted:

I do not think I have ever felt Christ so near as at the bedside of a boy who was dying of consumption in a Bermondsey slum.

(*Letters*, p. 171)

Bermondsey and Oxford's mission there had not then laid their full claim upon him, but they were influencing him already. Modern writers like Galsworthy had troubled him with their 'impatient contempt of Christianity, because it claims so much and does so little'. He describes a vexing polarity between 'modern philanthropy, which is so contemptuous of religion [as to be] founded on nothing at all', and 'Christian theology of the rigidly orthodox kind', whose 'mental attitude ... we of A.D. 1909 cannot honestly adopt' (*Letters*, p. 148). Dr Stansfeld's humble mission, especially its work amongst the spirited but desperately disadvantaged youngsters of Bermondsey, embodied the combined practicability and spirituality of 'the crucified life'. 'We *are* all members of one family,' Dr Stansfeld often told the boys of Bermondsey and the chaps from Oxford. Such a vision of relatedness naturally appealed to Donald Hankey, who was signing many of his letters to Hilda 'Fraternally yrs.' even before he knew anything of the OBM with its touchingly idealistic slogan *Fratres.* Brotherhood appealed to his own experience–it implied a social posture that was immediate and down-to-earth but at the same time broadly ideal.

Now an orphan himself, Donald was under little pressure during these years at Oxford to conform to family expectations or requirements. Though he might lecture Hilda about the fetters that inhibit respectable upper-middle-class life, that was good-natured banter; the two of them continued to see things generally eye-to-eye. He assures her that his 'philosophy' does not quite apply to her circumstances in Eldon Road, Kensington; Hilda's independence is hardly threatened by the social world she inhabits. Donald touches again on a subject they have canvassed before:

> I quite agree with you about marriage in general, but I would almost go further, and say that some people are devoid of a certain faculty or–*je ne sais quoi*! I think I must be without it. I never feel that way about people. . . . I want to be alone, in order to catch the tones of silence.
>
> (*Letters*, pp. 164–5)

These remarks, with their brotherly frankness couched in the idiom of well-bred reserve, may in fact take us close to the limits of Donald's own self-understanding at the time. But the final sentence of that letter to Hilda–*I want to be alone, in order to catch the tones of silence*–does seem genuinely *de profundis*, voicing the persistent and enduring desire of a man who felt himself otherwise a stranger to passion.

*

If the most decisive learning experience of Hankey's Oxford years was his discovery of Dr Stansfeld's medical mission in Bermondsey, the most accomplished piece of work he produced at that time must have been an essay he wrote on the Atonement. Titled *The Cross*[3] when it was published posthumously in 1919, this essay is no mere academic exercise, by no means unconnected with Donald's discovery of Bermondsey. Though ostensibly a discourse, in layman's terms, on the theological meaning of Jesus's suffering and death, it attempts to expound that meaning as it imposes a view of life—indeed, a way of life—upon the believing Christian. In other words, it is Hankey's lay sermon whose text might as well be Dr John Stansfeld's phrase describing what he was proposing to those Oxford undergraduates he recruited to Bermondsey: 'the crucified life'. Hankey's biographer refers to *The Cross* as 'a little masterpiece'. Perhaps it lacks the originality and intellectual rigour to sustain such a description, but it does occupy a crucial place in Donald Hankey's attempt to bring his religious convictions—and his abiding scepticism—into working relationship with his complex sympathies for the lot of the very poor.

Hankey's two-part sermon contemplates the Cross first as a symbol, then as a principle of action. This division also corresponds to a distinction Hankey elaborates between Jesus as teacher/prophet and Christ as Saviour. The Cross embodies Jesus's acceptance of the difficulty inherent in His teaching and also His perfect faith in its truth and power (*The Cross*, p. 19. [Subsequent numbers in parentheses here refer to pages in the 1919 edition].) Crucifixion, in the world's eyes, was 'the most ignominious death—the death of the slave' (12). In so dying, 'Jesus reached the nadir of worldly failure' (14), but thus He demonstrated 'His contempt of men's values' (17), of 'outward respectability' and 'worldly success' (12, 13). His teaching is by *deed* as well as by *word*. Jesus 'was not weakly senti-

---

[3]Hankey, D. (1919) *The Cross*. London: Andrew Melrose Ltd.

mental' (16); His love 'was combined with ... a power to face the sternest facts of life' (16, 17). 'In dying on the Cross He showed that there was no limit to service'; those who accept Him 'must be ready to give their lives for the same cause' (14, 15). 'Fearless' is a notably recurrent word in Hankey's depiction of the Christ-like character.

Thus the Cross calls all Christians to the cause of serving others, to addressing in the spirit of sacrifice the world's injustices. Hankey does not regard innocent human suffering as merely a fact of life endured by the unfortunate, much less divine punishment visited arbitrarily upon the bulk of mankind. It results from the wrongs that people do to other people and that followers of Jesus's example must strive to undo. 'Who is saving the world?' Hankey asks and then answers:

> Those women who, in the Spirit of Christ, go by their sympathy to raise the wrecks of womanhood that have been ruined by men. Those who, in the Spirit of Jesus, share the troubles and sufferings of their employers; ... ordinary men and women who in a quiet and unprofessional way help to undo the wrong that others have done. These are the body of Christ.
>
> (34–5)

The Church, then, is 'not the Roman, Greek, Anglican, or Free Church, but the company of all those in whom the Spirit of Jesus dwells' (31). 'Established by the blood of the martyrs' (38), its work is accomplished 'not by costly ceremonial, by well-trained choirs, by eloquent sermons,' but by 'those servants of Christ who gladly bear His Cross' (39, 41).

A traditional view of the Crucifixion as effecting the appeasement of God's wrath is an affront to divinity and a failure to relate Jesus's sacrifice to human needs:

The sacrifice of the Cross was not a transaction which altered God's attitude towards man: it was the revelation of an eternal fact–that God is Love, and that where there is imperfection love means suffering, and that in this suffering of God lies salvation.

(42)

Hankey does make a few gestures in the direction of abstract theology and attempts at times a more high-flown intellectual perspective. He acknowledges God as 'the creative Principle which . . . can save the world and bring order out of chaos, good out of evil' (26). He does regard the Crucifixion as the formal complement to the Incarnation and its conceptual resolution: 'In the Incarnation God entered humanity. In the Crucifixion that divine humanity was taken up with God' (26–27). He does describe the death of Jesus on the Cross as 'no mere solitary event', but as a crucial intervention of God into history, whereby an otherwise 'vicious circle', or 'endless chain of causation where sin is always breeding sin', becomes the perfect circle of 'His imperishable goodness' (28). But these are flourishes in an otherwise homely and down-to-earth exposition of what in America was becoming known as 'the Social Gospel'.

*

Armed thus with a far from original yet not quite conventional form of Christian faith, Donald Hankey took the next formal step towards a vocation within the Church by entering the Clergy School at Leeds. First, however, he treated himself to an extended holiday spent mostly in a journey to Africa that included a return to the island of Mauritius.

Orde Browne, Hankey's friend from their service as fellow-officers with the Royal Garrison Artillery in Mauritius, had invited Donald to visit him in British East Africa, where Browne was now in charge of a colonial station at Embu, north of Nairobi near the foot of Mt Kenya. Judging by his letters (the bulk of them to Hilda), Donald undertook this adventure in a buoyant holiday spirit. He was feeling 'riotously fit' (*Letters*, p. 204), especially when he reached Africa, and he was also doing his best to be an entertaining correspondent for Hilda, who was convalescing from surgery. The Donald Hankey of these letters is the rather typical young upper-middle-class Englishman abroad, sending his elder sister rather supercilious impressions from shipboard and ports of call. The things he enjoys are predictably 'jolly'; those that strike him as outlandish or otherwise deserving of censure are classified as 'funny', signifying good-natured toleration and mild disapproval. More than willing to be impressed by the exotic, Hankey is not slow to register disappointment with drabness, to pronounce upon the dismal look of colonial intrusion, even to dismiss what he judges the worst of it— Nairobi from the wayfarer's perspective—as 'a hideous little galvanized iron town' (*Letters*, p. 216). As for the human element, Donald's sense of the ridiculous is frequently in play. The self-importance of inflated officialdom and even more the absurdity of miscellaneous Europeans on their travels—the vulgarity of some, the pretentious airs assumed by others, and the smugness of newly established colonials ('the bungalow side of the business' [*Letters*, p. 217])— particularly attract his amusement and mild scorn.

Hankey does not exempt himself: he belongs in the class of 'respectable prig', whose chief vice is an excess of circumspect self-consciousness. 'But of course if your ancestors were bankers,' Donald reflects, 'you cannot be naturally impulsive, any more than you can expect the son of—say—a country gentleman, whose ancestors' sole interests have been the chase and the bottle, to be cautious and rational' (*Letters*, p. 194). On the other hand, Hankey is not sorry to find himself admiring the qualities of 'a fat, rather vulgar-looking "Italian"' whom he meets coming up to Nairobi from Mombasa (*Letters*, p. 193). There is no 'side' to such a 'frankly [childish] pagan with his generosity, barbarian courage, and [presumably] loose morals' (*Letters*, p. 194). 'He is not likely to lead me astray, and he is more likely to teach me his virtues than his vices' (*Letters*, p. 195).

After meeting up with Browne in Nairobi and having completed an uncomfortable drive as far as Fort Hall, Donald appears, during the three-day march from there up to Embu, to have pretty well surrendered to the fascination of his surroundings:

> We travelled in great state, with fifty outrageously savage porters, three spearmen (or 'Moran') in feathers, shields, and crimson cloaks, a few native police, and innumerable gun bearers, etc. The Moran are most beautiful people. I mean to paint a picture of one some day.
>
> (*Letters*, p. 197)

Much as he relished the experience, Hankey's way of registering his feelings may have left a mixed impression. According to his biographer, who had access to Orde Browne's recollection of the visit, Donald could not be persuaded to learn so much as a simple word of the native speech 'and poked fun at most of the local characteristics'. Yet Browne also claimed that when his friend left 'my native spearmen were far sorrier to see him go than they had been in the case of other men who should have been far more popular with them' (Budd, p. 49). What this report suggests is the contrast between Hankey's social persona as a young tourist in unfamiliar situations and his response at a deeper, quieter level where, if one may apply the words of a poet, 'strangeness made sense' (Philip Larkin, 'The Importance of Elsewhere').

For Browne, Donald was a guest to be entertained; and the two of them played the pianola, drank the case of claret Hankey had brought as a gift, and met the neighbours. There was game shooting, including a strenuous but unsuccessful safari in search of elephant; but Donald was not handy with a rifle and disliked killing for sport. He much preferred to watch the spearmen dance–which he pronounces, in a phrase knowingly borrowed from Browne, 'awfully good value' (*Letters*, p. 198) – and to listen to their 'weird chants' while the glow of the fire intensified the darkness and made it all seem 'awfully like a dream' (*Letters*, p. 199). It was not to get acquainted, much less to feel at home, that Donald came to Africa but to taste strangeness. By no means reclusive, indeed acknowledged by those who knew him best to be lively company, Hankey nonetheless found his most characteristic role not as a forward participant but as a detached observer. So much, after all, is implied by the name he chose when he came to write the essays that brought him fame: 'The Student'. Studying his surroundings in the form of watercolour sketches, though as always Donald disparaged his success with paint, was therefore a particularly welcome pastime.

Sketching ... has this virtue, that it does instead of *company*! If I had sufficiency of paints and paper I could live quite comfortably on a desert island!
(*Letters*, p. 220)

That could be another way of 'listening to the silence'.

After leaving Kenya, Hankey made several stops along the coast of Madagascar and enjoyed long walks through idyllic tropical scenery, observing handsome Madagascans,

62

eating excellent food. He sailed on to Mauritius and found it 'as beautiful as ever' and Bishop Gregory, with whom he stayed, even more admirable than he remembered him to be. Donald repeatedly refers to the priest's 'mellow' judgement and general cast of mind. The two men had been reading many of the same religious books, especially those reflecting 'the Modernist School of the Roman Church' (*Letters*, p. 229), and although the Bishop is quoted by Hankey's biographer as describing his young friend's views to have been 'indeterminate', their conversations seemed 'delightful' to Donald, full of shared interests and congenial points of view. Fresh from Oxford, Donald was especially pleased that he and Dr Gregory had belonged to the same college, and he relished the older man's recollections of Corpus Christi and the notable men who had been his friends there. In a letter to Hilda addressed 'Bishopscourt, Moka, Mauritius, Sunday, Nov. 27, 1910' Donald leaves no doubt that he is having a splendid time:

> We *are* enjoying ourselves. *Ain't* we just! Oh my!
>
> (*Letters*, p. 229)

Other pleasures besides his host's ripe judgement and extensive library contributed to this enthusiasm; there was also the Bishop's cook, not to mention his well-ordered household and its exquisite furnishings. Convinced though he was that a religious vocation was a call to sacrifice, Donald could not be displeased by this modest but elegant preview of the life of a celibate clergyman.

In a letter to Bernard Hartley, Donald conveys these good feelings. 'It is awfully jolly being here again,' he assures 'Tartles' (*Letters*, p. 228). But he thinks also of the interests he and this young college friend share, and he indulges himself in some generalizations about national traits and how these are reflected in various branches of European

Catholicism. Many aspects of the Roman Church had long appealed to Hankey, and he acknowledges to Hartley his partiality to the flattering *sympatica* and devout Catholicism of the Creole ladies in Madagascar. But he then holds forth about 'the other side' of his experience in that French environment: 'their natural scepticism—or rather atheism. It seemed to take all the beauty out of life.' The French, Hankey informs his friend, have not evolved a true Catholicism but have 'tried to make a cult of the Republic' (*Letters*, p. 225).

I am really glad to have stayed in that French place, because it made me realize as I had never done so vividly before how completely atheism takes from life all that I find beautiful, and yet how it can retain more than all the cant and priggishness and dogmatism and vulgarity which are apt to disfigure 'popular religion.'

(*Letters*, p. 227)

Confessing to a strong element of agnosticism in his own outlook, Donald acknowledges great difficulty in 'expressing spiritual things in terms of the material' (*Letters*, p. 227). The otherwise ineffable bridge between these seemingly contradictory realities remains always for him the figure of Jesus.

'I went to Africa to think things over,' Hankey wrote in 1915 (to Canon Cremer, April 1915, *Letters*, p. 360). Little in the way of concentrated thought appears in the letters from that five-month sojourn; but the fresh perspective, especially as it bore upon previous experiences, braced him for the next stage: the Clergy School at Leeds. Also during these travels Donald had been avidly reading William James's *The Varieties of Religious Experience*. James's pragmatism (which Hankey refers to as 'The Philosophy of Common Sense') appealed strongly to Donald and inspired him to test 'the truth of a thing' by asking not 'is it logical?' but 'does it work?' (*Letters*, p. 214). Anyone bound for clergy school might be particularly wellserved by such encouragement to trust in his own experience. There are no published letters from the time Donald Hankey spent at the Leeds Clergy School (February to June, 1911), but what he did say in other places about those five months or so makes clear what it showed him of 'parochial life at close quarters' (*Faith or Fear?*, p. 14). He remembers being 'violently put off being ordained by what seemed to me to be the evasive teaching and the attempt to substitute devotional discipline for honest thought' (letter to Cremer, 9 April 1915, *Letters*, p. 360). He confessed to his friend Barclay Baron, Warden of the Oxford and Bermondsey Mission, that all he learned at clergy school was 'a horror of clerical shop, clerical professionalism, clerical phraseology, and the clerical manner, also clerical timidity, fear of truth, and disingenuousness' (quoted in Budd, p. 52n). Donald quickly grew impatient and weary in this stultifying atmosphere; by April he was expressing 'an ardent desire to do some hard work of a troublesome and tedious kind, to own someone else for taskmaster, to suffer some sort of servitude' (quoted in Budd, p. 52). By June his discontent was near its limit: 'A term nearly ended,' he writes in his journal of 14 June. 'How little done! More slackness, increasing lack of self-discipline. Even reading has suffered.' From the hell of clergy school the 'crucified life' he had sampled in the Bermondsey slum reasserted its appeal. 'I am to go to Bermondsey for a year from July 7. I hope to learn that freedom from self is to be gained by the service of Christ and the tending of His lambs' (quoted in Budd, p. 54).

Hankey's biographer asserts, without citing his evidence, that the appearance of J. M. Thompson's book *Miracles in the New Testament* in the middle of 1911 strongly influenced Donald's decision regarding the clergy school and ordination at this time. Rev. Thompson's argument that a constructive Christian theology need not cling to a belief in the strictly miraculous would have reinforced Donald's sense of Christianity as a way of life rather than a belief in strange happenings. In Budd's sketchy and rather evasive account of Hankey's misadventure at the clergy school, there is a reference to an exchange of letters between him and the school's principal in which Donald's impatience with authority on the one hand and the principal's failure to appreciate the younger man's sincerity and depth of feeling on the other produce a regrettable impasse. The principal declared that anyone holding Hankey's views was not an appropriate candidate for ordination. Donald, for his part, was the more convinced that 'no gospel for the working man' could be learned from such people in such a place, 'that the life of a clergyman offered after all no prospect of usefulness to me' (*Faith or Fear?*, p. 14).

Hankey's experience at the Leeds Clergy School plunged him into the midst of the intensifying dispute within the Church between the authority of traditional belief and the spirit of intellectual and scientific questioning that was gathering strength to challenge it. Hankey's biographer thus characterizes him as a theological pioneer, a man ahead of his time whose view of the Church would be championed (though largely unacknowledged) by numbers of more learned and expert churchmen who came after him.

But to accept that assessment would be to see Donald Hankey as the son of but one parent: Robert Alers Hankey, withdrawn from the world and occupied mainly by an absorbing but amateurish interest in liberal theology. Donald was, after all, more his mother's son; his inheritance from her was the desire to push past the distractions of theological controversy and put the teachings of Christianity into effective practice. In *The Lord of All Good Life* (1914) Hankey would criticize the Church for its detachment from the things that immediately and practically concerned the average Christian. 'Even in theological college,' he writes, 'the teaching is often neither candid nor practical' (quoted in Budd, p. 57). His quarrel with such colleges, based upon his own experience at Leeds, is but incidentally doctrinal; more essentially, he accuses the Church in its 'clerical professionalism' of triviality and irrelevance and, by implication, of aloofness from the world of critical human needs:

> Hours are devoted to proving that chasubles were or were not used in the Elizabethan Church. ... But very little idea is given of the great truths by which the Christian ought to live. ...
>
> (Budd, p. 58)

Though by no means the embodiment of false doctrine, Donald's father was surely a personification of irresponsible detachment, of something worse than literal absence. The elder Hankey sought truth, but did his quest make a solid difference? The seeker remained indifferent to whatever practical human implications might be claimed for those truths. So unsurprisingly, a paternalistic Church full of authoritative pronouncements did not greatly move Robert Hankey's youngest son; it was the Mother Church—a church of unpretentious but tangible ministering presence—he longed to serve.

In his letter of 9 April 1915 to Canon Cremer, Rector of Seaford (who had written admiringly of *The Lord of All Good Life*), Donald speaks from the heart of his effort to achieve 'a sort of synthesis between the teaching of the liberal theologians, and the teaching of life as experienced in as wide a sphere as possible' (*Letters*, p. 361). In a sense the antitheses from which such a synthesis would need to be fashioned originated for Donald Hankey in the contrasting natures of his two parents and in their diverse influence. Robert and Helen Bakewell Hankey were both gone, but the opposing claims of their son's divided nature—of the meditative, self-absorbed, self-indulgent Donald Hankey and of that other Donald Hankey who craved the ecstasy of painful service—remained to be acknowledged and somehow negotiated.

4

Bermondsey and the Outback (1911–1914)

Early in July of 1911 Donald Hankey cast his lot with the Oxford and Bermondsey Mission. Looking back at the course of her brother's life Hilda considered Bermondsey to have been 'the forcing-house of his development' (*ASIA, II*, p. 2). The Leeds Clergy School had disillusioned him and he was through with it. He would never completely abandon the idea of eventual ordination in the Church of England, but he expected that his 'modernist' views might make ordination unlikely. His plan was to stick it out in Bermondsey for a year and then see how things stood. He wanted to subject himself to hard physical work and even wondered whether something like a 'Railway Mission in Canada' might not 'make more of a man of me' (*Letters*, p. 234). In the meantime, he already had enough experience of Bermondsey to know it would be no holiday. Much about his surroundings there he found repellent; work for the OBM was often discouraging and uncongenial. But he was determined to seek 'freedom from self' by plunging into 'the service of Christ and the tending of His lambs' (Budd, p. 54). That the lambs in the noisy streets and foetid alleyways of Bermondsey were a particularly rough and ragged flock made their tending the more worthwhile.

It is unclear whether the vivid and valuable account Barclay Baron gives of Hankey's arrival in Bermondsey refers to his first visit to the OBM while he was still an undergraduate or to the beginning of his residency in midsummer of 1911. Baron recalls Donald as something of an apparition:

> On the night he came, mysterious, unheralded, his fellow-residents decided uneasily that he would never fit. His eyes, one grey, one brown, were disconcerting, his accent very 'Oxford,' his clothes too well cut for this casual company.
>
> (*The Doctor*, pp. 167–8)

Baron may have inadvertently conflated Donald's initial undergraduate venture into Bermondsey and the later and much more extended period, but he must have known him about as well as any of the Oxford 'missionaries'. The two helped each other on club productions of Shakespeare, and Baron's work as Warden of the OBM ensured frequent and varied contact with all of the Oxford residents. He alludes to Donald's 'fastidious taste in books and food and wine'; he recalls Hankey's painting in watercolours, his 'cello playing, his writing of verses 'which he rarely showed to anyone'. The boys in the Decima Club—the one among the Mission's several boys' clubs which Donald helped to manage—could not resist ragging so 'unlikely' a specimen of Oxford eccentricity, but Baron records that 'they ended by giving him their whole confidence'.

> 'You Oxford chaps think you know us,' said a very astute Bermondsey officer to the Warden a year later, 'but none of you understand us like Donald.'
>
> (*The Doctor*, p. 168)

Donald himself believed he knew the reason for whatever success he had in commanding the respect and affection of his young club members. In April 1916 he wrote a letter to an army chaplain who, in admiration of

Hankey's war essays, had written to him for counsel as to how he might better reach the soldiers to whose spiritual needs he was expected to minister. Donald's reply draws primarily upon his experience with the boys in the Bermondsey Mission. He describes what he refers to as an 'accident' that caused those products of a wretched life in south London to take him seriously at last:

For some idiotic reason—I really couldn't say just what it was— I dressed up as a tramp one day, and spent a night in a casual ward. I didn't do it for any very worthy motive, and I didn't mean any one to know about it; but it got round, and I suddenly found that it had caught the imaginations of some of the fellows, and I realized that if one was to have any power over them one must do symbolic things to show them that one meant what one said about love being really better than money, and all that sort of thing.

(*ASIA, II*, pp. 157–8)

Of course, in writing this letter, Donald was framing his own experience in a way that would encourage the chaplain to undertake whatever 'symbolic things' might improve his credibility with men in combat. Hankey is candid in sizing up his night in the doss house and its accidental benefit. It belongs with subsequent instances of 'a most gigantic reward of goodwill for actions which cost very little, and which were not always done from the motives imputed' (*ASIA, II*, p. 159). He cites it as a strategy that works rather than the result of some noble prompting. Nonetheless, the whole incident sheds its light upon Hankey's personality and perhaps even illuminates some deeper reaches of his nature.

At the beginning of his Bermondsey adventure, Hankey lived among the other young Oxford residents in their

71

settlement at 60 Riley Street. Later he lodged by himself or rather, as Barclay Baron specifies, 'in one of the most rickety and vermin-ridden courts with one of his married club officers', a man named Tom Hewitt (*The Doctor*, p. 168). According to Baron, this change of quarters occurred 'after a few months', but there is a letter to Hilda dated 'August 9, 1912' (announcing Donald's imminent departure for Australia) that is addressed from 60 Riley Street. So perhaps he did not move in with the Hewitts until he returned from Australia early in 1914 to reside in Bermondsey until the outbreak of the war and his enlistment in the army that August.

Hankey's service in the Oxford and Bermondsey Mission coincides with what from many points of view was the heyday of that university settlement/mission. Though its physician-founder John Stansfeld had relinquished leadership after his ordination, he still exerted an influence as vicar of St. Anne's Bermondsey. A change of name, from The Oxford Medical Mission to The Oxford and Bermondsey Mission, reflected the fact that, by the time Donald Hankey knew it, the Mission no longer functioned as a clinic and dispensary. At the same time it was invigorated by a growing spirit of integration affecting both the university and the local elements of the Mission. Dr Stansfeld's chief disciples and successors to his leadership saw the connection of Oxford to Bermondsey as increasingly one of mutual benefit, as more truly fraternal. Many of them wished to involve themselves more fully in the life of the neighbourhood and in some instances to become more or less permanent citizens of Bermondsey.

Barclay Baron was one such. A stylish writer with a flair for drawing, 'Barkis', as he was known around the Mission, worked as a journalist but was to become prominent in the YMCA and in Toc H. Another was Alec Paterson, 'A.P.' or 'Alec Pat', a remarkable man who never served as the

OBM's official head but who was acknowledged as Dr Stansfeld's *de facto* lieutenant and heir of his authority. In 1911 Paterson published a humane, lively, and acutely-observed study of Bermondsey life titled *Across the Bridges*, one of the best books ever to be written about the urban poor. He taught in a local school without compensation, gave generously of his skills and energy to the activities of the OBM, and when war came enlisted as a private soldier. Rising to the rank of captain, Paterson was gravely wounded and cited for bravery. At the war's end he returned to live in Bermondsey for many years and continued to participate in the affairs of the OBM to the end of his life. Sir Alexander Paterson is remembered as a reformer of the Borstal Service and a world renowned penologist.

An extraordinary generation of variously gifted and high-spirited Oxonians carried on Dr Stansfeld's work, followed his inspiration, cherished his example, extended the influence of his vision, and evolved a more egalitarian basis for perpetuating what he had brought to Bermondsey. The list of those connected with the Mission in those years is distinguished, including two future Archbishops of Canterbury (Geoffrey Fisher and, from a somewhat earlier time, William Temple), numbers of other notable churchmen, artists, musicians, writers, civil servants, politicians. Donald Hankey knew and was known to many of them. But he was not living in the London slums to enjoy the company of a memorable few of the best and brightest. Relieved not to find in the OBM much of the 'forced piety' and 'forced heartiness' that repelled him amongst the 'pi-squad' at the university, Hankey nevertheless remained wary of a common-room atmosphere, even at its most stimulating and uplifting. His declared aim was to lose himself, but to hard work and in serving the poor, not to the commanding personality of someone like Alec Paterson.

The Annual Report of the OBM for 1911 records that by the end of July Donald and another 'Oxford Fratre' were hard at work wielding picks to prepare for the Senior Camp at Camber Castle in Sussex; so he was quickly absorbed into the Mission's diverse activities. An extant poster indicates that on 31 August (1911) 'D.W.A. Hankey, Esq.' took part in a 'Farewell Concert' at the St. Olave and St. John Institute in honour of three local members of the Mission clubs who were emigrating to Australia.

Donald emphasized that he went to Bermondsey 'as a learner, rather than as a teacher' (*Faith or Fear?*, p. 14), but that describes his manner and suggests little of his actual function. In fact he *did* teach. He tried instructing the boys in French, but found his own command of that language was not sufficient to guarantee that rascally fourteen-year-olds would learn it. He and Barclay Baron initiated a Shakespeare Society, the members of which read through and then set about staging one of the plays—*Julius Caesar* seems to have been their first such undertaking. A comprehensive list of his duties at the Mission and at the Decima Club left his sister Hilda 'breathless' (*ASIA, II*, p. 27). Eventually he discovered his true niche in giving simple but well-judged talks to the boys preparing as candidates for confirmation (*The Doctor*, pp. 169–70), talks he would incorporate as the basis of that part of his book *The Lord of All Good Life* devoted to 'a Study of the Greatness of Jesus'. 'To the end,' Barclay Baron recalls, 'he remained a paradox, always an individualist and yet a wonderfully sympathetic friend, immensely gay and active among his beloved boys but often a lonely man still fighting a secret battle' (*The Doctor*, p. 169).

The secret battle to which his fellow missionary refers but leaves otherwise unexplained must certainly point to Donald's effort to overcome—firmly, decisively—that besetting fault of self-consciousness of which he repeatedly accused himself: 'I hoped that by living in Bermondsey I should lose my self-centredness, and become interested in other people and their point of view and needs' (Budd, p. 66). On yet another level Hankey's 'Battle of Bermondsey' involved a struggle against his aversion to the sheer physical oppressiveness of the place: its squalor, its inescapable noise and stench, its comprehensive ugliness, its manifold discomforts. From the actual battlefield in 1916 Hankey cast his mind back to this place and confessed, in a passage already cited, that his initial impressions of Bermondsey were almost viscerally negative on all these counts.

More broadly, the struggle was with his own class identity. K. G. Budd, his biographer, puts it fairly in saying that he aimed at 'nothing less than [to become] "declassed"' (Budd, p. 71). Only by so doing could he make himself fit for ordination according to his own conception of a clergyman as one who successfully stands outside the social spectrum. 'I think that a priest—or a Christian for that matter—ought to be almost classless,' he told his Oxford friend Hartley (*Letters*, p. 241). He emphasizes that he is not looking towards 'social reform', but to 'greater humility' (*Letters*, p. 240): the radicalism he champions is not political but *emotional*; the root change it advocates is not a change of system but a change of heart:

I don't mean 'despise the dukes,' but 'love the dustmen.'

(Letters, p. 241)

By facing the challenge of Bermondsey Donald was deliberately putting himself in an uncomfortable situation. He did feel that to gain the trust and genuinely to appreciate the point of view of the working man he must experience the conditions under which such men lived, and in several ways Donald tried this. He became in Bermondsey, and later on his voyage to Australia, not so much a missionary as a 'social explorer'. This category of men and women, emerging a generation or so before Donald Hankey, has been perceptively likened by Peter Keating to geographical explorers such as Speke, Burton, Livingstone, and Stanley. They were a various assortment of adventurous individuals who lowered themselves into the 'abyss' of urban poverty and unprecedented strangeness to learn at first hand something of that uncharted social territory, that 'unknown England' inhabited by the poorest of the poor.[1] Hankey's expedition to Bermondsey was consciously undertaken to test himself and to seek a 'cure' for self-centredness and class prejudice 'on the principle that if you want to make a boy swim, you should throw him into the water' (Budd, p. 66). An aspect of this desperate venture was Hankey's insistence that abnegation was merely a means to a further end. 'I want to be quite clear—and I think you understand,' he told his sister, '—that whatever I do I shall do for gain. I don't believe in asceticism or renunciation or anything of that sort' (Letters, p. 243).

But naturally this struggle to free himself from class involved complications. Hankey told his friend Bernard Hartley that living and working in Bermondsey had convinced him that 'an era is coming when "the gentleman" will no longer exist' (Letters, p. 234). A more conventionally sentimental or less honest man might have added, 'and good riddance!' but the fact was—though it stood in his way—that Donald Hankey's tastes in most things remained very decidedly those of a gentleman:

---

[1]Keating, P. (ed) (1976) *Into Unknown England, 1866–1913: Selections From the Social Explorers*. Fontana/Collins.

The thing which I feel prevents me working properly as a teacher of religion, or a priest, is that dress and gastronomics mean so much to me, to say nothing of immunity from the *necessity* to work, and from all discipline except what is self-imposed. This makes real sympathy with men of other classes difficult.

I value my education, my good taste, my ability to mix comfortably with the upper classes. I don't want to lose it.

(Letters, p. 253)

Indeed, a number of what he continued to regard as the distinctly gentlemanly attributes belonged, in his mind, among the essential Christian virtues: 'absence of self-consciousness, consideration of others, contempt of public opinion, and honour before life' (*Letters*, p. 235).

But surely Donald's uneasy sense of this inner conflict, which pitted his human sympathies against not only conventional standards of respectability but even his personal idea of a gentleman, touched upon still deeper issues. Somewhere at the heart of the matter, it appears certain, lay the question of whether and how his sexual nature could possibly be involved. The years we are now considering belonged to a time when the attitude of the English public towards homosexuality could be summarized, as E. M. Forster summarized it,[2] in two plain words: ignorance and terror (*Maurice*, 1971, p. 255). Forster, whose novel *Maurice* takes as its action date the year 1912, reveals the emotional climate of that period as an amalgamation of fixed and determined Englishness on the one hand and the particularly queasy after-effects lingering from the Wilde scandal of scarcely twenty years earlier. 'I

---

[2]Forster, E. M. (1971) *Maurice*. W. W. Norton & Company Inc.

doubt it,' responds another character whom Forster's eponymous hero has asked whether the law criminalizing homosexuality is likely ever to be changed. 'England has always been disinclined to accept human nature.' Then comes the clincher:

> Maurice understood. He was an Englishman himself.
> (Maurice, p. 211)

Homosexuality, Maurice himself admonishes a school chum early in the novel, is 'the only subject absolutely beyond the limit as you know, it's the worst crime in the calendar' (p. 59). But then the truth comes to him: 'I have always been like the Greeks and didn't know' (p. 65). Later, his struggle to overcome both ignorance and terror are tellingly contextualized in Maurice Hall's disclosure to a physician friend that 'I'm an unspeakable of the Oscar Wilde sort.' To which, of course, there is only one response a friend, a professional authority, and an Englishman can properly make: 'Rubbish!' (p. 159).

Whatever Barclay Baron may or may not be intimating in his characterization of Donald Hankey as 'a lonely man ... fighting a secret battle', his careful words about Donald's attachments among the Bermondsey working class suggest a sexual element, uncertain, unresolved, unacknowledged, not fully comprehended, perhaps on Donald's part all but entirely repudiated:

> After a few months he had left the residents' little colony and gone down the street to lodge in one of the most rickety and vermin-ridden courts with one of his married club officers. This was not done as a penance—he inveighed against that—but out of sheer affection. To this Tom Hewitt, ignorant, consumptive

and rheumatic, as to bed-ridden Tom Graves, he fully revealed himself and became to them all in all.

(The Doctor, p. 169)

Only one of Hankey's published letters is addressed to either Graves or Hewitt. The 'Dear Tom' of that letter, written 10–12 November 1912 while Hankey was *en route* to Australia, is identified by Miller the editor as Tom Graves (though it sounds as if it could have been written as appropriately to Tom Hewitt, especially with its reference to 'you and your wife'). It reveals genuine tenderness towards a sick man but does so in an idiom whose plainness seems somewhat studied and even condescending, suggesting a relationship of the sort Forster describes as 'precarious, idealistic and peculiarly English' (*Maurice*, p. 251):

> Just a line to let you know that I am getting on all right. I wanted to tell you that your friendship had meant an awful lot to me and that you have taught me some things which will make a difference all my life. If we do not meet again in this world, it will be my prayer that I may go to the same place as you in the next.

(Letters, p. 259)

Hankey's biographer devotes a certain amount of attention to Tom Graves and identifies him as 'a Bermondsey working-man and a friend of Donald Hankey' (Budd, p. 72), but he figures mainly as the protagonist in a touching and rather detailed story of how he forfeited his job in a tannery out of loyalty to his foreman by taking the blame upon himself for that other man's sloppy work (Budd, pp. 72–3). About Tom Hewitt Hankey's biography says nothing, though certainly Hewitt's was the 'little flat in a dull tenement house' where, in the spring of 1914, Donald wrote *The Lord of All Good Life* and which Hilda Hankey describes having visited in the company of a cousin. Hilda found Donald's sitting room light and pleasant, decorated with colourful and amusing mementos of his travels, but she was not shown his bedroom because it was cold and damp. Tom Hewitt is not mentioned by name; but in fact Hilda rather oddly identifies the man's role in that most unusual domicile:

> Here the Student [i.e., Hankey] lived like a lord—for Bermondsey! For he possessed two flats, one for his 'butler'—a sick-looking young man in list slippers, and his wife and family—and the other for himself.
> ('Something about "A Student in Arms",' in, *ASIA, II*, pp. 25-6)

In the week or so before Hankey penned the shipboard letter to 'Dear Tom', he wrote to Hilda two long and confiding letters (6, & 9 November 1911). There is a postscript in the first on the subject of 'marriage':

> To say the truth, the number of young women I have met who have any interest for me at all could be counted on the fingers of one hand. . . .
> I know that I think and read too much, and am not human enough. I know I do miss a lot by not enjoying dances, etc. But I think I am built that way.
> (*Letters*, 255)

In the second he thanks Hilda for having sent him H. G. Wells's book titled *Marriage*, and launches into a discussion of men and women (he had also been reading *Anna Karenina*) and from that to a comparison of himself to his brothers, with the emphasis on Hilda's favourite, Hugh:

I loved and admired Hugh ... who could never be an
example to me any more than a whole man could be
an example to a lame one.

(*Letters*, p. 257)

Then he confesses to Hilda 'how strongly I felt my personal
failure at Rugby and Woolwich':

> My whole life, from the day I went to Wathen's [day
> school] until the day I went to Oxford, was poisoned
> by the bitterness of feeling myself a failure, deservedly
> looked down on. It was that which made me so
> devoted to my pre-Oxford friends, X [which would be
> Browne] and Fleming. They saved me from despair by
> appreciating me in spite of my failure! That is why I
> could have married (at that time) any one who had
> buttered me!

(*Letters*, p. 258)

His brother Hugh's dashing, manly, chivalrous example
made Donald see all he himself did and was in the dim
light of inadequacy, of failure. The ever-competent and
dependable brother Maurice, less brilliant than Hugh, only
added firmness and weight to this burden. Marriage,
Donald is hinting to his sister, would under those circumstances have been a desperate refuge, a flight of self-decep-
tion. He adds what can be read as a more obscure yet
bolder hint:

> From the day I went to Oxford until the present day, I
> have been progressively more and more happy,
> because I know that I have been useful and that I have
> been loved.

There is an intensity in that which he himself almost
dismisses, yet he will not unsay it:

81

All this sounds awful; but it is the truth.
Your aff. brother,
Donald W. A. Hankey

The next day he writes his sentimental letter to Tom (Graves?) telling him their friendship 'will make a difference all my life'.

Despite indications it would be wilfully obtuse to overlook, there is hardly enough in the record to support firm and comprehensive conclusions about Donald Hankey's sexual inclinations, to say nothing of the nature of his attachments. But Donald's own perplexity and self-dissatisfaction regarding these matters are palpable. Ignorance, bewilderment, and anxiety are evident even in so well-disposed a young man; those qualities do appear in what he writes when it approaches the realm of sexual feeling. Easy about so many things, he was not at ease with himself concerning these feelings. Apparently his attraction to men who were far below him on the social scale was psychologically intertwined with his simultaneous compassion for the unfortunate and his envy of their seemingly freer ways. Somehow the transgression of class barriers may make achievable—or anyway make 'thinkable' as a kind of metonymy for it—the sexually risqué. Forster again (and Wilde himself) comes to mind, at this point in connection with the relationship between social disparity and sexual attraction. Hankey's penchant for disguise also belongs to these interrelated involvements with otherness—in the context of the repressive codes of social superiority. But at all events one cannot forget—because Hankey himself was unable to forget—that he was, in his own words, 'a gentleman branded'. He felt the cost of this, but it was not as if there were any real choice.

*

In recounting Hankey's announcement of his departure from Bermondsey for Australia in the summer of 1912, Barclay Baron makes it sound impulsive, even quixotic:

> ... he walked into the Warden's room with a typically abrupt, 'Well, I'm leaving.' To the dismayed rejoinder of, 'But why, Donald? We can't spare you,' he simply answered, 'Because I love this place too much—it's become self-indulgence and that's not good for me.'
>
> (*The Doctor*, p. 168)

But in the previous September Donald already seemed clear that his plan was to stay with the OBM for only the year, after which he would probably seek some hard physical work overseas (*Letters*, p. 234). His complaint at that earlier point had been that fits of depression, 'almost misanthropy', were spoiling his work at the Mission, not that his fondness for it made staying there a dangerous temptation. Donald's departure from Bermondsey fulfilled his previous intentions, but if Barclay Baron's account may be trusted he left in a spirit that may have surprised even him. Somehow life in Bermondsey had come to exert a claim on his personal feelings to which his conscience would not let him yield.

In any event, Donald was bound for Freemantle by mid-October 1912. He had several purposes in mind. One, perhaps foremost, was to experience physical work as he had found it difficult to do in England, where his manner and his Oxford accent were obstacles at every point. Then there was the scheme of establishing somewhere in Western Australia a training farm where lads from the alley-ways of Bermondsey, orphans perhaps, would be able to find a healthy environment and a hopeful way of life. Finally, and this was a fall-back alternative which in the end (and, to be sure, from the beginning) best suited Hankey's nature and gifts: he could turn to journalism and write about prospects in Australia for some publication at home.

The outback as a new beginning for refugees from the urban slums was by no means a novel idea at that time. Some local members of the OBM had tried it, and there was a growing literature on the subject to which Donald had ready access. Then too, Australia—though a world away—would not be entirely strange to him. It was his mother's birthplace, and his parents had met and lived some of their married lives there. Australian relatives had regularly visited the Hankeys in Brighton, and of course Donald looked forward to reciprocating. Much as he obviously liked being on his own it was an advantage, which other eligible places like Canada lacked, to have 'down under' close connections within relatively easy reach.

There was a degree of secrecy involved in Donald's plans for departure; he asked his Oxford friend Hartley to 'be discreet' as to whom he told. 'I must keep it dark until my escape is accomplished,' he wrote, with what to be sure may have been an air of mock stealth. But he was serious about not taking too many people into his confidence; his 'programme' included more things than he might actually succeed in accomplishing, 'and I don't want my failure to be public property!' (*Letters*, p. 240). Perhaps Donald felt that the less some of his close connections knew of his plans the better; to Hilda he expressed gratitude for her 'being so nice about the whole thing'. He concedes that his emigration is in some respects a selfish act. 'This year at Bermondsey has been an awfully happy one,' he tells her; but he goes to learn, to gain *more* of everything, which— paradoxically— he cannot get unless he does without 'a certain number of things for a time' (*Letters*, p. 243).

Comfort was certainly among those things Donald Hankey expected to live without when he took what he refers to as 'steerage accommodation' on SS *Zieten*. He guesses there must be 600 third-class passengers of whom he is one of the 109 who share the same sleeping quarters (*Letters*, p. 247). However, as he reports comically to Hilda, he found the others on board 'disappointingly aristocratic!' North country men are wearing their Sunday best; the 'lady' he sits next to at meals has made a hobby of economical world travelling. Having tricked himself out as a working man in bandana and denim trousers, Donald discovered himself to be 'almost the worst dressed person there!' (*Letters*, pp. 244–5). Nevertheless, by the time the ship had reached the Bay of Biscay Donald was finding the voyage 'a pretty unpleasant experience'. Many of those crowded together in common quarters were sick on the floor and the ship was too low in the water for the portholes to be opened for ventilation. He mentions, without apparent satisfaction, that among the hundreds of third-class passengers there are 'only half a dozen shots at gentlemen' (*Letters*, p. 247); in the heat the men's collars were coming off at a good rate. 'There are some *very* nice men and boys, though,' Donald admits. Among these admirable working types he mentions in two successive letters to Hilda 'a lovely little Cockney from Southwark', all pluck and humour and cheerfulness, with 'the ugliest face and awkwardest manner you ever did see' (*Letters*, pp. 247–8).

In the midst of all this 'very great mixture' (*Letters*, p. 254) Donald managed to write some of his most frank and thoughtful letters to his sister. He tells her of his last evening in London before leaving England, an amusing dinner with an unnamed friend whom Hilda would evidently know, on which occasion Donald surprised himself by talking unusually well. He reports having found his friend 'much improved by being really and truly in love, with apparently a very nice girl with a strong character' (*Letters*, p. 246). There follow thoughts on that familiar subject between Hankey and his sister: marriage. To many men—and to many women as well—marriage means what it was in St. Paul's eyes, he tells her: 'a renunciation of the heroic and an acceptance of the prosaic' (*Letters*, p. 246). It is rare that either partner finds in marriage a means of fulfilling individual aspirations, though when that happens, he concedes, it is 'about the best thing in the world' (*Letters*, p. 247). Some of these thoughts were nourished by his reading, apparently on Hilda's recommendation, of H. G. Wells's latest novel, *Marriage* (*Letters*, pp. 255, 260-61). That book would have illuminated for Donald how marriage tends to narrow the focus of many a man's life, concentrating his benevolent impulses upon affections and interests closest at hand. Marriage, Wells's novel warns, involves difficult choices that make the kind of selflessness Hankey admired all but impossible to achieve. It might of course result in an ideal alliance, the combination of qualities that leads to high and disinterested goals; but more certainly, so Wells suggests, marriage imposes an obligation to attend to the more immediate sphere of personal consequences. *Marriage* so captured Donald's interest that he finished it in a single day. It 'fitted in well' with his heavier reading: *Anna Karenina* in a French translation (*Letters*, p. 261). He is particularly struck by Levine's determination, in having been disappointed in love, 'to marry a peasant and become one' (*Letters*, p.256). It occurs to him that 'the combination of a man and a woman is really much more effective than either singly' (*Letters*, p. 261).

'Yes,' Hankey replies to something Hilda has written, 'you could have come with me, but you would have hated it.' The notion of Hilda and himself presiding over an Australian training farm for Bermondsey youths was to remain appealing. It might be a way to achieve Levine's declassé dream without the necessity of marriage, but he senses that would require too great a social adjustment for Hilda. 'To say the truth, I think that the difference between women of different classes is almost more marked than that between men' (*Letters*, p. 256).

Some way of achieving nobility of spirit that would incorporate honest humility—the essential qualities of Christianity—and to manifest such qualities in a classless, sexless romantic idyll seems to be the impossible nature of Hankey's personal vision at this point. The two ideal figures Donald mentions in these letters, written midway between home and his antipodeal destination, underscore that impossibility by being so decidedly creatures of invention—from the polar realms of popular fiction and personal mythology. One was Mr Peggotty from *David Copperfield*, a natural gentleman domiciled with his sister, whom Hankey cites as 'representative of a type [which] has been produced out of most unpromising material and in the most adverse circumstances' (*Letters*, pp. 251–2). The other is Hugh Hankey, or rather Hilda's heroic memory of their eldest brother, whom Donald himself claimed to have 'loved and admired' but 'always as a demi-god—a glorious being of another order.' The qualities of both these contrasting male exemplars were clearly beyond Donald's attainment: Mr Peggotty's precisely because his Dickensian simple-heartedness was inimitable, especially by a self-conscious and educated person like Donald Hankey; Hugh's, as his admiring youngest brother explains it, because 'a whole man could not be an example to a lame one' (*Letters*, p. 257).

How far Hankey would have been able to go in describing his own 'lameness' is impossible to say. He associates it, clearly, with what he calls 'my *negativeness*' (*Letters*, p. 257), by which he did not mean simply a dismal or pessimistic outlook. He identifies it with 'over-sensitiveness', a 'sense of failure', a 'need for philosophical consolations'. It stands in marked contrast to Hugh's (and Maurice's) success in 'becoming positive'; and Donald always felt drawn towards his other brother, the ever-shadowy Clement, as sharing some of his own negative nature. Certainly for Donald it meant a *lack* of something, some quality or capacity assumed to be a necessary element in male adequacy, something essential to a 'whole man'. Further than that Donald could hardly go, since he knew what was missing only by his sense of its absence. But it was the subject of marriage that brought on these references to 'a certain faculty or *je ne sais quoi*.' 'I think I must be without it,' he had written in his Oxford days. 'I never feel that way about people' (*Letters*, pp. 164–65).

*

Donald made his voyage in the company of Jack Reeves, 'a Bermondsey lad', the editor of the *Letters* notes, 'whom Hankey helped to settle in Australia.' He tells Hilda that Reeves 'is an excellent companion' (*Letters*, p. 244), and though Donald's references to him are few, Jack's presence must have stimulated the thinking about social class that is so evident in Hankey's shipboard letters to his sister. 'This voyage is doing a good deal of what I wanted,' he informs her, 'and I certainly do not regret it in the least' (*Letters*, p. 254).

When the *Zieten* docked in Ceylon, giving its passengers an interval on shore, Jack Reeves figured in what could have become a serious misadventure.

> We had a day in Columbo, and I got an attack of extravagance, and drove Jack out to Mount Lavinia, where we found most of the first-class passengers having tea on the lawn. I, however, was feeling extra-ordinarily good-tempered, and we carried it off very well.'
>
> (*Letters*, pp. 261–2)

So far, so good; but then the two young men resolved to go bathing in the surf and encountered 'a beastly current'. Donald discovered Jack could not swim. 'We were really within about ten aces of being drowned,' he informs Hilda; but, as he concludes his account of this 'bathing incident' with proper British *sangfroid*, 'I managed to make for some rocks, and got him on shore with no damage beyond a few scratches' (*Letters*, p. 262). During the war Hankey would repeatedly disparage his capacities as an officer, but this close call in the waters off Ceylon suggests he had some of the qualities required to lead men into battle.

Hankey's letters tell us little of the subsequent fate of Jack Reeves. After saving his life in Ceylon, Donald appears to have rather lost patience with his Bermondsey companion once they reached Australia. Other than a complaint to Hilda about an unnamed person who might well have been Reeves having turned out to be a disappointment, there is no mention of anyone resembling Jack until the following April. Hankey is describing to Hilda his travels to various points in Australia: 'The boy I told you about behaved very idiotically, loafing about towns and stowing away from port to port. I found him in Sydney last week, and sent him off to the Dreadnought farm with another stowaway. I hope he will stay' (*Letters*, p. 293).

Evidently Jack Reeves did not stay—at least his was not a permanent emigration. In the *Oxford and Bermondsey Mission Report* for 1918 his name appears on the 'Roll of Honour' along with that of Donald Hankey and 126 other *'fratres'* who were killed in the war.

In announcing his safe arrival in Western Australia, Donald declares at the outset that 'things have not turned out a bit as I expected' (*Letters*, p. 262, Perth, 5 December, to Hilda). That phrase, whether uttered hopefully or in dismay, sounds the key note of his entire adventure down under. To his surprise, he found a woman in charge of the labour bureau where Donald applied for assignment to some hard work in the bush. She sized him up as so patently English, and so much a 'gentleman', that no farmer or foreman would tolerate him. For the time being, so this lady advised, Hankey would do better camping out with half a dozen other men——evidently a group of freelancing workers-for-hire—doing as little or as much as suited him. His next few days must have been a trial of strength and spirit. By train and by bicycle, hastily equipped to cope with the desolation and heat of the bush in December, Donald found the work gang after what added up to some 90 miles of weary trekking. They were more unwelcoming than he could stomach, and he there-fore appealed to a homesteading couple who had given him tea the night before. Not only were 'Mr and Mrs L____' 'very charming', they were even 'very short-handed' (*Letters*, p. 266). Donald pitched his tent on the Ls' ground and became their hired hand.

Being taken up by the Ls was rare good luck for Donald Hankey. He found the hard work he wanted—nine-hour days full of it—and got to know two people whose strug-gles to make a farm in that desolate yet strangely beautiful wilderness won Donald's deepest admiration. Quickly this feeling focused upon the wife. Mr L, who had been a research chemist and left England in an effort to regain his health, had an interesting background and family connec-tion, but of him Donald has little to say. However, Mrs L, whom Donald describes as 'the kindest of women', rather surprisingly 'used to be a keen Church worker in Bermondsey' (*Letters*, p. 267). In her, so his letters both to and about her suggest, Hankey made a friend for life. He marvels at her burden of work, both within their shack of a house and wielding an axe clearing their fields. 'She has emerged unsoured and smiling from the life here,' Donald writes to Hilda in praise of Mrs L (*Letters*, p. 270).

In the same letter Donald reflects broadly on the aristocracy and the newer moneyed classes, on the failure of the landed gentry to understand the needs of an industrialized population, of the sources of 'Honour'–that prize virtue of 'gentlemen'–and the need to foster it as a corrective among the bourgeoisie, of the positive moral value in the 'cult of the useless' perpetuated by the public schools and the universities (*Letters*, pp. 269-70). As often happens to people finding themselves in a distant place, Donald's unfamiliar surroundings produce fresh thoughts from abroad. He sees some things about the social composition of his native country with a new clarity.

Hankey gives himself a holiday and catches the train to Freemantle for Christmas. Straight from the bush, and looking it, he is directed to an inexpensive hotel. It is late and being tired he does not entirely realize until morning what a disreputable place he is occupying, 'full of dirty plates, glasses, and linen' (*Letters*, p. 272). 'The result,' as Donald writes to his cousin Dorothy from the up-scale Palace Hotel in Perth on Christmas Eve, 'was, of course, reaction.' He buys some new clothes and luxuriates in the amenities of the 'Palace': a hot bath and some surprisingly good French cooking. He is feeling 'extraordinarily well' (*Letters*, p. 273) and can truly relish the rigours of farm life from the vantage point of this brief interval of self-indulgence. His pride in doing useful menial work by no means diminishes his appreciation of nice things and creature comfort (*Letters*, p. 296).

But Hankey did not view Australia uncritically, though his reservations are seasoned with characteristic humour. He quickly formed a dislike of Australian men ('They are beastly, cocksure, and dogmatic') and sounds a bit cocksure and dogmatic himself in pronouncing the remedy: '*There are not enough good women here*' (*Letters*, p. 274). 'Out of defiance,' as he puts it, he is attracted to the idea of being a parson among these people. 'I would like to flout all their ideals openly, and make them angry' (*Letters*, pp. 274–5). He is perhaps more serious in a letter written but never posted to the Bishop of Western Australia, whose Christmas day sermon Hankey heard during his holiday in Perth. It is not His Lordship's sermon that prompted this letter but rather features of the service which Hankey found by turns meaningless and unhelpful to the ordinary lay person. That he would have second thoughts about mailing such a letter is perhaps as characteristic of its author as the fact of his having written it; good manners and a taste for dispute were equally part of his nature. In any case, the incident shows that Donald's new surroundings had not distracted him from a customary preoccupation with the failings of his church.

Donald had earlier told Hilda that the opportunity of this sojourn to Australia was a lucky chance for him. Now he repeats those sentiments to his cousin Dorothy, mentioning the value of 'time in which to think and pray' and an urge to launch some major undertaking, 'whether by the pen or otherwise'. Its heat and flies notwithstanding, life in the bush could tempt him permanently, but he feels 'responsibilities elsewhere' and the condition of his liver requires a better diet (*Letters*, p. 284). From Kalgoorlie ('a perfectly beastly place') he writes more appreciatively of Australian men, their regard for the honour in hard work and contempt for dilettantes ('like myself, I fear') and for genteel ways and pretensions (*Letters*, p. 285). His reactions to both the country and its people continue to be mixed. Compared to Mauritius and Madagascar, Western Australia is savourless; 'an infusion of some O.B.M. spirit would do no harm.' That thought, however, is accompanied by the wish 'that something could be done for Bermondsey people with this cheap land.' As for his own future, Donald vacillates between the many challenges in London and staying in Australia. 'No doubt my course will be indicated. It generally is, if one leaves it alone' (*Letters*, p. 287).

After three months in the bush, Hankey began a series of excursions that made him more broadly acquainted with the country. As he travelled, he looked back on the prolonged experience of hard manual work and he read a life of Tolstoy that confirmed his conclusions about the value of simplicity in life but also the impossibility of fully escaping the influence of one's upbringing. Physically he did not claim much benefit, but he tells Hilda he found prayer easier and felt less of 'this fatal shallowness' (*Letters*, p. 289). It showed him, he admits, that such work is not what he is most fit for in the long run. The lesson of humility is to accept the limits of one's abilities and to make a contribution by working at what one does best. In his case, Donald supposed, that may well be writing, and he began a series of articles for English readers on 'Australian Life'. These appeared in the *Westminster Gazette* for successive weeks from 26 July to 29 August, 1913. Hankey's six articles address different aspects of English emigration to the Australian hinterlands. He said they were originally intended for the *Oxford Economic Review*, and it is evident Hankey was aiming at the kind of sober readership that would expect a knowledgeable, objective, and practical-minded treatment of the subject.

Hankey writes as an Englishman to his fellow English and he assumes a strong interest in empire. Australia ought to concern not only potential settlers but also any who value its links to the mother country. For English immigrants Australia offers great possibilities, Hankey emphasizes; but more than that, it poses a stern test of character. Cheap land is its appeal, but there is no quick and easy way to wealth; honest work, under conditions discouraging to any but the most resolute, is all that will succeed with either the land or its people. 'Australia will not get the right sort of emigrant until she advertises the difficulties as well as the opportunities of life on the land and ceases to paint everything *couleur de rose*'[3].

In the article titled 'The Population Question', Hankey puts forward a racial view that, however deplorable, is hardly surprising. He refers to a general opinion that the country should 'be adequately populated with a white race as quickly as possible in order that the white community already there may not be swamped by Asiatics' (1 August 1913, p. 1). 'As a Christian,' Hankey insists, 'I do not believe in the eternal antipathy of the different races of men,' and there is no reason to doubt the sincerity of his claim. He welcomes 'the time when all shall be one people in the Kingdom of God' and notes that 'many rationalists (i.e., non-believers) have a corresponding ideal.' The argument he offers for the urgency of white immigration is, of course, economic: he accepts as incontestable the proposition that Asians live 'at a cheaper rate' than Europeans; therefore, to avoid a decline in the living standard of the existing European inhabitants, their continued numerical dominance must be ensured. Hankey denies he is claiming that Europeans have 'superior standards', only that they cannot 'live as cheaply and frugally' as Asians. But he does argue that 'white people who believe that their civilization is the highest in the world and the best for humanity, are justified in trying to plant it securely in this great Continent where it is the first in the field.' Australians, at any rate, cannot be blamed for so believing; history must decide the issue (1 August 1913, p. 1).

The population of Australia, as Hankey considers it,

---

[3]Hankey, D. (1913) 'Australian Life ... I' *Westminster Gazette*, 26 July, p. 2.

poses two basic problems and offers two different solutions. Southern Europeans, who can better thrive in the climate, should be recruited for the tropical regions in the north, Hankey urges. He accepts the familiar assumption about northern races in the tropics, but includes a curious explanation that may have seemed cogent to him for personal reasons: It is not that Englishmen cannot work in the tropics but that they 'tend to become sterile' by living in that environment. 'Scientifically,' so he contends, 'the greater intensity of the ultra violet rays of the sun have a pernicious effect which nature neutralizes by means of the pigment in coloured races' (1 August 1913, pp. 1–2).

'I did not invent these views,' Hankey troubles to tell his readers. 'They were propounded to me by an Australian statesman who is not only a patriot but a scientist' (1 August 1913, p. 2). Whatever his source for such ideas, this claim of a 'scientific' connection between a tropical climate and lack of reproductive capacity amongst northern races living in the tropics might have seemed particularly plausible to the unscientific Donald Hankey. His health in more obvious ways had certainly been damaged during his time in Mauritius, and here was a welcome explanation for the absence of sexual appetite he had obliquely confided to Hilda. He had generalized it as an inability to *feel* strongly, puzzled over being 'devoid of a certain faculty' (*Letters*, p. 164), suffered a sense of failure he likened to lameness in the presence of whole men (*Letters*, p. 257), and accused himself of not being 'human enough' (*Letters*, p. 255). The notion that a tropical climate had inflicted upon Donald himself a kind of emasculation might serve as an explanation preferable to a burden of anxiety and guilt.

The more temperate regions of Australia did not require the importation of darker-skinned southern Europeans; there, as Hankey saw it, the problem was that Australia's need to settle its rural areas did not match well with England's urban surplus. Already Australian town workers were beginning to resent the influx of more highly skilled 'Pommies' of urban background and with urban skills. 'Townsmen who emigrate to Australia will not benefit the country, nor in most cases themselves'.[4]

With England's townsmen not wanted and her rural workers too few to spare, 'if Australia is to continue predominantly British,' Hankey asserts, 'it is to the boy that we must turn.' He means boys sixteen or thereabouts from the city slums, boys like those in the Decima and Dockhead Clubs, *fratres* of the Oxford and Bermondsey Mission. Hankey describes the hard and virtually hopeless conditions of their lives in the mean streets; he praises those salient virtues that survival under such conditions requires and in some respects promotes: 'infinite adaptability', cheerfulness, fierce loyalty, unfailing generosity.[5]

Subsequent articles in the series develop Hankey's other suggestions for Australian immigration. He recommends Australia to English public-school boys of the right sort, and *vice versa*. These are not to be confused with the 'Jackeroo'—slack young 'gentlemen' with little ambition and many bad habits, family 'black sheep' most likely, who have been shipped 'down under' by their families who are willing to pay expenses in the hope such young prodigals will gain maturity or at least keep out of harm's way. 'For this kind of "gentleman", needless to say, Australia has no use'.[6] But true English gentlemen, without snobbery and not averse to dirtying their hands, are a valuable import for the Commonwealth. Hankey tells of a farm hand who had

---

[4]Hankey, D. (1913) 'Australian Life ... II' *Westminster Gazette*, 1 August, p. 2.
[5]Hankey, D. (1913) 'Australian Life ... III'. *Westminster Gazette*, 8 August, p. 2.
[6]Hankey, D. (1913) 'Australian Life ... IV'. *Westminster Gazette*, 15 August, pp. 1-2.

risen to become a farmer himself lecturing him on the glories of Socialism but concluding by saying, 'mind you, a country without an aristocracy is no damn good' (15 August, p. 2). Claiming less authority concerning the prospects in Australia for women, Donald concedes that English domestic servants would have a difficult adjustment to more freewheeling ways, but suffragettes would thrive. Also he is confident that poor-law children would be well received.

After the initial article, the remaining five of Hankey's reports from Australia ran on the front page of the *Gazette* and were apparently a success. Their author is making an earnest attempt to contribute positively to British settlement in rural Australia and especially to the development of its potential as a better future for lads from England's teeming streets. Hankey is acting on his recently expressed conclusion that one helps most by working at things one is best fitted to do. Whatever might or might not come of later attempts to make a place for himself, and for needy youths, in this forbidding yet appealing land, he will at least have spoken from authentic if limited experience and had his honest say.

Hankey's attempt to know Australia and to decide what part it might play in his future took him to many places: Sydney, Brisbane, Adelaide, Broken Hill. The country gives him a new perspective on his conventional social instincts and on how religion has prevented these from dominating him. Writing to Hilda, who is soon to meet him in Australia and accompany him home, he refers—not for the first time—to his tendency to be 'cautious and unenterprising' and 'to keep within the indicated restriction of convention and caste.' But his religion—which was never so much the church itself as it was his mother's example of acting on one's principles—has always had a 'widening influence' on him. This conflict between a cautious nature and more daring beliefs has at times involved painful struggle; but the results, Donald puts it decisively, 'were far beyond my wildest dreams'. Bermondsey, he says, brought him unhoped for happiness and friendship—and he is not thinking of his fellow Oxford missionaries. Australia, however, has presented a harder challenge; he feels he has struck a bedrock of social prejudice in his nature with which he had to compromise (*Letters*, pp. 293-4). The nature of this impasse is suggested in a letter from Brisbane to his cousin Dorothy admitting that 'conventions hinder'. There are 'Bermondsey fellows' in Adelaide he wants to meet 'in a perfectly friendly way and on equal terms'. But he will be accepting hospitality with his mother's relatives there; and, as he flatly writes, 'it can't be managed' (*Letters*, pp. 298-9).

Having confronted the limits of his 'adaptability', Donald declares himself prepared for ordination. 'If I can first write a book with my layman's freedom I shall be ready if they will have me' (*Letters*, p. 294). But still he puzzles over the question 'whether the donning of a clerical coat' will mean the end of his effort to escape from those confining instincts of caste. The conditions of his own nature are one thing, the requirements of the church another: 'I *don't* want to be even the best of conventional parsons' (*Letters*, pp. 295-6).

Returning to the Ls' farm from his travels, Donald finds the place transformed by the season and by some welcome improvements. The dusty ploughed land is now green with springing crops, the well is in operation, and Mr. L has built Donald a little 'bush humpy' with an iron roof to replace his tent. 'These quiet times in remote places appeal to me no end. One can do such a lot of thinking' (*Letters*, p. 295). He cannot finally abandon the freedom he feels with these people and in this out of the way place.

Hilda arrived in July; presumably Donald met her boat

and they spent much of the time before their departure together visiting relatives. He did not take Hilda to the Ls' homestead near remote Tootiken. No doubt the difficulty for the Ls in accommodating such a guest ruled out their meeting, but as if to compensate somehow for even so blameless a social slight, Donald does share with Mrs L the admission that 'I find staying with relatives extremely trying.' Within the constraints of a letter he attempts to tell her something straight from the heart: '[I] long for the freer life in Bermondsey or Tootiken.' The conventional gentleman in Hankey will not allow him to let that juxtaposition of squalid Bermondsey and the Ls' farm stand unqualified, so he adds in parentheses: '(pardon the comparison! They are only alike in that one respect)' (*Letters*, p. 301).

Donald's letter to her from Broken Hill (enclosing some photos he took in Tootiken) mentions his possible return to Australia 'in eighteen months'. 'Perhaps,' he adds lightly, 'as curate of Noora preparatory to being rector of Merriden, and finally Bishop of Adelaide!' (*Letters*, pp. 300–301).

But on 1 September, as the SS *Macedonia* takes him further from that farm in the bush, Donald writes again to this kind woman asking her if he could revisit the Ls for a month the next September. On his way home the plan for his future has been revised to include a preparation for the ministry in the form of a couple of months working in the mines at Broken Hill, preceded by 'some really hard axe work' on his friends' Tootiken farm to toughen his hands and muscles (*Letters*, p. 301).

Brother and sister stopped briefly in Ceylon and had a more extended visit to Mauritius, staying in the 'Government House'. Along with showing Hilda around the colony, Donald found time to preach a sermon on Dr John Stansfeld and the Oxford and Bermondsey Mission. That part of London would be his home for the first seven months of

1914, and he was turning his thoughts in that direction and to the book he wanted to write in an atmosphere free from social constraints and his future vows to the church. His cousin Dorothy had sent him some remarks on ordination, and from Mauritius he responded. He takes a positive and determined view of the ministry; it is a matter of the opportunity a person has for teaching 'an idea of what Christianity aims at being', also of the prestige and authority of the church. In another eighteen months— Hankey is thinking of the time he needs to write his book and to revisit Australia—he hopes to stand for something, to *be* something 'not generally found in the ranks of the clergy'. Within those ranks, however, Hankey feels he will have access, as an official part of the comprehensive church, to 'a full and many-sided "body of Christ"' to which no individual can singly aspire. Yet that fullness implies a crucial, even a predominant role for the laity, he tells Dorothy, if it is truly to embody the true idea of Jesus as 'the Lord of *all* good life' (*Letters*, pp. 304–5).

Hankey had thus come upon the title of his book; that was a commitment and at least a beginning. This same letter from Mauritius—the scene of his initial illumination— also voices what will be that book's basic assumption concerning the grounds of meaningful belief: 'All the *really* important doctrines of Christianity are expressions of experience and are amenable to proof or disproof by experiment.' This is Donald Hankey's version of the pragmatism he had appropriated from William James. Take the 'fundamental doctrine' of loving one's neighbour as oneself:

The only way of proving or disproving this is to try to love one's neighbour and see whether as we achieve that we do not also achieve a power of faith and a power to pray. ... To sum up, I hold that 'It doesn't matter what you believe unless it's going to alter your whole view of life.'

(Letters, pp. 305-307)

At least the bare outlines of Hankey's course of action, the future direction of his life, seem laid out at last: a return to Bermondsey, concentrated work on a book that will freely develop his most essential religious thoughts, a period—perhaps as much as a year—of a workingman's life in Australia while the church decides the issue of his ordination. In line with those plans, as he explains to Mrs L, he will leave England to return to Australia early in the coming August. However, that fateful month was to bring something unanticipated to Donald Hankey—and to several million other souls. 'But of course,' as Donald adds in that letter to Mrs L, '*"l'homme propose, Dieu dispose"*' (*Letters*, pp. 301-2).

5

Out of Dark Shadows (1914)

Donald Hankey's published *Letters*, the primary source of
what can now be known of his life and character, includes
nothing from the time between his return from Australia
and his enlistment in the army at the outbreak of war in
August 1914. No letters survive from the more than nine
months during which Hankey produced the book he felt
he was born to write and his life took one of its most
decisive turns.

They were, to be sure, busy months in which he may
have had little time for letter writing. His urge for self-
expression was being satisfied to a large degree by the
book on Jesus and the church that was now pouring out of
him. And in any case his sister Hilda—kindred spirit, confidante, and correspondent-in-chief—was close at hand. Not
as close as either may have wished, but near enough to
make many letters seem hardly necessary. The two must
have been in touch by telephone or even 'wire', nor would
Donald have denied himself time away from his writing and
his duties with the Bermondsey Mission to frequent Hilda's
home out in comfortable Kensington. Hilda herself, when
their cousin Dorothy could accompany her, occasionally
ventured upon the alien fascinations of her brother's
adopted neighbourhood and gathered first-hand impressions of his self-imposed exile. Nonetheless, it is hard to
imagine Donald Hankey writing no letters of substance—to
Oxford friends like Hartley, to absent members of the

Oxford and Bermondsey Mission, to 'Mrs L, Tootiken, Western Australia', or to his other siblings and close relatives–in the spring and early summer of that fateful year.

His voyage home in the company of Hilda had been punctuated by visits to Ceylon, Mauritius, and Madagascar. Donald needed a period of relaxation and self-indulgence after the rigors of the bush and so drastic a separation from the creature comforts he admitted having missed rather more than he expected. He also needed a carefree time to brace himself for a return to Bermondsey and a resumption of his life working evenings at the Decima Club, teaching Bible classes, rubbing elbows with poverty and squalor, and renewing friendships with some of the club members, friendships that more than anything else brought him back to that part of south London. Moreover, it was as if he was drawing a long and easy breath of sea air before settling down to work on the book he had been promising himself he would write when he felt ready. Now was the time.

It would not have taken Hankey long to pick up his work with the Oxford and Bermondsey Mission where he had left it to visit Australia. The residents from Oxford were an earnest and close-knit group, and though Donald always stood apart from them, they valued his way with the boys– not so much in their more boisterous activities but in their quieter, more receptive moods. During this second period of residence in Bermondsey Donald did not live settlement-fashion with the university contingent, others of whom had by this time also decided to live less separated from their Bermondsey neighbours, in smaller groups or singly. Hankey's address was 196A Weston Street, a short walk down Elim Street or Long Lane, through a narrow alleyway, and into Decima Street where his boys' club was located. Hilda has described the lodgings he shared with Tom Hewitt and his family, Donald's sitting-room appearing pleasant and cheerfully decorated with dancing shields from East Africa, 'barbaric looking' dolls (nearly naked) from Madagascar, brass ornaments from Ceylon, and some of his own watercolours (*ASIA, II*, p. 26). Hilda found nothing unsuitable in what she saw of her brother's arrangements, though, as she noted, they were a far cry from her own 'sunny little sitting-room ... looking on to a leafy back garden in Kensington, where Donald often sat and smoked and wrote' (*ASIA, II*, p. 25).

Busy as he was with weekday evenings in the Decima Club, Sunday services at the Mission, and miscellaneous charitable duties around the neighbourhood at odd times, Hankey was still able to give concentrated effort to thinking through the subject of his book, with the result that finally, as he puts it, 'in a burst, in six weeks, without any consultation of authorities or any revision to speak of' (*Letters*, p. 321) he completed *The Lord of All Good Life*.[1] The genesis of this work went back a long way in Hankey's young life, perhaps as far back as his struggle with religious doubt in Mauritius, certainly to his theological studies and discussions with other students at Oxford, and to his disappointing experience at the Clergy School in Leeds, as well as much subsequent thought derived from both Bermondsey and the bush about the condition of the Church of England. More immediately, it was the product of his work with the boys in the Decima Club of the OBM whom he was preparing for confirmation. After much seemingly futile effort, the writing in that brief interval came easily to Donald and he obviously took much pleasure in the experience itself. As for the finished work, in spite of his natural modesty he made no

---

[1]Later Donald described it as 'an attempt to express in simple language and for simple people a Modernist Gospel'. Hankey, D. et al., (1916) *Faith or Fear? An Appeal to the Church of England*. Charles H.S. Matthews (ed)., p. 15. Macmillan and Company, Ltd.

secret of his pride in it. 'The book I regard as my child,' he wrote to a friend. 'I feel quite absurdly about it; to me it is a sudden vision of what a lot of obscure things really meant. It is coming out of dark shadows into—moonlight' (quoted by Hilda in *ASIA, II*, p. 24).

Published by Longmans, Green and Company in October of 1914, *The Lord of All Good Life* bears the subtitle, 'A study of the greatness of Jesus and the weakness of His Church.' As that suggests, Hankey's book divides into two parts; no doubt it is the first half, a simple but not unimpressive consideration of Jesus's life, character, and moral authority, that owes most to Donald's attempts to make sense of Christianity for a number of adolescents from the tenements and back streets of south London. The result may not be a sophisticated essay in Christology, but neither is it merely a young persons' guide to the brave and loving nature of Jesus. Making a convincing case to street-savvy boys in the Decima Club was, after all, no mean challenge for any Christian apologist. An account of Jesus that could command the serious attention and lively sympathy of such an audience might not be subtle or learned, but it would have to measure up to a fairly exacting standard of intellectual honesty, clarity, and common sense. Obviously, Hankey believed that was an appropriate standard for the book he dedicated 'to the laity of the Church of England'. 'It is,' he confesses, 'the book of a nobody—of the obscurest of laymen. It has no weight of scholastic or ecclesiastical fame behind it' (1914, p. 7). His aim is 'to think clearly' even if the result is unorthodox or perhaps heretical, in the belief that such thoughts are shared by great numbers of ordinary church members, earnest and open-minded, who have little relish for controversy or respect for dogma. He speaks to and for those who, in Hankey's words, 'feel that in Jesus Christ and in His Church, and at the quiet service on a Sunday morning early, there is power and love and life for which they are in sore need' (1914, p. 7). (The page numbers in brackets here are all from this edition.)

Part I, titled 'Jesus of Nazareth: His Life and Work', consists of thirteen short lesson-like chapters that seek to regard Jesus from a reasonable but receptive point of view—*without prejudice*, in so far as that might be possible, as to the nature of His divinity or the supernatural elements in His story. As the Lord of all good life, the dominion and appeal of Hankey's Jesus is broad, by no means limited to those whose belief is narrowly literal. It is not, for Hankey, a question of what Christian faith obliges one to affirm about Jesus, but rather what acceptance of Him as Lord entails and makes possible in the effort to live what may be called a truly good life. Predictably therefore, he side-steps questions concerning the status of miracle, particularly the central one of Resurrection; more surprisingly, perhaps, he makes no reference at all to the Christmas story, with all its power of sentiment and richness of symbol. Hankey's first chapter on 'The Birth of the Lord Jesus and His Growth' will only say that what can be supposed of Jesus' early life must be inferred from what we see of Him later (p. 15). As 'a common village boy, and yet a boy apart,' the central fact about the young Nazarene, what distinguishes Him from other children, was His love of God, His absolute acceptance of God as His Father. Unlike others, it was not hard for Him to be good, but He saw this was not so for others (p. 16).

The portrait of Jesus that Hankey offers, then, is not built upon miracle, though it by no means overlooks the presence of mystery. The depth of His impression upon Simon, 'who, though he was older than Jesus, loved Him with a love he simply could not express' (p. 17), and the conviction of John the Baptist at the sight of Jesus point to powers that defy ordinary explanation. Hankey's concern, however, is not to explain those powers but to note how Jesus understood them: not as the basis for a grandiose personal claim, but as the sign He was called to a particular Work. 'He was the Son of God. He believed it. But all that that meant was that with a son's obedience, and with a son's confidence, He would be about His Father's business' (p. 24).

That business was broadly to prepare the way for the Kingdom, which Hankey makes clear involved Jesus's saving gifts, distinct yet inseparable: His teachings and His example. Hankey's book does not expound Jesus's teaching at great length; there is another Book, a sure and comprehensive guide, where these are preserved. Mainly he seeks to underscore an essential theme of those teachings: 'that the unseen was more real than the seen, the spirit than the flesh' (p. 26). Jesus's message about the nature of the Kingdom, unlike that of other prophets, incorporates that fundamental idea: it is not of this world, yet neither is it something far off, since He spoke as one who already possessed it. Those who enter the Kingdom and experience the joys of its new life do so by means of faith, love of God, humility and purity (p. 32). It is not the realm of the prig or the snob, not a narrow and exclusive place of a narrow coterie of the Select or Chosen. For the person of true faith the world becomes much bigger, he is 'a citizen of the great world, an inheritor of the earth in the fullest sense' (p. 39). As for purity, Hankey insists, 'it is not the same as conventional morality,' not a code of respectable behaviour but 'a quality of the heart' (p. 39). Donald's generous sense of Jesus's teachings affords little sympathy for those whose self-proclaimed purity is their justification for condemning human weakness and misdeeds born of misfortune. 'There are many cases where theft of a straightforward kind should trouble the conscience of society more than that of the thief' (p. 40).

Hankey explicitly contrasts his picture of Jesus with Swinburne's 'pale Galilean', a Lord of stern prohibitions and life-sapping repressions. Jesus' true power consists, in Hankey's words, of 'The Holy Energy of Love' (p. 41), not a negative but a positive force, 'more than a mere shrinking of the sensitive and aesthetic soul' (p. 40).

The authority of Jesus's teachings, and also their efficacy, derive from the perfection of His character. Its corner-stone, Hankey finds, is Jesus's love of God, which implies absolute trust. So the temptations Jesus overcame in the wilderness reduce to that one all prophets face: the temptation to require some 'objective sign', to seek the validity of His calling not in perfect faith but in His own demonstrated powers (p. 24). The mark of complete and loving trust is humility, the opposite of the false prophet's 'blasphemous self-assertion' (p. 24). Further, the truth of what Jesus said— His teachings and the assumptions on which they rest—is 'proved', Hankey contends (following the 'pragmatic' test he had adapted from William James), by the quality of the result produced. This 'result' was nothing less than 'a character more noble, more admirable, more potent to inspire love and devotion, more free, more harmonious, more complete than any other in the history of the world' (p. 43). One might object to a certain circularity in the argument: We affirm the principles because they produced a perfect individual whose perfection we credit because they reflect these principles. But Hankey's assumptions concerning Jesus—assumptions having to do not with the alleged facts of His life but with qualities associated with His presumed personality—are, after all, the assumptions on which Hankey's entire position rests.

Few indeed would find the Jesus who emerges from the pages of Part I of *The Lord of All Good Life* anything but appealing. It is a comfortable rather than a particularly penetrating, original, or unsettling characterization, entirely in keeping with Hankey's declared purpose 'to set down what he believes a great many people think' (p. 7). Part II, his account of the church's failure to live up to its ideal definition as 'the body of Christ', is a more prickly performance and reveals a side of Donald Hankey that was all but glossed over in the adulation accompanying his posthumous renown as 'A Student in Arms', author of that pious piece of hero-worship 'The Beloved Captain'. Hankey had a serious case to make against the established church and wished to state it publicly as a layman (and, as it turned out, as a soldier in the ranks) before taking the plunge of seeking ordination. He still believed his future lay in that direction, and in fairness to both himself and the church he wanted to make it clear by his analysis of that church's weakness just what sort of clergyman, if given the chance, he would become. 'Of all Churches, save the Church Catholic and Invisible,' he was to write early in 1916, 'I am a discontented critic' (*OBM Annual Report for 1915*, p. 14).

Hankey imagines the church as an organism, drawing its life from the great heart of Christ ever beating at its centre. But His life-giving blood cannot circulate freely; the various organs and members of the body that is the church 'fail to work in harmony with each other, and many seem numb and dead' (p. 102). Hankey applies this metaphor to Christendom as a whole, but his discussion of 'the Church: Its Ideal, Its Failure and Its Future' is directed 'with special reference to the Church of England.' Elaborated in the subtitle of this part of his book is Hankey's claim for it as 'the orthodoxy of a heretic, and the catholicism of a Protestant'. There is rather a lot contained in these words. To begin with, the English church itself is, from one point of view, an orthodoxy, yet to the Papal church it is heretical. Hankey's church may be considered historically Protestant, but the faith it affirms is ultimately universal, 'catholic'. On either side of these opposing pairs is the ideal church (the church as the true body of Christ) on the one hand and on the other the actual church, which fails and falls short of that ideal. Beyond that—and more clearly in line with Hankey's critical intention—the paradoxes he cites apply to him personally in his relation to that church. He acknowledges that his opinions, both in some matters of belief and in respect to the conduct of the church, make him an outsider; yet he feels in harmony with everything the church ideally represents. He is adopting the role of a 'protester'; but in so doing he advocates the church's proper 'catholicism', its claim to belong to everyone who accepts it.

Christianity, for Hankey, is not doctrine but *spirit*, the acceptance of Jesus's example and authority in pursuing a good life. Such a 'truly Christian spirit' is often to be found, he notes, more in the streets than in the churches and chapels, which cater to the rich and respectable. Consequently, all are not equally welcome in God's house, and like the Pharisees many within the church have made the mistake of confusing respectability with holiness. 'In short, English Protestantism fails to embody the personality of Jesus Christ' (p. 106).

In contrast to a true catholic inclusiveness, Protestantism, as Hankey sees it, seeks to separate the wheat from the chaff by applying the tests of 'orthodoxy', 'respectability', 'loyalty', and 'clothes'. The laws and conventions of society are its criteria; but such 'morality' is not holiness, it is negative as holiness is positive. 'Morality is ice, holiness is fire' (p. 108).

Hankey includes a fairly standard criticism of Roman Catholicism. It is a church of dogma, of the philosophizing of Christianity, of vestigial paganism; it teaches 'many things that have no relation to experience or life' (p. 114); 'in trying to include the world [Catholicism] became

110

worldly' (p. 117). However, those reservations do not overshadow his admiration for that church's embrace of the full social spectrum. This admiration points up Hankey's indictment of his own church: its failure effectively to transcend the English class system. When he writes that, in order to be more of a living limb of the body of Christ, Protestantism must be made more catholic, Hankey is thinking not doctrinally but socially (p. 109). Even his objections to liturgical practice have their basis in his passion for making Christianity more truly accessible to the poor and more meaningful in their everyday lives, so that the church would belong to them as much as to those who presently dominate it.

> If the services and teaching of the Church were made more simple and practical, it might cease to be ruled by the upper classes.
>
> (p. 147)

Hankey notes the church's partiality to hymns using the language of warfare and other reflections of the church militant. But in such calls to arms there is vagueness as to the nature of the enemy. He enumerates the enemies that Jesus knew: 'meanness and cant, callousness and cruelty, coarseness and lust, tradition and conventionality, riches and class pride, physical and moral cowardice' (p. 144). Familiar as it may be, the list reveals the essence of Hankey's particular outlook, the natural way he incorporates with vices and social evils those elements of life, usually regarded as morally neutral, that seem to him complicit in the panoply of human wickedness. It is his way of suggesting the true enemy is within the church itself and especially within its privileged ranks. 'The Church as a whole is interested in the preservation of class distinctions, of the rights of property, of traditions and

111

conventions' (p. 146). Its endorsement of or virtual identity with an upper-class ethos results in the church's sentimental and essentially unchristian view of poverty:

> We are willing to do things for the poor; but we are not willing, we are shocked and grieved, when the poor try to do something for themselves. As soon as labour begins to organize itself our sympathies are alienated.
>
> (p. 146)

Hankey never fully overcame the prejudices of his own upper-middle-class; he could not stomach Shaw, much less more radical socialists. So his welcome to organized labour as an ally in the fight against Christ's real enemies is all the more striking:

> We may legitimately think that our ally is not always wise; but we ought at least to appreciate the fact that it is an ally, and that in intention it is on the side of the angels.
>
> (p. 146)

His personal situation, as a son of privilege and a potential priest himself, played into Hankey's criticism of the clergy. His conclusion that 'the Church must cease to be identified with one particular class before it can be free to fight' (p. 147) leads him to regard the social status of the clergy as the crux of the problem.

As things stand, priests are expected to be gentlemen and this must somehow change. The ideal of a genuinely classless clergy would require a rule of celibacy, since it is his opinion that marriage inevitably makes a man a member of a particular class. But to look at the matter realistically, Hankey believes, is to abandon such an ideal: 'We cannot

112

contemplate a celibate clergy, for that means an immoral clergy or an inhuman clergy' (p. 148). Consequently, the best alternative would be a conscious policy of recruiting from the widest possible range of the social spectrum in order to achieve at least a balanced representation if not a truly classless ideal. 'We are convinced that it is only by having a clergy of all classes that the Church can escape from identification with a particular class,' he asserts (p. 148). He is offering here a prospect for the Anglican clergy that would be a kind of ecclesiastical extension and application of the example Donald and his associates were forgeing in the Oxford and Bermondsey Mission.

Part II of *The Lord of all Good Life* addresses other matters of Christian belief and practice—the evil of war, the inhuman cruelty of legal imprisonment, a relaxing of the church's position on divorce, the meaning of Jesus's sacrifice as 'the Way of Salvation'—but Hankey's dominant concern is his advocacy of a church free of the blight of class discrimination. In the process of reform in that direction, Hankey concedes there may be a loss of 'social influence'; but that would be a temporary loss for the sake of a more desirable good, an ultimate gain in freedom. In the meantime, for all its present bodily weakness, the heart of the church, the love of Jesus, remains for those who humbly seek it, a source of life and strength ('Conclusion').

As Donald worked these ideas into his book, life in Bermondsey and its Mission became increasingly absorbing. Hilda was astounded by the variety of her brother's activities. She mentions a 'multifarious list of duties that left me breathless when I saw it' ('About a Student in Arms', *ASIA*, *II*, p. 27). And as he found himself more useful to the Mission and its club life, more deeply engulfed by the life of the neighbourhood, and more truly fulfilled by his writing, Donald began to experience a feeling he had not known since the death of his mother: in this formerly alien

113

and repulsive slum world he was feeling himself at home. So much is clear from what Donald wrote later–as a commissioned officer–for the 1915 *OBM Annual Report*, by way of a brief tribute to the Mission and its place in Bermondsey:

> The Colonel tells us that the Mess is our home. It isn't mine. . . . Home is the place which one dreams about: the place where one hopes to end one's days. ... If anyone asks me where my home is, what part I come from or where I belong, I answer 'Bermondsey.'
> (*OBM Annual Report*, 1915, pp. 13-14)

One of the things that must have added to his pleasure as a diversion from both his book and the Mission was another fortuitous outlet for his writing. Barclay Baron, by this time the Warden of the OBM, became editor of *The Challenge*, a liberal Church of England magazine that began publication on 1 May 1914. Baron drew upon the talents of some of his fellow OBM members for the first numbers of that journal– Alec Paterson, already making his mark in prison reform, Alfred Ollivant, author of *The Royal Road* and *Owd Bob*, and Donald Hankey. *The Challenge*, as its name suggests, sought to throw down the gauntlet to more traditional elements of the church. This aggressive if not adversarial stance may be seen as part of a general surge of rebellious energy that showed itself among young Englishmen in the spring and summer of 1914, before the outbreak of war in August.[2] But spirited as it was, in its own terms, Barclay Baron's *Challenge* would rank rather low on the scale of belligerence compared to something like Wyndham Lewis's *Blast*, which appeared the following month.

---

[2]See Hynes, S. (1990) *A War Imagined* pp. 7-10, London.

Donald contributed to 'The Open Forum' a letter on poverty and the clergy ('Holy poverty is a great power, compulsory poverty is not') and published a report on the condition of 'The Church in the Australian Bush'. He must also have been an author of a mildly playful piece published under the name 'Donald Alers' in a series devoted to 'The Church beyond the Seas'. The item in question is titled 'The Kikuyu at Home' (22 May 1914). 'Alers' was of course the family name Donald shared with his siblings, and this clearly seems to have been Hankey's work, drawing as it does on the kind of experience he had in British East Africa and reflecting his interests and sentiments. The tone is facetious, flippant, even stained by racial insensitivity. One can imagine Hankey, along with Barclay Baron himself, and other young Oxonians indulging in some sophomoric high-jinks under the solemn camouflage of the church periodical 'Barkis' was editing—perhaps supplying last-minute 'filler' for its pages.

So as Donald's time in Bermondsey extended into that 'golden summer of 1914' which Englishmen who survived The Great War would long recall, some as a poignant goodbye to all that, some as the fading of a cruel illusion, he was among friends. Though never entirely gregarious, he took an active part with Barclay Baron and Alec Paterson in conducting confirmation classes and in other good works. Added to the satisfactions of having spoken his mind in a book that was being published, a book that truly pleased him, these were moments to savour. Donald, however, was restless. His promise to return to Australia, pledged to himself and mentioned in his correspondence with Mrs L, became a resolve and he booked passage for an August sailing. In the summer of 1914 Donald believed his quest for a less selfish, more genuinely sacrificial bond with people far below his own social status had to take him elsewhere. That, indeed, was how things were to turn out,

115

but in no way that Hankey as he prepared to sail again for Australia could possibly have foreseen.

Early August found Donald Hankey on the South Downs in Sussex, by himself and probably dressed as a farm labourer. This habit of occasionally disguising his class status—a form of 'going native'—we have seen before. The night he spent in a casual ward 'dressed up as a tramp' (*ASIA, II*, p. 157) was, as Donald himself intimates, a crucial instance; the voyage to Australia as a steerage passenger had involved a more extended change of identity. He was known to seek occasional escape from his OBM colleagues and the boys at the Decima Club by 'dressing rough' to lose himself in the country. The fruit harvest was coming on and casual workers were needed. In any case, Hankey thought he was leaving England soon and he must have wanted, as a kind of secret goodbye, to connect himself with its rural beauty. It had been one of his chief delights as a child to ramble in what he called 'the country of my boyhood' near Brighton (*Letters*, p. 362). The neighbourhood of Stoughton in Sussex would have been close, without being too close for his purposes, to these childhood haunts. In that village Donald somehow got the news of England's declaration of war against Germany and Austria-Hungary. He cancelled his booking to Australia and—at some point having applied for an army commission—on Friday, 7 August he walked to Chichester and caught the train for London. Budd quotes the plain but excitement-charged account in Donald's journal for that day:

Find that Kitchener has called for a hundred thousand recruits under thirty [Donald qualified under that limit, but by less than two months]. Decide to apply. Dare not withdraw application for commission till accepted lest fail in medical. Inspect recruiting offices. Hopeless

116

crowd. Some been there all day without getting in. Dine at Club.

(Budd, p. 98)

Of course that was Donald's posh gentlemen's club, not the boys' club he helped to manage; and it is significant that the call to arms brought him not immediately back to Bermondsey but away from it. Presumably, he might have enlisted in the Queen's 22nd Regiment, popularly known as the 'Bermondsey Boys', with whom many members of the OBM, prominent among them Alec Paterson, marched off to war. Several factors must have contributed to Hankey's line of action. His immediate application for a commission suggests the influence, direct or more subtle, of his elder brother Maurice, now a Lieutenant-Colonel in the Royal Marines and—more importantly—since 1912 Secretary of the Committee of Imperial Defence. When it came to military service, Donald quite naturally looked to family tradition and his own personal experience, which meant accepting the responsibilities of a commissioned officer—accepting, so to speak, the role usual for patriotic gentlemen. Also, as the journal entry quoted above makes clear, a commission would remain an option in the event that his dodgy liver prevented him from passing the medical examination for enlistees and joining the rank and file.

But none of these considerations can explain why Hankey, once he decided to take the king's shilling, did not make of his enlistment a more direct gesture of comradeship with his Bermondsey cohort. It is as if he was merely carrying out in a new direction the separation he had supposed would take him to Australia. It seems an instance of Hankey's penchant for the harder, less likely alternative that he would reject both the possibility of a commission and the familiar company he would surely have found

117

among the Bermondsey Boys. At 6 a.m. on Saturday, 8 August Hankey again presented himself at the recruiting office in Whitehall. He disliked revealing the facts of his past, but he hated still more lying about them. The examining doctor wondered aloud why such a man, a university graduate and a product of a military academy, with honourable service as a subaltern overseas, would not prefer to accept a commission. 'Gentleman Rankers', as Kipling referred to men from public schools and universities who enlisted as common soldiers, though far from unheard of, were generally considered a particularly strange lot. By 11:30 that morning Donald Hankey's enlistment was complete. He became a private soldier in the 7th Battalion of the Rifle Brigade and withdrew his application for a commission.

Given the extreme needs of the new army Lord Kitchener was raising, previous military experience such as Hankey's marked him at once. Within a week he was given the rank of sergeant. At the recruiting office he had explained that 'as possible parson I want experience in ranks', and no doubt it would have suited him to remain a private. But Donald did not mind his sergeant's stripes. Perhaps his age and manner seemed less odd in a non-commissioned officer, and though unfamiliar with infantry units he felt as competent as most NCOs in drilling his men. The important thing was that he remained with the ranks, not consorting with other gentlemen in the officers' mess but essentially among the lads. He had what he wanted: he was counted among ordinary people and shared most of their common hardships and extremities, yet he could also assert a degree of leadership and guidance. Below the officer class at least, this was a citizen army, in fact a predominantly proletarian one. Within the rigidities of military discipline Hankey could feel relatively free of the taint of personal condescension in setting an example and in giving help and counsel and even comfort. From many standpoints this was better than managing a boys' club in Bermondsey. Naturally, he could not ignore the regular role the army required of him as a sergeant; but with luck he could mediate between humble men and the rigid authority above them. It would be no mere gesture or affectation to share their hardships. The yearnings that made him still look towards a vocation in the church were thereby largely fulfilled. Unlikely as it may seem, as a sergeant in the Rifle Brigade Donald Hankey had found his ministry.

From Aldershot, where the brigade had gone into barracks, Sergeant Hankey wrote to Hilda on 24 August, telling her, 'This is doing me no end of good in every way' (*Letters*, p. 312). Hilda herself came to the opinion that the early part of her brother's training period 'was certainly the happiest time of his life' ('About "A Student in Arms"', *ASIA, II*, p. 29), and his other letters from those months suggest an uncommon degree of wellbeing.

I had a very jolly letter from Maurice last week, in which he asked me to make an effort to attend the christening of Michael in uniform! ... I have been told [by Maurice?] that I shall never make a good N.C.O., but should be an excellent officer! Well, I could never be the ordinary sealed pattern N.C.O.–but I think I have my uses. ... After all, this is not quite the ordinary sealed pattern army.
(*Letters* [to Hilda, 18 September 1914], pp. 313-14)

Even though he was new to the infantry, his military duties were not entirely strange; Hankey encountered no particular difficulty in settling into them, and in fact army life itself must have almost 'gone without saying'–it figures so little in his published letters from that time. Instead–and this is surely a contributing element in Donald's contentment—he is enjoying first the prospect of his book's appearance and then the absorbing pleasure of responding to the various reactions of his friends and other readers to *The Lord of All Good Life* after it was published in October, with its author identified as 'Donald Hankey, Sergeant, Rifle Brigade'.

Responding to Tom Allen, a fellow member of the OBM who must have ragged him good-naturedly by letter about having thus identified himself in a religious book with no ostensible connection to the nation's military crisis, Hankey is apologetic but unrepentant. 'Put it down to aesthetic deterioration due to low company if you like!' he offers; yet the opportunism of publishing, so soon after war's outbreak, in the guise of a ranker-in-arms does not really embarrass him:

> But honestly, if one writes a book, and believes that there is something in it of value, one does want it read so that it will have a chance of proving useful.
>
> (*Letters*, p. 320)

Though written by a civilian, part of its meaning in the literary career of Donald Hankey derives from the fact that *The Lord of All Good Life* appeared as the work of a soldier. This clearly was an element in both the favourable and the unfavourable attention the book received; more than that, it must have played a significant part in the formation of that authorial persona which was to become famous as 'A Student in Arms'.

Donald had enjoyed writing his book, and he also enjoyed writing *about* it—to members of his family, to friends from his past who discovered the book and wrote to him of their interest in it, and to other readers whose reactions, whatever the accompanying reservations might be, signalled some sort of like-mindedness. To Hilda he made it extravagantly clear that 'for me the book is my life's work' :

> It represents the conclusion of my thirty years of living, thinking, speculating, experimenting. It is the best part of myself. I feel that if I were to die tomorrow I could say 'Now Lord, lettest Thou Thy servant depart in peace. ...'
>
> (*Letters*, p. 318)

To his cousin Dorothy he sent warm thanks for her encouraging praise and explained that his chief reason for publishing the book was that *balance*—the due consideration of opposing sides of controversy—was so hard to achieve by mere discussion (*Letters*, pp. 314–15). In a lengthy reply to Jane Robertson, a friend of Hilda's who had sent him admiring comments on the book, Hankey expatiates with obvious self-satisfaction on its 'pragmatic' approach to religious questions and on 'the great struggle for the survival of the fittest' in such matters, on 'the formation of "the higher synthesis"' (*Letters*, p. 312), his inherent modesty engaged in an almost desperate contest with authorial pride:

> I don't know whether all this will seem rather contemptible, or quite unintelligible to you, or whether you can find a pantheon in which you can find it a corner.
>
> (*Letters*, p. 329)

Although Donald naturally set store by his work's intellectual respectability, he also liked describing it as 'not altogether abstract theory', but 'a good deal founded on experience' (*Letters*, p. 314). Mrs. L in far off Western

121

Australia received a copy of Hankey's book with a letter telling her that it 'represents the summing up of a lot of puzzling and experimenting' (*Letters*, p. 323). Acknowledging the letter of Rev. Arthur Hankey of Brighton (a distant cousin) he again alludes to the designation 'Sergeant, Rifle Brigade' appearing on the title page and explains—while owning up to a degree of 'humbug' in so identifying himself—that 'I did it mainly to make it clear that I really was an ordinary layman' (*Letters*, p. 315). So he was particularly pleased to tell his friend Tom Allen that the book 'has gained favour with such various people as a sceptical doctor, my sister's cook, and Alec Paterson' (*Letters*, p. 320). Above all, it was an average, earnest, somewhat sceptical but not unsympathetic churchgoer's point of view that he wished to assume as he urged readers in the direction of more confident and serviceable faith.

This has been my great effort [he tells a reader, who characterized himself as 'agnostic in certain ultimate issues'] —to find out what really were the beliefs which made a real difference to one's outlook and character. ... I don't know that I am very much more certain than you are. ... As regards the church, one often despairs. ... What I want is to dethrone the rulers of it, and flood out the pew-holders with new blood, of the sort which gets the door slammed in its face at present.

(*Letters*, pp. 338–40)

Winston Churchill, Hankey informs this Canadian reader, 'has put something of the same sort in his 'The Inside of the Cup'.' He told Hilda that he wished he could muster the 'cheek' to send Churchill a copy of *The Lord of All Good Life* (*Letters*, p. 326).

Riding high, though he had no illusions that his book would be widely read, the author was hardly more than mildly irked by adverse criticism. He knew what he had and had not aimed at, and was not surprised to be patronized by some and lightly dismissed by others. He guessed at the identity of an unfriendly reviewer for the *Oxford Magazine*, a don one of whose lectures Donald remembered attending. It was bad luck on them both, he joked to Hilda, that the reviewer had to read the book, and that he had to sit through a dreary lecture. Yet the Oxford don's misfortune was the greater; Donald stopped attending after the initial lecture, whereas in order to review *The Lord of All Good Life* the don must have had to suffer through most of the entire book (*Letters*, pp. 319–20).

The review in *The Times Literary Supplement* (5 November 1914) reflects how Donald's decision to identify himself as Sergeant Hankey of the Rifle Brigade influenced the critical reception of his book. It is a fair enough assessment, sympathetic to Hankey's call for a church less conscious of class, more truly Christian and more genuinely effective in pursuing the aim of a good life for all. *The Times* review quite justly emphasizes the absence of exceptional originality in the book's 'honest and mostly common-sense notions of the Christian faith and its meaning'; but it suggests (with a touch of the supercilious) 'that Sergeant Hankey did not acquire his sense of style in camp or even in the barracks, and to that extent he must not be taken as normal but as an extraordinarily interesting exception.' Altogether, the reviewer in his innocence makes more of the author's place in the military than a reader of Hankey's book ought to—makes what is an incidental and belated aspect of authorial identity a major consideration in evaluating the work and in divining the particular 'needs' it was intended to meet. The sergeant-author is praised for having so appropriately judged what, when it comes to religion, 'the normal need' among soldiers is likely to be.

The Times reviewer's conception of Hankey's book as a kind of Christian primer for the men in the ranks is after all unknowingly in accord with the author's own hopes. He had written it to reflect the outlook and address the interests of a *civilian* rank and file within the English church. Those who read *The Lord of All Good Life* as a book for soldiers, sensitive to their condition and concerned with their spiritual needs, may have denied it a larger place, a broader significance. But as Hankey himself said, this was not the ordinary sealed pattern army; it was to a great extent Bermondsey writ large and as such it represented those too little thought of by the established church. Their fate had now become, for better or worse, that of the entire nation.

6

In the Ranks (November 1914 to May 1915)

Feeling good about his book, reasonably comfortable in his duties, and well disposed towards his company officers, Sergeant Hankey moved with the Rifle Brigade from barracks at Aldershot into billets in the nearby Surrey village of Elstead. From late November until the brigade entered its next training phase at Borden in February, Donald spent a blissful interval, a time of the most unalloyed happiness he ever knew.

Elstead struck Donald as 'a nice straggling old place', and the surrounding country—'all woods and lakes and bracken and heather' (*Letters*, p. 317)—could hardly have been more appealing. He was billeted at Firs Cottage along with two very congenial riflemen. It was the home of an Irish lady in her seventies, a Mrs Coppin, who received seventeen shillings and sixpence per week for each man she housed. All three guests took their meals with the cook-housekeeper and the maid. But Mrs Coppin recognized Sergeant Hankey to be an unusual lodger—a cultivated university man with charming manners and a playful sense of humour—and she quickly made a pet of him. That good woman arranged bridge foursomes and tea parties at which she introduced her sergeant to some of her more distinguished neighbours. Donald enjoyed these particular benefits, but he also relished the company at the Woolpack, a 'Dickensy' village pub in whose parlour he and the other sergeants often enjoyed a pint and a pipe in the early evenings. Mrs Coppin was delighted to find Donald such a contented home body; after his death she sent the *Spectator* her affectionate recollections of him. These give us a picture of Donald in what for him were almost ideal circumstances, leading a life that suited him so perfectly its clearly temporary aspect must have made him savour it all the more.

On duty both Donald's superior officers and the men under him tolerated his shortcomings as an NCO and appreciated his earnest efforts. He was sufficiently occupied in ways that had purpose without being unduly stressful. There was time, off-duty, to write and smoke in his room at Firs Cottage, to socialize with his fellow lodgers, to entertain Mrs Coppin with amiable chat. He also found time, according to Mrs Coppin's account, to enter more informally into the lives of both the villagers and his own men. She does not use the term 'pastoral', but that word comes to mind in connection with what by this time had become Hankey's relation to those around him when the opportunity was present. From others in Elstead or in surrounding cottages Mrs Coppin gleaned reports of the unobtrusive 'work' her sergeant carried on as a leisure activity:

His life at Elstead was a living example of all that was good and admirable; sympathetic, sensitive, loving all that is pure and beautiful, his labours without ceasing were not very much noticed by men. ... Mr. Hankey ... used to go into their cottages for a talk round the fire; ... he was so interested about their sick children, or some other of the family, and then one realized that they had gained an insight into a better and different kind of life.

(*Spectator*, 9 December 1916, p. 728)

It was Mrs Coppin's impression that Donald's influence among the men in the ranks bore the same stamp. 'How he loved his Bermondsey boys (many of whom marched to enlist with him) and the Rifle Brigade boys! His heart yearned after them.' Her aside here referring to Bermondsey recruits is unsupported by any record, but it indicates that the mistress of Firs Cottage had incorporated into her idealized memories of Donald Hankey some of his actual history at the Oxford and Bermondsey Mission.

Such a life as Donald led at this period seemed to him 'a bed of roses'. He felt himself 'extraordinarily well treated' on every hand, seeing more evidence of human kindness and good than he had thought possible 'even five years ago' [i.e., before Bermondsey] (*Letters*, p. 335). The contrast between his tour of duty as a subaltern in Mauritius and his present circumstances as a sergeant could hardly have been more striking. So much of his time in Mauritius was spent idly looking for ways to improve himself or participating in the life of the officers' mess. Central to his current well-being, no doubt, was his enjoyment of the correspondence still being generated by his 'parvum opus', as he called *The Lord of All Good Life*. His letters reflect a particular involvement with two matters that had caught the interest of the book's readers: the social views underlying much of the author's criticism of the church, and the question of how a Christian should feel about the war.

Hankey's aunt read his book and charged him with being a 'democrat'. Donald replies good-naturedly, accepting this characterization 'only in a limited sense' (*Letters*, p. 333). Though sceptical of the notion of 'blood' as implying 'congenital superiority', he does concede to some people 'of really good birth' a certain 'fineness' that must be regarded as '[n]ever anything but splendid.' Its mark is a socially valuable disinterestedness of view that, owing to their circumstances, removes true aristocrats from the 'baser ambitions and pretensions of the "climber"' (*Letters*, p. 333).

> Oddly enough, the man who is so aristocratic and wealthy as to despise or rather ignore social position and wealth often has most in common with the honest manual labourer who can never hope either for position or wealth.
>
> (*Letters*, pp. 333-4)

Hankey's sentiments, at least those he reveals to 'Auntie Mie', far from being aggressively democratic, seem almost feudal. Is it not the 'manual labourer's' hopelessness—that is, his necessary acceptance of his place within a fixed class structure, without prospect of more just alternatives—that earns him Hankey's sympathy? The disinterested aloofness of the 'fine' aristocrat and the passivity of the 'honest' labourer are in any case both preferable, in Hankey's view, to 'the intermediate class' with its 'pretence and hypocrisy ... striving after the outward symptoms without any appreciation of the inner spirit' (*Letters*, p. 334). He concludes in a postscript:

> I think that an aristocracy whose motto was *noblesse oblige* would be splendid. Failing that, I incline to favour a democracy with the O.B.M. motto, '*Fratres*'.
>
> (*Letters*, pp. 335-6)

Perhaps that way of putting it would mollify a particularly respectable aunt, but in fact the prospect of brotherhood moved him more deeply, as well as holding out more solid hope, than did occasional fineness amongst the aristocracy. When the feelings of a family member were not involved, and when his social conscience was focused

128

upon what he knew at close range within the life of the church instead of being vaguely directed at the broad and abstract concept of class, Hankey could sound less conciliatory, almost fierce, as when he told his Canadian reader he wished to 'dethrone the rulers' of the church and 'flood out the pew-holders with new blood' (*Letters*, p. 340).

Not surprisingly, readers of *The Lord of All Good Life* were especially alert to whatever its author was thought to be saying or at least implying on the subject of war. Since it had been written before the outbreak of hostilities, the book addressed the moral question of war more or less abstractly. In responding to some readers, Hankey continues to explain his version of a Christ-like view of violence in general, but he also treats the question in terms of his sense of the present conflict, a resistance to Germany's aggression. 'I must try and think out my position on the question of Christianity and war more carefully,' he writes to one of Hilda's friends who had admired his book (*Letters*, p. 345).

In that work, so he now claims, he sought 'to repudiate the entirely wishy-washy and sentimental and hypocritical campaign against war which I thought was giving a false idea of Christianity' (*Letters*, p. 341). He recalls having told his Bermondsey boys in a confirmation class that one need not always turn the other cheek; there were rare occasions on which 'it was a duty to kick the other fellow' (*Letters*, pp. 340–41). To Hankey the thought of inflicting pain and death is 'more revolting than the idea of suffering wounds and death'; but 'the law "thou shalt not murder" is nothing. The spirit "thou shalt not hate" is everything' (*Letters*, p. 350).

Though he reflects a widespread national self-righteousness, Hankey was never among those who represented the present conflict with Germany as a 'holy war' any more than he approved of vengeance or placed any emphasis on the war as upholding the 'national honour'.

I believe quite honestly that as far as this nation as a whole is concerned ... this is a war without hatred. But I don't believe that any friendship or brotherhood is possible between any other nation and Germany until Germany has been defeated in war.

(*Letters*, p. 350)

War, then, seemed to Hankey 'a solemn duty'. Its aim was not to punish Germany but to save it 'from a false ideal and philosophy'. 'England as a whole,' Donald wrote in March of 1915, 'is fighting in the hope of making friendship possible' (*Letters*, pp. 350, 351).

But even before he sees the face of war with his own eyes, Donald has surmised that those who fight it do so not out of high principles but in desperation. 'When one enlists one thinks of dying for one's country, and before long one feels that one's business is to live and kill for it' (*Letters*, p. 340). When he had experienced combat first-hand, especially during that brief time left to him after the horrific slaughter on 1 July on the Somme, Donald's sense of the enormity of mass warfare makes the abstract issue of a proper Christian attitude towards the taking of life almost irrelevant. Slayer and slain alike were mere victims of a nightmare which had outwardly transformed modern existence. Christianity as 'the love of all that is good and wholesome in life' (*Letters*, p. 341) still asserts its claims, but for Hankey those claims had increasingly to do with that narrowing but still essential sphere of interpersonal conduct where the good and wholesome had not been entirely overwhelmed. His detachment—what he sometimes condemned in himself as emotional coldness—was that of one who puzzled and pondered upon experience even as he lived it. Such a feature of temperament stood him in very good stead. It kept him sane and functional while he survived the fighting, and it provided him with the qualities he needed to construct the persona that brought him brief fame as 'A Student in Arms'.

Hankey's characteristic detachment was uncommon enough to strike almost everyone who knew him, but there was something else in his passive, yet hardly pacifistic, attitude towards the war that he certainly shared with many young Englishmen. The reviewer of K. G. Budd's biography for *The Times Literary Supplement* [126: 1931] describes Donald Hankey as 'among those to whom the War came almost as a moral and spiritual relief'. Whatever lay behind that feeling, in Hankey's case it enabled him to put aside a number of troubling personal things: his quarrel with church and churchmen, his uncertainty about his own fitness for the clergy, his struggle to sort out his declassé sympathies and his class prejudices and habits, and—comprehending these matters—the likely pressures both from older siblings and within himself to set his course more firmly in the direction of a career and a family. Until war's unimaginable actuality revealed itself, it could be understood and accepted as a simple duty, not only virtually inescapable but clarifying, even reconciling. This would have been true even if Hankey had not found in army life the chance he was searching for to serve and guide simple men, men who appeared really to need him, and moreover to lose himself in their midst.

Some time in January Donald's tranquillity was disturbed by bad news about his Bermondsey friend Tom Hewitt. His wife wrote to say that Tom was dangerously ill in Guy's Hospital. The letter reached Donald at lunchtime on a Friday; he went straight away to his sergeant major, who granted him a weekend pass, and by five o'clock he was at the headquarters of the OBM in Long Lane looking for a bed. Apparently none was available, because Donald went on to Rotherhithe (where other club officers had digs) and ended up spending what he confessed to Hilda was 'quite an amusing weekend really', meeting a wounded Belgian refugee, dining at Frascati's then on to the Alhambra, and gabbing with his friends till all hours. According to the report he gave his sister, it was not until Sunday afternoon that he visited Tom Hewitt at Guy's, staying with him only until it was time to catch the 5:30 return train. Tom seemed 'a good deal better than I expected', but Donald offers the judgment that 'he hasn't much to look forward to this side of the grave' (*Letters*, p. 337).

Tom Hewitt's condition was even more precarious than Donald supposed. He died only a few days after Hankey's visit, on 21 January in Guy's Hospital. The death certificate, which spells his surname 'Hewett', records his age as 27 and the cause of death 'Mitral Stenosis', a rheumatic heart condition involving narrowing of the mitral valve. Its typical symptoms, which Hewitt may have been suffering for several years, are breathlessness and a marked lack of stamina and would readily account for both Donald's and Hilda's perception of 'poor old Tom' as a chronic invalid— perhaps assumed to be a victim of tuberculosis, since in his part of London that wasting disease was notoriously rampant. 'Caretaker' is the occupation given on the death certificate; the address of Hewitt's residence and also of his place of employment (evidently in a building he attended to in some fashion) is 196a Weston Street. That was also Donald Hankey's Bermondsey address before his enlistment in the army in August of 1914.

If one takes at face value Donald's report to Hilda of his weekend pass, it leaves the uncomfortably mixed impression of a young soldier (but Donald at 30 was mature for a recruit) hastily responding to the distress of a sick friend and former housemate, who yet fritters away most of his time in London as if it were merely a chance for a night out on the town. Yet after all, he is writing to his sister who expected to hear from him or perhaps even see him that Sunday and deserved an explanation as to why he had disappointed her. Donald, the tone of his letter suggests, was therefore writing with two conflicting aims. On the one hand, his excuse for having let down his sister must be made to appear convincing ('events on Friday took an unexpected turn' [*Letters*, p. 336]); but on the other, Donald may well have felt it prudent to reassure Hilda that in visiting this unfortunate young man from the slums of Bermondsey he was not exactly rushing to the bedside of a particularly intimate friend ('Poor old Tom, . . . he is a very nice old thing, . . . and I believe he is a great deal fonder of me than I ever have succeeded in being of anyone but myself' [*Letters*, p. 337]). We know from Hilda's own description of the menage her brother shared with the Hewitts that Donald had given his sister so sketchy an impression of his living arrangements there that she believed Tom to be her brother's 'butler' (*ASIA, II*, p. 26). In the January 1915 letter from Elstead, Donald seems at some pains to portray his relationship to Tom in a condescending light. It is 'the faithful Tom' he feels duty-bound to visit; the sergeant major's permission to take leave is portrayed almost as if it were an off-hand response to some merely half-uttered wish from Donald ('You can have a pass if you like, boy!' [*Letters*, p. 336]). For Hilda's benefit, evidently, Donald makes the attachment between Tom and himself clearly stronger on Tom's side than his own.

It makes me feel extraordinarily grateful to Providence that I should have had the luck to have people fond of me like that; only it also does make me feel horribly shallow and theatrical; because I really haven't got very deep feelings. I wish I had much deeper ones; but I don't seem to be built that way.

(*Letters*, p. 337)

But there is reason to suspect otherwise; Donald's feelings for Tom Hewitt may have been deeper than he was prepared to admit. This would be even more likely if, as I believe, the editor of Hankey's letters misidentifies the letter Donald wrote on his way to Australia as having been addressed to one Tom Graves. That letter is dated the day after he told Hilda he had been 'progressively more and more happy, because I know that I have been useful and that I have been loved' (*Letters*, 258), and in it he assures 'Tom' that his friendship had meant 'an awful lot' to him, that 'Tom' 'taught me some things which will make a difference all my life' (*Letters*, p. 259). If this was in fact Tom Hewitt, the friend with whom Hankey shared for a time his quarters in Bermondsey (and the allusions to this Tom's ill health and to his wife support the conclusion that Hewitt is the Tom in question), shallowness and theatricality do not seem qualities that apply to Donald's part of that friendship. Accusing himself of shallow feelings was Hankey's usual way of saying he is confused about them— or aware of something possibly unconventional in his emotional constitution, something in him that does not follow the approved prescriptions of class and of sex. Stressing his own gratitude for Tom's affection as a way of stating that his own feelings do not match it may have reassured Hilda and served to account both for his dash to Bermondsey and for the way he actually spent the time there. But a phrase like 'I don't seem to be built that way' betrays some fundamental uncertainty about his own nature, something beyond a mere acknowledgement of casual flightiness.

The question of Tom Hewitt's place in Donald Hankey's life remains a puzzle. The social disparity between the two men must always be factored in when considering both Hankey's allusions to Tom and his sister's recollections. In most respects Hilda is vague about this obscure young man, but on two matters she seems rather pointed: Tom was married when Donald knew him, and the nature of his connection with her brother was that of a personal servant. As for Donald himself, his letters reveal nothing as to when or from whom he learned of Tom's death. The January report to Hilda about seeing him in hospital contains his last published reference to this unfortunate friend.

In any case, a sergeant's duties and the diversions of Elstead tended by and large to put any troubling personal questions in abeyance. Donald's relations with his men were defined by regulations and governed by routine; the vexing subtleties of class were simplified in the army by the rigidities of rank. And with his landlady, Mrs Coppin, Donald could and did form a friendship that suited both his inclinations and his experience. With her he was free to be boyish and playful, gentlemanly and reserved. With women—those to whom he was related or who were older or safely married—Donald seemed most at ease and was ever at his likeable and affectionate best. Such a woman as Mrs Coppin would and did respect his need for privacy, understand and admire his compulsion to seek out and help the less fortunate, play to his whimsy, his courtliness, his sense of fun:

> ... straightaway one's affections went out to that fine, tall, stalwart young soldier, whose eyes searched into the inmost depths of the soul, then twinkled with kindness, friendliness, and all the fun of the thing, as he greeted us with the voice and words of the cultured, true-hearted Christian gentleman he was.
>
> (*Spectator*, 9 December 1916, p. 728)

By the time Donald was moved out of billets and transferred to the dreary Borden Camp he and Mrs Coppin had agreed on a kind of informal mutual adoption. Somewhat juvenile on Hankey's part, and sentimental, this arrangement between a man of thirty and a woman in her seventies was, for all that, genuine and important, a serious pledge of mutual affection. As Donald explained, he was an orphan and Mrs Coppin had no one else. He visited her on leave and wrote to her faithfully the rest of his life, addressing her as 'Grandmamma' and signing himself 'Your loving grandboy'.

In one of his early letters after the move into the 'Guadeloupe Barracks' at Borden Camp Donald tells Mrs Coppin that Elstead remained one of the 'four places in the world where I feel at home' (*Letters*, p. 351), the other three being Tootiken in Western Australia, Port Louis in Mauritius, and Bermondsey. Each of those four places embodied a 'spiritual treasure': Tootiken was where Donald encountered 'noble self-sacrifice, generosity, endurance' in the person of Mrs L, 'one of the best women I have ever met'; Mauritius was where he overcame religious scepticism; Bermondsey meant 'heroism, and patience, and brotherly love, and true religion pure and undefiled'; 'Elstead,' Donald wrote of his life at Mrs Coppin's, 'spells kindness— the charity which "hopeth all things, believeth all things", and thinketh no evil' (*Letters*, p. 352).

Borden, on the other hand, 'spells slave-driving, which isn't my job and isn't going to be'. He was equally outspoken to his cousin Dorothy. 'This is the abomination of desolation mentioned in Daniel the prophet.' Far from any town, the camp was 'simply miles and miles of huts full of soldiers and mud and lice' (*Letters*, p. 344). But he recognized a positive side to the physical unpleasantness: active combat was the immediate next step, and 'Elstead [has been] so pleasant that one feared a change.' The conditions of Borden were so dismal that almost any change was welcome. 'I hate fear,' Donald added, bracing himself for what lay ahead 'out yonder' (*Letters*, pp. 344, 345).

The contrast between a pastoral life at Elstead and the misery of Borden Camp was not entirely a matter of the physical environment. It had to do with Hankey's most acute—perhaps his only—experience of hero-worship, an experience that resulted in his resigning his sergeant's stripes in order to transfer out of his company and also inspired the piece of writing largely responsible for his forthcoming fame as 'A Student in Arms'.

'The Beloved Captain' became Donald Hankey's most popularly admired essay. It was a tribute to the memory of Captain Ronald Montague Hardy of the Rifle Brigade, who as a lieutenant was Hankey's platoon commander through the months at Aldershot and Elstead. About the time the company moved to Borden, Lieutenant Hardy was promoted to captain but was not given command of 'D' Company. Unfortunately, the captain put in charge was Hardy's antitype, a man Hankey despised as 'an egoist . . . who has a craving for power, popularity, recognition, etc. In slang, a "swanker" and a bit of a bully' (*Letters*, p. 356). As training for the trenches neared its completion Hankey 'got gradually worked up to such a pitch of nerves I could not stand our captain any longer' (*Letters*, p. 357) and traded in his stripes for reassignment to 'C' Company in the brigade (*Letters*, p. 378).

That 'change of status' (about which Hankey found 'everyone' to be 'kind and considerate' [*Letters*, p. 358]) was accompanied by a lift in his spirits. The brigade moved from Borden back to Aldershot and prepared to leave for France. As he anticipated the ordeal of combat and its dire chances, Donald wrote the usual round of letters to those who were closest to him. Even allowing for the obligatory cheerfulness such messages convey, these truly seem the product of a contented and unanxious mind. To his cousin

Dorothy he described his gratitude that 'this best gift of human friendship has been simply poured in on me, and I would not swap it for anything' (*Letters*, p 358). 'In a war of this magnitude and difficulty,' he told his sister Gertrude, 'the chances of coming back are not very great. But I have no anxiety on the subject.' He assures her that he faces the future 'with a great deal of interest' (*Letters*, pp. 362, 363). There was time for several visits, both in London and at the base, with Hilda. On 25 April he sends her what sounds like a considered goodbye:

> If I do survive the war I shall have gained immensely in every way by having been in the ranks; and if I do not, I feel that this is a good time to finish, when one is extraordinarily happy in many friendships, and when the world lies before one as an attractive place, full of promise and interest. I would not like to finish my life feeling disappointed and cynical.
>
> (*Letters*, p. 362)

Delayed departure creates a note of strain. 'We are now on the very verge,' Donald informs his Australian cousin Valerie. 'We are living in what we can carry' (*Letters*, p. 357).

In the brief commemoration she wrote as the concluding pages of *A Student in Arms, Second Series*, Hankey's sister Hilda furnishes a glimpse—prim and poignant as an old photo—of a last meeting with her brother before he departs for the front. Dorothy Gurner, their cousin, accompanies Hilda to Aldershot. At the station, the two women catch sight of Donald, now in his private's uniform, while he is still anxiously on the look-out for them.

> I am not tall and cannot catch his eye. It is like being at a play, watching him! All at once he sees me! Invo-

luntarily a sudden quick spasm of joy passes across his face, absolutely transfiguring it.

He smoothes it away quickly, for he is a Briton and does not like to show his feelings—but he has given himself away!

Dorothy and I shall never forget that look. And it was for *me*. ...

(*ASIA, II*, pp. 244-5)

Donald takes Hilda and Dorothy to 'a little tea place' where other Tommies are with their sweethearts. After tea they have a nice walk and sit beneath some trees. Donald picks two bouquets ... 'violets, hyacinths, and wild strawberry flowers—we have them still' (*ASIA, II*, p. 246).

When Hilda sees her brother again he will have been wounded and, as she makes clear (*ASIA, II*, p. 244), his face will have lost the boyish look she cherishes. But on that very English Sunday in May of 1915 'it is a lovely day, and we are very happy!' (*ASIA, II*, 245).

7

Into the Fire and Out of the Ranks (May 1915 to January 1916)

The 7th Battalion of the Rifle Brigade reached Boulogne on 20 May at a strength, according to the Battalion War Diary, of 30 officers and 907 in the rank and file. They set out for the front marching towards Belgium in weather so warm the men were allowed to throw onto the blanket wagons the great coats they carried with them. Even so, many fell out exhausted from the heat. But Donald Hankey was not sorry the battalion had not shipped over before the weather turned fine, and personally those earliest days on the march suited him perfectly.

> ... we have really had a splendid time, sleeping out in the long sweet grass of the meadows and occasionally getting a plunge in a pond, and drying oneself in the sun, which is one of the pleasantest sensations in life.
>
> (*Letters*, p. 363)

At Dranoutre the brigade was distributed through the 46th Division so as to assimilate the ways of trench life, and by Sunday, 30 May, the 7th Battalion's War Diary was already recording casualties.

In fact, Donald's letter of 2 June to his cousin Valerie just quoted was written 'in a trench about 100 yards from the Germans' (*Letters*, p. 364). That was his second day in the line. Hankey appears to have been writing with the understandably mixed aims of reassuring Valerie of his high spirits yet intimating that, if he has not quite 'seen the elephant' (as Americans in the Civil War came to refer to the strange horror of combat), he was close enough to sense its presence. The progress up to the front 'was more like a holiday camp than anything' (*Letters*, p. 363); and Donald describes the countryside and the people in the language of an appreciative tourist. He reports that 'comparatively speaking all is quiet just here' and he has 'not done any fighting yet', but in the same letter to his cousin he mentions having that very morning found a splinter from a machine gun bullet sticking in the skin at the back of his neck (*Letters*, pp. 364, 365).

To Mrs L in Australia Donald often represented himself as a bit of a stoic, given to wry humour that cannot (because intended not to?) conceal a touch of melancholy. Two days after his letter to Valerie he describes himself to Mrs L 'sitting in a trench with the bullets pattering round', and adds that 'it is rather rash to talk about "after the war".' 'One only has a sort of reversionary interest in one's own life!' Recalling the words of his father that it is better 'to rot in a trench than rust in a furrow', Donald goes on to cite this as a very selfish sentiment, explaining with uncharacteristic crudeness that 'to rot in the neighbourhood of a trench, as so many poor chaps are doing, makes it very smelly for the rest!' (*Letters*, p. 365).

Hankey is writing here to a woman hardened by life in the outback, but clearly his admiration for her included mutual affection. Even here he sounds a note of kindred feeling by telling Mrs L that trench rations remind him very much of the provisions at the Ls' station in Western Australia: bully beef, jam, and lots of milkless tea—absent the 'sumpy puddings' or 'damper' (*Letters*, p. 366). Hankey, one might hazard, is not indulging in self-pity, nor is he at this point actually revolted by his situation. A characteristic detachment—useful for a student, in arms or anywhere else—is evident in his mode of observation. It is marked by something one might almost call stern, but it is not without sympathy. Or at any rate his actual aim may not be to appeal to the sympathy of these women correspondents but to *direct* it more precisely. *Not for me!* Hankey seems to be urging. *Rather more to all these others!* To the poor chaps whose carcasses are left to stink, and also to all the survivors exposed to the sickening odour of what they themselves might soon become.

Donald's letters—to 'G' (his sister Gertrude), to Mrs Coppin, to his cousin Dorothy, to his young niece Nora Spelman—continue to strike the humorous, cheerful note. He describes his existence as that of 'a rather amateurish rabbit'. It is 'rather jolly' to be looking out of his burrow, nice to look back on when a sleepless night and an indifferent breakfast return one to the world of human danger and misery (*Letters*, pp. 366-7). 'We are always on the move and get plenty of variety'; yet Donald protests that there is nothing interesting to tell—'except what I am not allowed to say' (*Letters*, pp. 367, 368). Nonetheless, war's reality comes through. He describes himself in his present act of writing, resting his paper on the back parapet,

> looking over a peaceful scene of meadows deep in grass which no animal will eat, stately avenues of trees marking the main road along which no man may travel, and in the distance are the ruined towers of a fair city in which no man may dwell. Such is war at sunset.
>
> (*Letters*, pp. 368-9)

That is Donald Hankey's ironically lyrical rendering of what was becoming one of the most notoriously hellish sectors of the entire western front: the Ypres salient.

As June progressed Donald's battalion became more involved in the action around Ypres. Its War Diary is dated from Vlamertinghe on the 16th: 'Bombardment and assault on Bellevaarde Farm. 2:45 a.m.' On the 24th the camp was shelled; at 7:30 in the morning the battalion left to dig communication trenches east of Ypres. On the 29th it took over trenches between Hooge—site of an enormous mine crater, much contested as a strong point—and 'Belwaard' [Bellevaarde Farm?]. On the 30th two riflemen in Corporal Hankey's company were killed. These and other casualties were described as occurring 'in ordinary trench duty, mostly from shell fire.' The War Diary for July 1915 records a brutal month for the battalion, locating its operation at Hooge, then Poperinghe, then Hooge again, then Vlamertinghe, Zoave Wood, and finally, at the first of August, a rest camp near Hazebrouk. In its pages the death of Captain Edmund Hardy of 'D' Company (Donald's 'Beloved Captain') is recorded for 7.23.15—and Corporal D. W. Hankey is listed among the wounded of Company 'C' for 7.30.15. By that time 'the elephant' had become all too familiar.

Poison gas (chlorine, in this instance) had been used for the first time in the war on 22 April 1915 against French Zouaves in the Ypres salient.[1] Evidently Donald's unit came under gas attack on 1 July. In a letter to his cousin Dorothy dated 3 July thanking her for two different parcels of delicacies and tobacco he refers to 'a piping hot day in the trenches, with interludes of most alarming shrapnel and high explosive shells and gas shells.' Water is scarce; some of what Dorothy sent is thirst-raising (deviled turkey) but some is 'beyond all dreams' ('Oranges! a lime! lemons! apples!'). 'When the taste of gas is still clinging to one's

---

[1]See John Keegan, *The First World War* (New York, 1999), p. 198.

clothes and mouth, nothing could be better for taking it away than chutney' (*Letters*, p. 370). For Dorothy's benefit Donald expresses his gratitude in the form of a comic disquisition that jauntily plays off his acknowledged epicureanism against conditions at the front:

> The butter is very good too; but it is not a thing that appeals to me very much just at present. I like it cool and fresh, in a nice solid lump, with parsley round it, on a nice white dish. ...
>
> (*Letters*, p. 370)

There were other things besides edibles and smokables from home to turn Donald's thoughts from discomfort and danger. The editor of his *Letters* notes that during this period Colonel Maurice Hankey began to appeal to him to apply for a commission. A shortage of trained officers was, according to this source, the chief argument Maurice urged upon his younger brother. During an interval of relative respite in the middle of July, with his battalion assigned to work details laying telephone wire and digging trenches, Donald implies in a letter to Dorothy that his application is already in progress. He refers to the likelihood of being sent 'to a sort of school for aspirants for commissions' and, if successful, getting five days leave before assignment to duty as an officer. But in view of this prospect and, for the time being, out of the trenches and in relative safety, Hankey wonders 'why it is I am not severely content instead of utterly fed up!' (*Letters*, p. 372). Despite the obvious advantages of an officer's life, he had an inkling that the drastic change in status from corporal to subaltern would not really suit him.

Next day (16 July) he adds in that letter to Dorothy some thoughts of a rather different sort. 'I've been wondering whether I can't write something for Mr Strachey [editor of

144

the *Spectator*].' Donald doubts he has anything of much value to add to the glut of articles and selections about the war, but the idea must have seized him forcibly all the same. In a subsequent letter to Dorothy only ten days later he refers to 'The Cockney Warrior', an essay which, for some reason, he eventually published in the *Westminster Gazette* rather than in St. Loe Strachey's *Spectator*, where nearly all the 'Student in Arms' pieces were to appear. From the way he speaks of what he calls this essay's 'blatant war journalism' it is evident he must have written it and sent it off to Dorothy within those few days.

I don't know how far I believe it [he now writes disparagingly]. I don't think any of us love war; but we get on and do whatever has to be done—because one is in it and has no real choice in the matter.

(Letters, p. 373)[2]

The note of dogged resignation in this letter seems new and might reflect the impact on Corporal Hankey of the death of Ronald Hardy of 'D' Company—the man Hankey would later idealize as 'The Beloved Captain'—just three days earlier at the Hooge crater. Donald's initial hesitancy in writing 'The Cockney Warrior' stemmed from his sense that 'we haven't really done any fighting yet'. With the papers choked with war articles, hadn't everything been said? With the tedious sounds of the drill sergeant's

---

[2]In the published *Letters* covering this first period of Hankey's service at the front, Dorothy Gurner appears to fill the role more customarily taken by Hilda Hankey. There are no published letters to Hilda between 24 April and 6 August 1915 (though one can infer that Donald must have written even sooner than 6 August after he was wounded on 30 July). Perhaps the conditions of Hilda's own volunteer service at this time in some way interfered with the regular correspondence between her and her brother.

commands threatening to drive any original thoughts from his mind, would not anything he might write be hopelessly stale (*Letters*, p. 372)? Now, on 26 July, Hankey's reservations about the piece he has written have modulated into a suspicion that he is merely contributing to a false and jingoistic spate of 'war journalism'. The truth about war is beginning to work more deeply upon his sensibility.

Even 'The Cockney Warrior' offers more on its own quite modest terms than its author's doubts about it might suggest. It contrasts the public-school trained soldier, whose performance as a fighting man is confidently assumed, with lads from places like London's East End and their apparent unsuitedness to the demands of war. In effect, Hankey poses the question whether Kitchener's Mob—as that citizens' army recruited largely from the urban lower-middle and working classes was being called—will answer the nation's needs. This is a question many were anxiously asking and many more may have felt too anxious to ask openly, and it persists as the underlying issue of nearly all of Donald Hankey's war writing. A 'gentleman's education' in the public schools—perhaps most conveniently represented to the English mind by those playing fields at Eton where Napoleon's defeat was supposedly preordained—ensures the ready adaptation to war as a 'glorified form of big-game hunting' (*ASIA*, p. 87). One thinks of such extreme products of this ethos as the aristocratic Capt. Julian Grenfell, whose war poems and letters express an all-but pathological eagerness to close with the enemy in that most thrilling of blood sports. Hankey did not know Grenfell, who had been fatally wounded near Ypres earlier that spring; but Rugby School, Woolwich Academy, and Oxford, to say nothing of his own family upbringing, had made him familiar with those taught, as he puts it,

146

... to welcome danger, and to regard the risk of death as the most piquant sauce to life. ... to sleep on a hard bed, to endure plenty of fresh air, and a cold bath on even the coldest mornings. ...

(*ASIA*, p. 87)

The habits and inclinations of the urban working class are almost entirely opposite, this essay contends. Hankey's experience in Bermondsey is at the forefront of his characterization of the Cockney warrior: 'The Cockney is not brought up to see anything good in danger. ... Nor is he taught to welcome hardship.' His ordinary life is hard enough without making an adventure of discomfort and risk. The softer the Cockney boy's bed, the better he likes it; he sleeps with the windows tight shut. When changing for football, 'he generally only takes off his coat and puts on his jersey over his waistcoat' (*ASIA*, p. 89). Added to this, the Cockney is 'over-sensitive to pain' and not only to suffering but also to inflicting it. His boastful anger 'nearly always evaporates in wordiness'; he loves his home and is at a loss away from 'the sights, the sounds, the smells of his native London'.

He [is], in fact, the last person in the world that we could imagine going out with set teeth to hurt and slay the enemies of his country.

(*ASIA*, pp. 89, 90)

It is as if England's chivalry remains unquestionably intact, but its yeomanry—whose long bows and stout hearts won Agincourt—have apparently dwindled into a crowd of good-natured, self-indulgent oafs. 'We couldn't help wondering,' Hankey confesses, assuming the collective voice of a West End journal such as the *Spectator* or the *Westminster Gazette*, how the Cockney-in-arms would

147

endure the exile, danger, and discomfort of a conflict from which he naturally shrank. But experience, so Hankey claims, had laid to rest all such doubts:

> Well, he surprised us all ... and has given the world the amazing picture of a soldier who is infinitely brave without vindictiveness, terrible without hate, all-enduring and yet remaining his simple, kindly, jaunty self.
>
> (*ASIA*, pp. 90–1)

Of course the characterization is idealized and at the same time patronizing. But one should not discount Hankey's emphasis; the Cockney's lack of hate and vindictiveness is part of the 'surprise', and Hankey finds it the most striking as well as the most valuable. The Cockney warrior's view of his enemy translates 'a statelier word of charity, "Father forgive them, they know not what they do"' into a more comfortable idiom: '"the Bosches is just like us, they wants to get 'ome as much as we do; but they can't 'elp theirselves"' (*ASIA*, pp. 92, 91).

Lacking as he does true bloody-mindedness, and relatively indifferent to abstract patriotism, Hankey's Cockney was simply swept into war 'by a wave of tremendous enthusiasm'. Here the essay touches, though it does not firmly seize upon, the shattering pity of war. Such a soldier 'found himself swimming in a mighty current, the plaything of forces he could neither understand nor control' (*ASIA*, p. 92). Hankey refers to this condition of hapless victimage as a 'sacrifice of ... personality' and chooses to regard it as 'sublimely heroic' (*ASIA*, p. 93).

Passivity, a suppression of personality, was something Donald recognized in himself; but since there can be nothing deliberate about this particular sacrifice, it seems sentimental of Hankey to call it sublime as well as inaccurate to call it heroic. Perhaps Hankey was conscious of hyperbole at this point, because he draws back from it in

148

offering his reader by way of conclusion merely a thin and hollow chuckle over the condescending reassurance that the Cockney warrior must be granted his 'one prized luxury' which such 'real heroism' has earned him: the right to grumble (*ASIA*, p. 93).

*

The War Diary of the 7th Battalion of the Rifle Brigade for July 1915 makes grim reading. Inserted into the monthly log is a sheaf of some twenty pages, torn it appears from a smaller notebook of ruled graph paper. This section lists casualties for 30 July, only that single day, about 300 killed, missing, or wounded. Corporal D.W. Hankey B86 of 'C' Company is named on page 4 among the wounded. The narrative report of that day's action is both technical and confused, but in general it parallels and fills out the selective, impressionistic account of the fighting around the Hooge crater and Zouave Wood contained in Donald's essay 'The Honour of the Brigade' (*ASIA*, pp. 245–259). The War Diary confirms the essential accuracy of what Hankey insisted was 'not ... the whole truth, but ... an aspect of the truth. ... [F]act and fiction are mingled; but to the writer the fiction appears as true as the fact, for it is typical of fact—at least in intention' ('Author's Foreword', *ASIA*, p. 13).

On the night of July 29, having been building trenches under heavy mortar fire, Hankey's battalion was relieved and sent to the rear. His essay describes the difficulties of this period of trench duty, the continual danger from German attack, short rations, and particularly a lack of drinking water.

They had set their teeth and toiled grimly, doggedly, sucking the pebble which alone can keep at bay the demon Thirst.

(*ASIA*, p. 247)

149

When the battalion reached its rest camp near Vlamertinghe at 3:45 on the morning of the 30th it learned that the Germans had overrun the position it had just handed over to fresh troops. Within an hour it was ordered to prepare to return to the front lines. Hankey and the other exhausted men filled their water bottles, received rations and ammunition, and started their march back towards the guns. His essay describes the scene:

> The road was full of troops. Columns of infantry slogged along at the side. Guns and ammunition-wagons thundered down the paved centre. Motor dispatch riders flew past with fresh orders for those in the rear. The men sucked their pebbles in grim silence.
>
> (*ASIA*, p. 251)

Hankey's account of the ensuing battle that afternoon juxtaposes the confusion and slaughter against a captain's message to his men that the honour of the brigade—and the reputation of the entire New Army of which it was a part—demanded the recapture of their lost trenches. 'The day we charged,' Donald later recalled, 'I had no frantic desire to get at 'em.' But he claimed 'one great asset': that in dangerous situations his nerves were steady. 'The whole thing seemed so absurd, and I started off knowing quite well that I should get hit, and not minding very much' (*Letters*, p. 386). The British attack was to have come out of the woods and on to the entrenched Germans, but it was almost immediately halted by its own barbed wire and the waiting enemy machine guns. Platoon after platoon was fed into the woods, but none of the men got more than a few yards out into the clearing from which they were to rush the trenches.

Half a dozen men found themselves alone in the open ground before the German wire. They lay down. No

150

Second-Lieutenant Donald Hankey in his dress uniform, soon after receiving his commission in the Royal Garrison Artillery. Probably taken in late 1903 or early 1904, when Hankey was in his nineteenth year.

Donald Hankey at about age 20, before he resigned his commission and entered Oxford.

Donald Hankey as a farm hand in the Australian bush. Probably dating from early 1913.

Self-portrait of Second-Lieutenant Hankey representing his mock fear that his recent publishing success in the *Spectator* has made his head swell too large for his hat size.

Donald's impression of a colonel unexpectedly returning to the base after having been called back from leave.

Writing to John Barker ('Prester John') shortly before returning to the front (May 1916), Donald promises his friend (whom he never met in person) that 'some day we will meet if God wills, but it will be after the war.' 'What shall we be then?' he wonders, adding this wry sketch of himself as a maimed veteran down on his luck and Barker (a working man) as having struck it rich (*Letters*, p. 417).

one was coming on. Where was everyone? They crawled cautiously back to the trench at the edge of the wood, and climbed in.

(*ASIA*, p. 254)

One of these survivors had been wounded in the leg. That was Corporal Hankey himself. When, after dark, he crawls back through the wood he finds it 'choked with corpses' (*ASIA*, p. 257). Finally he is picked up, given field treatment, loaded into an ambulance, and eventually taken by train to a hospital. There, clean and sedated, the wounded man thinks of the open space between trenches full of unburied bodies, some he 'had known and loved'. 'Yet it was well,' the essay declares, with a flourish one suspects is innocent of irony; 'The brigade was saved. Its honour was vindicated' (*ASIA*, p. 258).

Much as a modern reader might be tempted in that direction, to claim a Falstaffian resonance for the word 'honour' here goes too far. Yet it is fair to think of Hankey the writer, the observer, and the sufferer responding to the episode at several different levels, assailed by and committed to its crushing actuality but nevertheless unwilling to deny it some nobility, some high meaning. Donald had not yet learned—and in fact he never entirely did learn—the lesson of later trench narratives: their flatness of tone, their scrupulous avoidance of abstractions and rhetorical gestures. The result is an account of battle in which stark first-hand experience seems to struggle with an older language and its grandiloquent depiction of war.

What was left of the 7th Battalion of the Rifle Brigade (the War Diary put its fighting strength on 1 August at 14 officers, 559 in other ranks) spent the next week resting near Hazebrouck and sorting itself out. On 2 August Sir John Keir, the Corps Commander, made an inspection and spoke words of official encouragement to the shattered

151

unit. But by that time Corporal Hankey was recovering in hospital and had written Hilda a chipper message reporting a wound in his right thigh from either a bullet or a shrapnel ball, 'which seems to have lost its way inside somewhere'. He follows exactly the regulation practice of making light of an injury, even to the point of doubting whether he will get a trip home out of the mishap (*Letters*, p. 374). Of course it proved to be a 'Blighty' wound, and not until late September or early October was Donald released from hospital care in England. By that time he was 'Lieutenant Hankey' and already deeply regretted having allowed himself to apply for a commission. He wished he had stayed in the ranks with the riflemen of his brigade.

His period of convalescence must have made Donald's future appear in some respects to return him to his past. He spent the early days back in England at the Royal Herbert Hospital in Woolwich, not far from the scene of his military schooling. Then he learned that his application for a commission had gone through and that would mean a return to his old outfit, the Royal Garrison Artillery. For a time he was in Shornell's VAD Hospital, in Abbey Wood, Kent. There is evidence this may have been where Hilda was serving in a Voluntary Aid Detachment;[3] if so, perhaps it was not only Donald's commission but the fact that his brother was the Secretary to the Committee of Imperial Defence that accounts for such a favourable hospital reassignment. In any case, there are also letters from that period addressed from Kensington, presumably from Hilda's house in Elston Road (though his brother Clement's family also lived in Kensington, at Launceston Place). Then his letters are again from 'Woolwich', but now from the

---

[3]*Letters*, p. 387. On 12 September Donald writes to Mrs Coppin from that hospital, saying that 'I am getting bored here, and I am afraid my sister finds me very grumpy.' Of course, this may refer only to a brief visit from Hilda.

Officers' Mess of 'E' Brigade Heavy Artillery, Royal Garrison Artillery, at Charlton Park.

Donald's wound had required a longer recuperation than he expected, but that gave him time to write. In mid-August he sent a letter to Captain Hardy's mother. 'Perhaps you will be glad to know,' he tells her, 'how one who was an N.C.O. in his platoon for about six months regarded him' (*Letters*, p. 378). Hankey may already have been thinking of her son as a possible subject of the essay he probably did not write until December. The letter strikes a particularly appealing note: heartfelt but tactful, neither self-conscious nor effusive. He addresses himself 'No 86 Corpl. D. Hankey,' giving his regimental number as one from the 'other ranks', and makes no mention either of his own wound or of having become newly commissioned. As a stranger, he does not presume to share in her grief or even to offer sympathy. What he tells her about her son has a personal and informative yet unembellished direct-ness that would make it both credible and welcome to a sorrowing mother.

> I was Captain Hardy's platoon sergeant, and it was the great change which followed his promotion which made me resign my stripes in order to go to another company. We loved him, I think, as no other officer was loved by his men.
>
> (*Letters*, p. 378)

Examples of Hardy's goodness are given, culminating in one generalization about his character: 'He had the prestige of an inherent nobility.' But then Donald checks his own presump-tion, yet in a way that underscores his feelings for Hardy:

> Somehow all this seems so laboured and so lame. What I want to say is simply that he had won the heart of

153

every man from the roughest pit-boy to the gentleman ranker and that every one of us was proud to be commanded by him.

(*Letters*, p. 379)

Moved by this letter, Mrs Hardy wrote her thanks and there was additional correspondence between them. Donald ventures a bit more concerning his personal admiration for Captain Hardy and asks the mother if she could spare him a photograph of her son. His careful disclaimer of anything in the way of actual friendship with the Captain manages to make its own strong claim: 'He was my officer, and I his sergeant—nothing more than that, except that he was also my hero, and I have not had many' (*Letters*, p. 381).

Hankey shows in many ways that the prospect of serving as a commissioned officer troubles him. This was his long-standing problem with conventional authority reasserting itself in a new form. Doubts of his own fitness to exercise authority, combined with an instinctive sympathy for the underdog, caused him to struggle against his decision to become once again an officer in His Majesty's Army in much the same way he had agonized over the possibility of ordination in the established church. To Mrs Coppin he writes revealingly about his current state of mind. Considering the limits of their acquaintance she seems a somewhat unlikely confidante; yet who was more familiar with Hankey in his now abandoned role as a member of the 'other ranks', able by age and experience to see to the other, younger men as he served *with* them though not quite *of* them?

Dear Grandmamma,—

I almost wish that I had not got my commission. I find that I don't really remember anything about

Gunnery, and I *do feel sorry* in many ways to leave the R. B. [Rifle Brigade]. There were some such extraordinary good fellows in it, and one feels rather a worm wriggling out of it–specially for something which is a good deal 'healthier,' as they say.

(Letters, p. 384)

Evidently Mrs Coppin's reply urged him to take a more positive view of his return to the officer class, but Donald clings to his misgivings, adding a note of self-mockery at his exchange of a hard and dangerous existence for a currently trifling one:

> Thanks awfully for your encouraging letter. I still think that it was a mistake for me to apply for a commission, and that if I had waited another ten days I shouldn't have done it. ... I am going up to town tomorrow [13 September] for the day, to see my dentist, banker, brother, tailor, bootmaker, publisher, etc.! It is promotion.

(Letters, p. 387)

Correspondence resumed with Canon Cremer, Rector of Seaford, who the previous spring had written to Donald about *The Lord of All Good Life*. Rev. Cremer had somehow learned that Hankey was wounded, and must have written not only anxiously but warmly. 'It goes without saying,' Donald assures him, 'that I accept the offer of your friendship most gratefully.' His letters to Cremer show no reluctance to talk about himself and his prospects–or rather his current uncertainties in that regard:

> The future–if there is to be a future for me on this planet–is as black and impenetrable as a London fog. ...

155

Describing himself as 'an unpractical dreamer', he mentions 'a certain facility with my pen' and 'a certain power of making people like me, specially boys: but I can't do much that is practical with my influence.' He vaguely projects a kind of alliance between 'the labourer and the gentleman' with 'a certain potentiality for honest idealism which I don't see much sign of elsewhere' (*Letters*, p. 389). This notion of a leadership role among working men—not 'over' them but in their midst—illuminates Hankey's reason why, as he puts it, 'I now bitterly regret having applied for a commission' (*Letters*, p. 390). Later, in a letter to Rev. Cremer dated 8 December, Donald becomes more confiding and direct: 'I am going to pour forth my soul, which will do me good, and you need not read it unless you want to. Know then that I simply loathe being an officer, and am seriously contemplating trying to relinquish my commission, with a view to re-enlisting.' Thereupon he launches into an extended account of what led to his present predicament: unsuited as an officer, alienated from his former service in the artillery, feeling he has betrayed his fellows in the ranks, yet already committed to a line of action he cannot now reverse (*Letters*, p. 396).

Enlisting, Donald explains, 'was a great success up to a point; but then there came a time of extreme boredom.' In that mood

... the tempter appeared under the disguise of the spirit of Duty, and told me that it was up to me to be an officer because I was such a fine fellow. I didn't really believe him; but I pretended to, and applied for an artillery commission on the understanding that I should not have to go home for training, but should be attached to a battery at the front.

(*Letters*, p. 396)

This version of his commissioning, tricked out as a mock temptation allegory, both conceals and confesses the probable truth. Donald's tempter—Duty personified—was his next oldest brother Maurice, who had served as a captain in the Royal Marine Artillery, gone from there into the Naval Intelligence Department, and in 1912 was named Secretary of the Committee of Imperial Defence.[4] Donald would not put the blame directly upon Maurice, but it was customary for the Hankeys to view the military as a profession; they were schooled for it, and the eldest brother, Hugh, had died a hero's death as an officer in South Africa. By conventional measures Donald had not been a success in his first commission in the Royal Garrison Artillery, and now he was going to waste in the ranks. The army badly needed officers, and this was a second chance. So for the time being Donald let the process of his eventual commissioning take its sluggish course. He is sensitive to having 'given a great many people a good deal of trouble in getting it for me, and I felt bound to abide by the result' (*Letters*, p. 397).

One of the things that particularly dismayed Hankey was

---

[4]In a letter dated 26 August Donald welcomes Maurice home from his fact-finding mission to the Dardanelles. After praising his brother's letters from that theatre of operations, he ventures some comments of his own on 'the qualities of the Australian soldier' (no doubt because the ANZACs were heavily involved in the Gallipoli campaign and because of the family's personal ties to Australia). Donald acknowledges that Aussie soldiers are considered undisciplined judged by English standards, but he defends this characteristic as in some ways producing a more effective fighting man than the English, who by and large 'are lacking in personal initiative' and are 'less aggressive'. Making the most of his greater intimacy with the ordinary ranker than Maurice can claim, Donald enlarges on this contrast. 'To a certain extent the system is responsible,' he asserts, 'though it is mainly a defect in character.' Despite Donald's high regard for his fellow Tommies ('The men will do anything—if they are told to. But they do it passively, wishing they hadn't got to'), he puts it bluntly to Maurice that 'in the New Army discipline has destroyed individuality.' This letter is accompanied by an editor's note stating that it 'was shown to the late Lord Kitchener who read it with great interest' (*Letters*, pp. 382-3).

being sent for training to the 'home establishment' of the RGA in Woolwich, whereas it had been his understanding that he would be returned directly to action as soon as he was fit for duty (*Letters*, p. 397). The artillery regiment might have met that condition had he not been wounded in the meantime and sent back home. Now that he was emerging from a hospital in the vicinity of the training centre for gunners at Woolwich, the alternative of assigning newly-commissioned 2nd Lt Hankey to a period of instruction in his unfamiliar duties before putting him under fire seems to have been a fully appropriate decision on the army's part. But to Hankey himself the more he brooded on his situation the more intolerable it seemed. After a brief visit to his former haunts in Bermondsey Donald wrote on 10 October to his friend Lance Huntington, who, too consumptive for military service, was managing the Oxford and Bermondsey Mission through its wartime difficulties. He praises Lance for his efforts at the Mission but makes no bones about his own dissatisfaction:

The accumulated misery of this place [Woolwich] is dreadful. It is a cold and draughty hut. My feet are frozen, and yet it is full of flies! Could anything be more horrible? It hasn't even the merit of being heroic—like a dug-out. ... I am so fed up that I am really resolved to make a bid for a transfer to infantry.

(*Letters*, p. 391)

And that is what he does, applying to Hugh's old regiment, the Royal Warwickshires. Then almost two months pass; Donald knows the Colonel of the Warwicks has given his approval, but for a time his application seems to have dropped from view. In describing his troubles to Canon Cremer in his letter of 8 December, Donald declares

158

that he is on the verge of relinquishing his commission altogether and re-enlisting as a private soldier in the infantry. There are plenty of junior officers, he tells Cremer; nor does he consider himself a particularly good one, 'being too democratic in my tendencies'. In the ranks, however, there is real opportunity for such a person as himself to exercise a positive influence 'from within'.

> Further, if I survive the war I shall be in a much better position for prosecuting the schemes and studies which are nearest to my heart if I am a private, and in close touch with men of the working class, than if I am an officer and a gentleman branded.
>
> *(Letters*, p. 398)

According to the editor of Hankey's *Letters*, he did in fact ask in writing to be allowed to resign as an officer so that he could rejoin the ranks. That letter, accompanied by a note from a Lt. Col. of the Royal Garrison Artillery to the effect that in his opinion 2nd Lt Hankey 'would make a valuable officer in this regiment or in the Infantry' *did* succeed in getting the attention of Headquarters. Lt Hankey's resignation was thereupon refused and his former application to transfer to the Royal Warwickshire Regiment was at last approved (*Letters*, p. 399).

*

From the earliest days of his recuperation and continuing throughout all the tedious and frustrating process that finally made him a subaltern in the infantry, Donald's work as a writer gained momentum and set him on the road to wide recognition. Hardly a week after he was wounded, and before being sent back to England, Donald is telling Hilda about two articles he has written with Mr Strachey and the *Spectator* in view. These were most likely the essays titled 'Of Some Who Were Lost and Afterward Were Found' and 'Flowers of Flanders', when they appeared early the next year in the *Spectator*. Donald described this latter piece as 'about lots of things, including parcels and religion and love of nature. ... Neither [article] could possibly have been written except by one who has been at the front' (*Letters*, p. 377).

Later that same month Donald announces to Maurice that the 'Acting Editor' of the *Spectator* has accepted one of his articles and that there are four others awaiting Mr Strachey's editorial decision. Subsequently he reports to Mrs Coppin that the *Spectator* has now taken three of the five pieces he has sent them. Feeling 'rather bucked up' by this success, Donald gives 'Grandmamma' Coppin a detailed outline of a projected series of five articles for the *Westminster Gazette*, which spells out many of the themes that eventually were to run through virtually everything Hankey wrote as 'A Student in Arms'. These projected essays, he informs Mrs Coppin, 'are really a study of Kitchener's Army as a Union of the classes in a common aim, and life' (*Letters*, p. 384). Such a characterization of his purposes, and the outline that follows it, are invaluable clues to what actually marks, or ought to mark, Donald Hankey's distinction among World War I writers. Had more of his readers been alert to anything other than a view of the war that satisfied popular patriotic sentiments, Hankey's preoccupation with the New Army as an inadvertent but valuable experiment in social harmony might have won him a different sort of reputation, even a more durable one. For unlike most popular writers during the war, Hankey's chief concern was not the military conflict itself. The raising of an enormous citizens' army, subjecting it to the common military experience and the drastic ordeal of combat, and testing traditional notions of class supremacy and leadership under such extreme and harrowing conditions was bound to transform the entire warp and weft of Britain's social fabric. Few writers saw this likelihood as early and as sharply as did the 'Student in Arms'.

After he had written out the skeleton of his projected series for the *Westminster Gazette*, Hankey confesses to Mrs Coppin that he 'felt almost as if I had betrayed my comrades by applying for a commission!' (*Letters*, p. 386). The series as such did not materialize, but the Student in Arms pieces he continued to write and submit to the *Spectator* through the latter months of 1915 drew significantly on the ideas foreshadowed in his outline. In December Hankey's short essays began to appear weekly in the *Spectator*. Immediately they made a strong impact. As must inevitably be the case, readers found in them pretty much whatever they wished to find. Most were looking for heartening confirmation of the staunchness and courage of the men in the trenches and many, no doubt, for religious piety directed at the experience of war. There was plenty in Hankey's work to satisfy such readers. The response to the anonymous Student's pieces was so positive that Donald's characteristic self-mockery could not disguise his satisfaction. Replying to Mrs Wathen, mother of his childhood pal Ronnie and wife of his Brighton schoolmaster, who either guessed or was told the identity of the *Spectator*'s soldier-contributor, Donald includes a derisive pen and ink sketch of himself in the uniform of a newly-commissioned subaltern (complete with swagger-stick) whose cap is ridiculously too small. Of course it is not Lt Hankey's status as an officer, but rather the praise he has received from the *Spectator*'s eminent editor, Mr St. Loe Strachey,[5] that has caused his head to outgrow its cap size.

---

[5] J. St. Loe Strachey (1860–1927) had been editor and proprietor of the *Spectator* since 1898. He was the cousin (some twenty years older) of the biographer, Lytton Strachey.

Donald is now moved to make Captain Hardy the subject of one of The Student's weekly articles; he sends a polite letter to Miss Hardy, asking for her mother's permission to publish a tribute to 'The Beloved Captain', which he encloses and which he thinks likely some readers will correctly recognize as a tribute to Hardy. 'It is not to make money or to increase my literary reputation that I want to send it [to the *Spectator*]... I feel certain that the article, however badly expressed, might, simply because it is a portrait, prove a source of inspiration to many' (*Letters*, pp. 401–402).

This letter to Miss Hardy is dated 19 December; Donald was by that time probably resigned to his status as an officer but was hoping at least to be reassigned to the infantry. Not least among those he hoped his tribute to 'The Beloved Captain' might inspire was its author himself. If he was not to remain in the ranks and share the lives of those he was drawn to, then those qualities of selfless leadership he loved in Captain Hardy would be his own conscious model for what an officer should be to his men.

Early in the new year Lt Hankey reported for duty with the 3rd Battalion of the Royal Warwickshire Regiment. Already his *Spectator* articles had catapulted 'The Student' into prominence as a commentator on soldiers at war,[6] and

---

[6] The appearance of the Student in Arms articles was closely contemporaneous with the protracted parliamentary manoeuvring and intense national concern over the question of whether compulsory military service should replace the volunteerism which had produced Kitchener's Mob—the New Army that was the essential subject of Hankey's essays. It is more than an incidental irony that by the time A *Student in Arms* was published in book form in the spring of 1916 the passage of two Military Service Bills had virtually marked the end of the 'Kitcheners' and the beginning of an army of conscripts. I think it fair to conclude that the heated issue of volunteerism vs conscription, by heightening public interest in the composition of the fighting forces and 'universalizing' the prospect of soldiering, contributed substantially to the extraordinary reception that Hankey's essays enjoyed.

several publishers indicated an interest in bringing them out in book form. To Andrew Melrose, one of the first of these, Hankey writes from the Isle of Wight, where he is now serving with his infantry battalion, confessing his inexperience in dealing with publishers but saying he would be pleased to receive an offer. Melrose responded quickly, and by the end of January, 1916 he and his new author are discussing possible titles for the book. Strachey of the *Spectator* has agreed to write an introduction.

There are many ways of explaining the popularity of the Student in Arms essays. One might simply say they appeared at a time when England particularly felt the need of them. The winter of 1915–16 was a critical and generally depressing period. In her novel *Non-Combatants and Others*, published in August 1916, Rose Macaulay catches the weary mood that seemed to possess the nation at the end of 1915, after the costly defeat at Loos and the manifold disappointments of the failed Dardanelles expedition, with the prospect of universal conscription a virtual certainty:

> The year of grace 1915 slipped away into darkness, like a broken ship drifting on bitter tides onto a waste shore. The next year began.
> (quoted in Hynes, *A War Imagined*, p. 129)

Those are the concluding words of Macaulay's novel. H. G. Wells's *Mr Britling Sees It Through* (published in September 1916) traces the war's effect on the home front from its beginnings in a 'blaze of moral exaltation' into the summer of 1915 when its 'dramatic quality' had dissipated and it had 'ceased to be either a tragedy or a triumph' (Wells, p. 282). By early autumn of 1915 England was engaged in what Wells characterized as 'a war that had lost its soul' (p. 351). Donald Hankey's essays did something to turn the focus of readers' attention away from general discouragement and immediate cheerlessness to their fellow-citizens in arms. He reminded them that, whatever unimaginable things might be happening to these absent men, besides being fondly missed they could still be thought about as vital members of the social body.

1915 had been a momentous year for Donald Hankey; he would not live out the next one. Wounded as a corporal, he had recovered, bid a reluctant goodbye to the life of a ranker in Kitchener's Mob, and become a second lieutenant. But a more important new identity was the persona he had created for himself as A Student in Arms. It would attach to him for the remainder of his life and throughout the years of his fame as a writer.

8

Recognition (February–May 1916)

Until he left England in May to go back into the line, Donald Hankey spent the early months of 1916 stationed at the Albany Barracks, Parkhurst on the Isle of Wight. He drilled a squad of recruits from Derby ('nice lads most of them' [*Letters*, p. 405]) and later became a 'bombing instructor', an assignment he found 'really quite amusing'.[1] Though he continued to regret having left the ranks to take a commission, he was feeling more contented as he adapted to his new role. 'I lecture and instruct, instead of walking about with a stick under my arm watching a sgt.' (*Letters*, pp. 416-17). Teaching appealed to him, and now with some practical experience to impart to his troops his separation from the common soldier was somewhat mitigated. 'Today we had a great time blowing up trenches, etc.', he writes enthusiastically (*Letters*, p. 417).[2]

---

[1]As it became increasingly recognized that the Western Front was essentially war in the trenches, and as the techniques of trench warfare evolved, 'bombing' (i.e., hand-grenade throwing) developed as a critical skill in the training of infantry. So much so that Christopher Tietjens, the protagonist of Ford Madox (Hueffer) Ford's war novels, complains that 'in the poor beastly trenches the Tommies knew nothing but how to chuck bombs. ... The rifle was obsolete!' Captain Tietjens, the traditionalist in all things, considers this the 'imbecile idea' of a 'civilian army' (*Parade's End*, Vol. I [*Some Do Not ... & No More Parades*], Signet Classics, 1964, p. 499).

[2]To John Barker, whom Hankey addresses as 'Prester John', identified by the editor of the *Letters* only as 'a working man with whom [Hankey] kept up a regular correspondence' but never met in person (*Letters*, p. 410n.).

Parkhurst hardly matched the idyllic conditions of Donald's billet with Mrs Coppin in Elstead, but there were genuine satisfactions. He found his duties not altogether uninteresting, and there was a purpose to some of them he could appreciate. In addition—indeed, most particularly—Donald was enjoying his success as an author and all that went with it: praise from Mr Strachey of the *Spectator*, who was becoming a strong advocate of his work, and a correspondence with Andrew Melrose concerning publication of his essays in collected form.

His letters to Melrose have about them the easy and modest confidence of a man who finds such a relationship as that between a seasoned publisher and a new but rising writer entirely natural and hugely satisfying. Donald confides comically that the most obvious title, *A Student in Arms*, has always seemed to him rather too suggestive of 'a baby in arms' and signals his willingness to change *in* to *under*. On the question of revealing his authorship he is indecisive; 'anonymity has its lure,' he admits, but he also makes the point to Melrose that though his name would not count for much 'it might count for a little'. Then on second thoughts he suggests that some among his fairly wide acquaintance 'might buy for the name' (*Letters*, pp. 407, 409–10). To Mrs Coppin he can venture a self-disparaging reference to his essays as 'a heterogeneous collection of stodgy stuff' (*Letters*, p. 405); but he knows better than to assume that tone with a man who has undertaken to publish his work. Instead, he banters with Mr Melrose (*Letters*, p. 415) about a novel he began sometime that spring, making light of the project yet obviously taking pleasure in discussing with his publisher his struggles in attempting fiction.

Hankey's letters from this period reveal both his many-sidedness and his own consciousness of this characteristic personal quality. A perfectly earnest student in arms, he

166

writes facetiously of himself as 'a theological journalist' (*Letters*, p. 428). Obviously grateful for Strachey's generous efforts in his behalf, Donald nevertheless describes this respected editor's 'Introduction' to his volume of essays as 'very buttery'. Up to a point, of course, we recognize here various manifestations of a harmless false modesty—the rags of vanity, one might say, worn inside out. It is the familiar stance of a certain kind of young gentleman, fond of praise yet always somewhat guarded about responding to it, perhaps rather too proud to show that the approval of others is a thing that needs to matter.

Yet Hankey is not merely a late-Victorian upper-middle-class university-bred model of 'good form'. He gives these familiar traits his own distinctive, self-regarding detachment. His published letters reveal him as a more than competent impromptu pen-and-ink sketcher—most tellingly given to the art of self-caricature. These drawings, scattered through his letters, tell us much about Hankey's sense of himself. They seem extremely quick and charmingly careless in their approximations but at the same time often marked by witty observation. Intended as they were for others' amusement, it would be naive to suppose that Hankey was telling anything like the whole truth about himself. They are products of practised self-ridicule, and as such are offered as exhibitions, not confessions. They show only as much of the artist—the man who holds the pen and makes us laugh—as he is prepared to put forward, only as much of the joke as he wants to share.

If, in these self-caricatures, Donald held at arm's length some occasional and deliberately clownish projections, he was, with respect to his serious writing, similarly conscious of the distinction between the actual self and the *persona* he was creating. In this case the distinction he registers is that between images of what the writer wished to be and his sense of what he truly was. On 22 January Donald shared with Mrs Coppin the good news that Andrew Melrose had proposed to publish the *Spectator* articles. A week later, in supplying that letter with a third postscript, he thinks to add a gracious thanks to 'Grandmamma' for her many kindnesses and her good opinion. Then he cautions her that should she ever see a side of him 'which is not the best' she must try to believe he has not deliberately sought to deceive her.

> I don't mean to suggest that I have any secret vice; but I fear that my thoughts are the best of me, and always have been. . . . I have always been able to write, and even to preach, far bigger and better things than I have ever felt or practised.

To this he then adds the point he has made on other occasions, to other friends: that he seems to inspire deeper affection than he is able himself to give. 'I am afraid that I am really rather a shallow person,' he concludes, but with the hope that 'thanks to a few friends I am not quite so shallow as I was once' (*Letters*, p. 406).

Just as his hurried drawings, for all their deftness, are by no means a full and accurate portrait of the artist, so the Student's essays give only a partial impression of the man who wrote them. They are the thoughts of a 'student' abstracted from that man's full identity in all its complexity and contradictions. This is hardly surprising. No doubt all writers feel something of this circumstance; no doubt one's full identity can seem more shallow, less adequate, than the idealized but in fact sketchy and selective 'self' one invents out of necessity or convenience. What is notable about Donald Hankey's case, however, is the way this disparity between the full (yet 'shallow'?) real self and the shadowy deceptions of the ideal produces in him both a sense of guilt, or at least unworthiness, and moments of delight. What he feels he should be and what he finds he wants to be are then ironically transvalued. The affection of others reminds him of his own shallowness; elevation in the ranks makes him feel disloyal to his former comrades; praise and acclaim for his writing prompts him to belittle his own work. The author of sober essays on the spiritual condition of Britain's men in arms, he larks with them in blowing up trenches and relishes teaching them the sheer fun of bombing techniques.

Donald regards the incongruity of his activities at this time with a conscious appreciation of their essential absurdity that suggests a new-found equanimity:

I am very busy at present on a bombing course, and also correcting proofs. ...

(*Letters*, p. 413)

I have begun a story! But now that I am a bombing instructor I don't get much time.

(*Letters*, p. 415)

Here I am, who really enjoy trench digging and am condemned to look ornamental and typewrite journalese, while fellows who love typewriting are made to dig trenches. ... It is most absurd.

(*Letters*, p. 411)

The puzzle of his nature and his persistent discontents had not been fathomed, much less resolved; still, he could live with that. St. Loe Strachey, the editor of the *Spectator*, whose acquaintance with Donald dates from these months, wrote that 'he was at bottom what Walt Whitman calls "a natural and nonchalant" person.' Although theirs could not have been a close or extended friendship, Strachey believed he knew Donald thoroughly and he saw what solid accomplishment had brought out in The Student, his characteristic detachment not registering as aloofness. 'Not

169

for one moment did you find in him the chill of sanctity,' the editor goes on to say. Then, turning again to literature, he applies the words of Stevenson's Long John Silver to Donald Hankey: 'He kept company very easy'.[3]

*

In April *A Student in Arms*—'my collected writings of the last six months', as Hankey described it (*Letters*, p. 416)—made its appearance. A book of military science, one might mistakenly presume from its frontispiece which shows a rather dour likeness of the author wearing a subaltern's uniform.[4] The artillery badges on his collar suggest Hankey posed for the photograph soon after receiving his commission in the RGA. The heavy brows, slightly protruding jaw, and broad moustache give no suggestion of the blithe and agreeable side of his nature. The book's twenty essays are preceded by Mr St. Loe Strachey's introduction and a brief author's foreword.

In his introduction Strachey stressed what he calls 'the note of originality', an emphasis that would strike many modern readers, seeing nothing eccentric or newfangled in Hankey's style, as wide of the mark. In responding to that characterization, the author's foreword attributes the impression of novelty to 'an unusual point of view, due to an unusual combination of circumstances'. This claim,

---

[3]Strachey, S L. (1922) *The Adventure of Living*, (pp. 486-7). New York and London.

[4]In an essay titled 'The War and Literature', Edmund Gosse had written in the autumn of 1914 that 'for the remaining duration of the war ... The book which does not deal directly and crudely with the complexities of warfare and the various branches of strategy will, from Christmas onwards, not be published at all' (*Edinburgh Review*, October 1914, p. 381). Though an exaggeration, such a narrow and unappealing prospect helps one understand why a volume like Hankey's was welcomed by the public, who were grateful to find the New Army discussed in its more human dimension.

170

though Hankey does not elaborate it, should be taken seriously. At the very least it means the essays that follow were written by someone who has made a close and thoughtful study of ordinary British soldiers, who knows their world at first hand, almost to the point of seeing it through their very eyes, yet whose own experience and background are quite different from theirs.

And—it would be well to keep in mind as we consider these essays of Donald Hankey's—the world he and the men he served with at least partially shared in common was worlds away from *ours*. In his indispensable book, *The Great War and Modern Memory*, Paul Fussell offers telling reflections on this difference, speaking of 'those sweet and generous people' who fought the war and who supported their sons and husbands and lovers in fighting it[5]. Conditioned as we have been by the cynicism—justified and unjustified—of our time, 'how can we forbear condescending', Fussell asks, to such innocence as we find in almost every aspect of life before The Great War—and indeed through a great part of that war? Our knowing smiles at the radical innocence of that lost world are 'not appropriate', insists Professor Fussell, speaking not only as a literary scholar but with some of the vehemence of a self-described 'pissed-off infantryman' from World War II. He drives home the point that from our perspective the literary scene in the year 1916—its stock of stylistic gestures and images, its repertoire of feelings and attitudes—'is hard to imagine':

There was no *Waste Land*, with its rats' alleys, dull canals, and dead men who have lost their bones: it

[5]Fussell, P. (1975) *The Great War and Modern Memory*, (p. 19). London: Oxford University Press.

would take four years of trench warfare to bring these to consciousness. There was no *Ulysses*, no *Mauberly*, no *Cantos*, no Kafka, no Proust, no Waugh, no Auden, no Huxley, no Cummings, no *Women in Love* or *Lady Chatterley's Lover*. There was no 'Valley of Ashes' in *The Great Gatsby*. One read Hardy and Kipling and Conrad and frequented worlds of traditional moral action delineated in traditional moral language.

(Fussell, p. 23)

Although Donald Hankey's literary horizon was less barren than that of many well-educated contemporaries, Fussell's point obviously applies to him. He was a self-styled 'modernist', but to Hankey that term had to do only with matters of religion or theology. Freud certainly and probably even Marx were beyond his ken. As for his taste in literature, he did read Wilde with some sympathy (G. B. Shaw with hardly any) and Conrad, but he was not even incipiently *avant garde*. Browning was his poet; the brothers Benson (A. C., the essayist, and E. F., the novelist) were favourites in prose. Of course he was steeped in Dickens and adored him; he quotes Tennyson and a somewhat obscure couple of lines from Keats that suggest a fairly wide familiarity with that poet. So Hankey's 'culture' was substantial though lightly worn, largely traditional without being stodgy. Certainly a man who actually *did* read Darwin and was absorbed in William James was not a hopeless Philistine.

Finally, it is probably of some importance to a reckoning of what Hankey brought to *A Student in Arms* that it was the work of a man who had crossed the great generational divide and belonged among those 'over thirty'. If we think of the most powerful literature of The Great War as reflecting the disillusionment that came in its later stages—or, as many have noted, after the appalling 1 July of 1916 on the Somme—Donald Hankey's first volume of essays is surpassed and overshadowed by the major war writing that followed it. And one of the most obvious things that explains this is simply the fact that Hankey's view of life and of himself was pretty well formed before he experienced the war and felt the shock of combat. He was at least half a generation older than most of those we regard as having produced England's finest World War I literature. The exception was Ford Madox Hueffer, who was Hankey's senior by eleven years. But Hueffer (or Ford, as he called himself after he abandoned his German surname)—exceptional in so many ways—had begun his part in the invention of the modern sensibility well before the war inspired him to write the set of four novels known collectively as *Parade's End*. Hankey, to be sure, had nothing like Ford's fascination for current literary activity or his access to contemporary writers and the general discourse of the arts.

In the autumn of 1915, while he was still recovering in hospital from his wound, Donald Hankey outlined in a letter to Mrs Coppin a five-part series for the *Westminster Gazette*. Apparently the undertaking was rather separate from the 'five effusions' he had by then already sent off to the *Spectator*. The *Westminster* was the publication where Donald's articles on the Australian outback had appeared, and perhaps he felt that a series organized around a central theme or subject would be more likely to suit that journal than Mr Strachey's *Spectator*. The few pieces he had by then placed with the *Spectator* hadn't the degree of cohesion present in his outline to Mrs Coppin. The five-part series he describes to her—though it never came to fruition in exactly that form—gives the reader of *A Student in Arms* a useful clue as to what lies at the core of that book and constitutes what is perhaps its strongest, most valid claim to 'originality'.

What Hankey was planning that autumn he succinctly describes as 'a study of Kitchener's Army as a Union of the classes in a common aim, and life.' Not a book about winning the war against foreign enemies or even about the forming of a rag-tag collection of civilians into an army of which the nation could be proud, but a consideration of how the national emergency required a class society to find an alternative vision of itself. Such a vision, born of necessity and realized in the extremity of an armed conflict, Hankey proposed to show, would produce not only honour and victory in war but greater justice and a brighter future for even the least members of the body politic.

'All classes were at one' is the slogan Hankey assigned to the first of these projected essays. It was to have described the crowds of men swarming to enlist, plunging themselves into 'a common life and work' (*Letters*, p. 385). This phenomenon, Donald wished to emphasize, was no mere 'wave of sentiment', but a profound commitment by every element of a disparate society to a simple objective. This commitment would require from these volunteers the acceptance of a common experience and the sharing in its sacrifices. Whatever part patriotic fervour played in the formation of what came to be called 'Kitchener's Mob', in Hankey's view the raising of that new army had a deeper, more durable meaning: it was an act of social solidarity.

The second essay would deal with 'the equality of the classes' as the practical consequence of mass enlistment. Ability and character, not privilege or previous class identity, would determine how the enlistees would ultimately fare, what roles they would come to fill. In the third essay Hankey planned to consider the officers as a 'super-class'. How he would develop this concept is unclear, except that he intended to suggest that 'the traditional [i.e., military] view of discipline did not succeed

174

altogether in this citizen army.' Apparently, and despite the authority of the officer class, the truly transforming social dynamic Hankey perceives in such an army is largely a matter of the 'other ranks'. Hankey wished to call the fourth essay in this series 'Men Wanted'. His aim there was to discover how the war itself 'completed the adjustment' away from a hierarchy of social classes towards a recognition of merit—not by rank but through a common acknowledgment of those who 'were always on the spot in a moment of crisis.' Men at war learn to see their fellows 'as God sees them' and to value and love them 'quite irrespective of their accents and manners' (*Letters*, p. 385).

The intended conclusion would pose a question for the future. At war's end, would 'the old artificial grooves' of class behaviour reassert themselves, or would 'a more unselfish and communal spirit' carry over into civilian political life? Cryptically, Donald suggests that the answer 'will depend on the women' (*Letters*, pp. 384–6).

That Hankey failed to proceed with this projected series along just these lines may be attributed to the success of his earliest 'Student in Arms' pieces for the *Spectator,* to the encouragement this gave him to range more broadly in the subjects he attempted. But he adapted his ideas for the five-part series to fit the subjects of some of the weekly *Spectator* essays. Two or three of those essays might well represent Hankey's final working-out of individual sections of the five-part study he projected. In any event, his abiding sense of the Kitchener army as the crucible of social transformation is certainly a critical ingredient in *A Student in Arms* as it appears in book form. Because Hankey looks beyond the crisis of war and its strictly military challenge to the question of what the effect might be on the fabric of English society, these essays stand apart from almost all other important writing the war produced.

The first essay (in the order given them in the book),

brief as it is, brings the social issue of a citizen army strongly to the fore. 'Kitchener's Army', as Hankey titles this mere three-page proem, assumes the collective voice and devil-may-care outlook of these early volunteers. It is a voice harking back to the well-remembered clamour Donald heard in the clubs of the OBM in south London— only still more diverse, in age and social background. 'We are a mixed lot–a triumph of democracy, like the Tubes' [i.e., the London Underground] (*ASIA*, p. 19). A rowdy crew, for the most part, full of cheek and confidence— contemptuous, if not quite oblivious, of the stark realities ahead. These realities Hankey admits to his portrayal of the New Army in its infancy as only a faint dissonance: 'Maiming, slaughter, blood, extremities of fear and discomfort and pain! How incredibly remote all that seems!' (*ASIA*, p. 21). As these recruits welcome their perilous adventure in the spirit of 'a great game we are learning', Hankey celebrates their diversity made harmonious by unity of purpose and equality of condition:

> Some miss their glass of claret, others their fish-and-chips; but as we all sleep on the floor, and have only one suit, which is rapidly becoming very disreputable, you would never tell t'other from which.
>
> (*ASIA*, p. 20)

The second essay, titled 'An Experiment in Democracy', develops this theme of the unity-in-diversity of this 'rag-time' army. It is actually a distillation of the entire five-part series Hankey had projected for Mrs Coppin. This was not the essay that stirred the greatest emotional response in the Student's readers. Other chapters—'The Beloved Captain' and 'The Honour of the Brigade' most particularly—came to be singled out for special praise, read aloud in barracks and club rooms, and widely treasured. But 'An

Experiment in Democracy' provides the clearest reason why Donald Hankey must be included among those who wrote significantly about England in The Great War. Of all the Student's studies this takes the richest account of its author's situation, draws most deeply from Hankey's own experience as a 'gentleman branded', who nevertheless felt the inclinations of a social explorer; someone to whom religion constituted the most valued sphere of life, but who detested the shows of piety and distrusted the claims of authority and orthodoxy. Donald often went out of his way to warn that what he wrote was better than what he was; of course that was a signal that his writing might be leaving something unsaid. In its way 'An Experiment in Democracy' is Hankey's freest, most outspoken essay.

As many other young Englishmen hailed the war as a personal adventure–an awakening from ignoble general lethargy, a chance to 'drink life to the lees' and perhaps seize individual glory–Donald Hankey takes here a quite different tack. 'The unprecedented had occurred,' he begins, contemplating the crowds surging outside the recruiting offices in Great Scotland Yard on that August day when he himself enlisted. He marks it not (like Rupert Brooke's sonnet 'Peace') as a histrionic leap into some vague form of 'cleanness', but a conscious concerted step towards a new social condition.

> For once a national ideal had proved stronger than class prejudice. In this matter of the war all classes were at one.
>
> (*ASIA*, p. 25)

The day of his own enlistment in the new citizen army, and its sequel, Hankey regards as less personally than collectively momentous; but he does so lightly–not facetiously, but with finely-judged humour. Before he and the other recruits relinquish civilian attire, their appearance strikingly belies the grave act of unity that enlistment represents. They are truly of all sorts: workmen, boys from the East End, clerks, mechanics, travellers, 'and most conspicuously well-dressed of all, gentlemen in their oldest clothes' (*ASIA*, p. 26). Donald does not put himself quite at the centre of this scene nor at any point in the essay, but we are aware of him as one of those 'other classes ... far less at their ease.' This group Hankey tellingly identifies as 'brought up from earliest youth to thank God they were not as other men', horribly embarrassed now to be divested of all the superficial accoutrements of their supposed superiority. Donald confesses himself one of these, proud to be free from 'the snobbishness of the suburbs', but as ill at ease as any. Even in the working-men's clubs he knew from the inside, he had been 'Mr Thingummy'; here he is addressed as 'mate'—a name he rather likes but wishes he looked the part. 'He felt as self-conscious as if he had arrived at a dinner party in a Norfolk jacket' (*ASIA*,, pp. 26–7).

Hankey's dependence on clothing to carry the emotional meaning of the enlistment experience is the essay's most inspired feature. Naturally but comprehensively the actual exchange of the variegated garb of class identity for the 'uniform' of army service makes vivid the loss and gain of such a transformation. Both his fondness for fine clothes and his various attempts to assume the identity of a common labourer—in the Australian bush and at harvest time in the fields of southeast England—surely enriched his feeling for all that is at stake, symbolically and psychologically, in such a change of dress.

But before this exchange of civilian clothes for the khaki of the common soldier, clothing figures in a still more revelatory moment. Here the universal and the intimate mingle, transcending yet also illuminating the social. It is

178

the one point in the essay where the anonymous 'gentleman' is indistinguishable from Donald Hankey and where his role is not only representative but, as it were, confessional. This is the moment 'when he sat, one of four nude men, in a cubicle awaiting medical inspection.' With the removal of every last outward mark of social identity and complete exposure comes something beyond self-consciousness. It involves absolute self-acceptance in the face of the irreducibly human:

> ... he did feel for that moment they had all been reduced to the common denominator of their sheer humanity; but embarrassment returned with his clothes and stayed with him all through the march to the station and the journey to the depot.
>
> (*ASIA*, p. 27)

For all the extreme difference in context and character, it is not farfetched to recall King Lear's pronouncements on nakedness. Hankey, afflicted with the reticence and prudery of his class and his era, can still come to a recognition and acknowledgement of unaccommodated man, 'the thing itself'. And how wry and modern and *un*Shakespearean that here the gentleman's lendings are not flamboyantly torn away but meekly and undemonstratively reassumed.

Hankey's predicament is not Lear's; no excess pomp in need of physicking, only a somewhat Prufrockian residue of decorum and inadequacy to be confronted. He recalls fighting for the prize of a verminous blanket at the depot. Along with the others he claims his six feet of floor space for sleeping. At daybreak his transformation, the erasure of distinction both cherished and loathed, seems complete:

> When he awoke the next morning his clothes were creased and dirty, his collar so filthy that it had to be

179

discarded, and his chin unshaven. He perceived with a shock he was no longer conspicuous. He was no more than the seedy unit of a seedy crowd. In any other circumstances he would have been disgusted. As it was, he sought the canteen at the earliest opportunity and toasted the Unity of the Classes in a pint!

(*ASIA*, pp. 27–8)

It is a particularly fine touch that Hankey registers his assumption of a conscript's life and the clash between his gentlemanly sensibility and his long-held and deep-seated yearnings in such specific terms. The khaki uniform itself, which other enlistees' accounts invariably disparage as ill-fitting and uncomfortable, furnishes a culmination of what Hankey calls 'the symbolism of clothes'. Donning the uniform consecrates the step that has already been taken; everyone's civilian accoutrements—'emblems of class distinction'—are deposited on a common rag-heap. By its very simplicity the occasion has about it, in Hankey's sensitive and resourceful treatment, an 'almost religious solemnity'. 'It was the formal beginning of a new life' (*ASIA*, p. 28).

Of course it is not a life of undifferentiated equality, but opportunities for these recruits are virtually the same; merit and 'native tact', rather than social class, are the basis of whatever preeminence emerges. To be sure, commissioned officers exist apart as a 'super-class'. They are 'an offence against democracy', survivals within a democratic citizen's army of 'the ancient religion of the army of aristocracy'. That is how Hankey regards military discipline, which—like other religions—'has its mysteries, its hierarchy, its dogmas, and its ritual' (*ASIA*, p. 30). As for the dogmatic and ritualistic features of this archaic religion of military discipline, Hankey is fairly scathing; but he tempers his account of the super-class by allowing that most officers possess sufficient scepticism and humour not to take their own exalted positions too seriously. In the trenches the religion of military discipline tends to lapse, Hankey contends; in the rest camps behind the line it reasserts itself strongly. By and large, actual experience of war brings the best men to the fore. Common dangers and discomforts tend to weld even officers and men more closely together. 'They learn to trust each other, and to look for the essential qualities rather than for the accidental graces.' In the stress of combat men see one another more as they must be in the eyes of God:

> Out there, if anyone dared to remind you that Jim was only a fireman while you were a bank clerk, you would give him one in the eye to go on with.
>
> *(ASIA,* p. 34)

Hankey's view of the citizens' army is coloured by his egalitarian longings, but his first-hand experience gives it substance. Much of what he sought in Bermondsey and in the outback was largely realized in Kitchener's Mob.[6] A citizens' army—at least in the ideal, and based on his service in the 'other ranks'—though far from a perfect world, might be the means of bringing such a world closer. What will the men who serve in it learn from this volunteer army? Hankey looks beyond the war and is tempted to prophesy:

> In those days there shall be no more petty strife between class and class; for all shall have learned that

---

[6]Of course it must be recognized that the recruitment of the New Army—especially those formations known as the 'Pals Battalions'—took account of the often marked aversion of many enlistees to being herded with men of different (i.e., 'lower') social background. Donald Hankey seems to have been relatively oblivious to this fact about the volunteer army.

they are one nation, and that they must seek the
nation's good before their own, ... In those days there
shall be no false pride, for all have lived hardly, all have
done dirty and menial work, all have wielded the pick
and spade, and have counted it no dishonour but
rather glory to do so.

(ASIA, p. 35)

What had long been Donald's personal fantasy thus
becomes his social hope. But he concedes the likelihood
'that men will slip back into the old grooves'. Hankey
concludes his essay by unexpectedly turning his attention
to 'the women of England'. The role they play, he suggests,
may be decisive. Only in a limited sense does he consider
women as an emerging social force. Indeed, Hankey
suspects that women are all too likely to reassume the
function of benign but reactionary guardians of 'the
ancient ruts' to which English society at large will be
tempted to return when peace comes. The positive hope
he places in women has little to do with the suffrage
movement; it consists rather in a more widely diffused
'vision of national unity' and charitable instincts more
broadly directed than heretofore (*ASIA*, p. 36). He is not
thinking of the Pankhursts and their ilk but of the women
he knew personally—all admirable and by no means cut to
the same social pattern, but hardly models of militancy: his
sister Hilda and his cousin Dorothy, Mrs L in the Australian
outback, and his 'adopted grandmother' Mrs Coppin.

As 'An Experiment in Democracy' makes clear, it is not a
military victory over the central powers that Hankey looks
to as the ultimate vindication of Kitchener's New Army.
Although military victory is the ostensible objective, a
social—perhaps a moral—transformation would be the
greater triumph. One suspects that Hankey's readers were
more anxious to be reassured that the citizens' army could

defeat the Germans than to be told their sons and husbands were learning the lessons essential for a better social order. Nevertheless, they were naturally concerned in a general way about the moral effect army life and the experience of war would have on those who had volunteered to face the enemy. The essay on 'Discipline and Leadership', though weakened by a somewhat equivocal conclusion, is a thoughtful extension of the subject of the 'New Army' as a social laboratory. 'The difference between the old and new Armies is not at all unlike the difference between the Roman and Reformed Churches' (*ASIA*, p. 41), suggests the Student, having studied theology and church history, but also drawing on his experience as an academy-trained subaltern in the Royal Garrison Artillery long before his enlistment. In both the Regular Army and the Roman Church, Hankey contends, 'discipline is strong and procedure stereotyped', and for that reason the personal qualities of the individual leaders within both institutions are not so severely tested—are not the basis of authority—as in the Reformed Church and in 'Kitchener's Army'.

In the old Regular Army it has always been recognized that all officers and NCOs could not be expected to be born leaders of men. The whole system of military discipline has been built up with a view to relieving the strain on the individual. The officer's authority is carefully guarded by an elaborate system designed to give him prestige.

(*ASIA*, p. 41)

Under this traditional system it is the machinery of discipline, extending from the highest ranks all the way to the most junior lance-corporal, that confers and sustains authority. Such a system, Hankey acknowledges, makes the Regular Army a marvel of efficiency.

Theoretically, the same 'law' with an equally high standard of discipline governs the 'New Army' raised from hoards of civilian recruits. 'But as a matter of fact it is quite impossible to enforce such a system in practice' (*ASIA*, p. 43). The new formations lack tradition, lack the dominant presence of a majority of veteran troops inured to rigid conformity, taking orders from a seasoned cadre of non-commissioned officers whose status and function have been 'bred in the bone'. The regular soldier in the ranks had sold himself to his country for a term of years and his feelings did not have to be considered. Conditions in a battalion of the New Army are entirely different. Its recruits are 'full of pernicious civilian ideas about "liberty" and "the rights of man".' Further, the good will of those already enlisted is vital to the sustained success of recruiting efforts as the war continues (*ASIA*, p. 44).

Under these virtually unprecedented circumstances, the very basis of authority has shifted, as Hankey views it, from 'discipline' to 'leadership'—from a rigid, impersonal mechanism of obedience to a system that must rely essentially on 'the inherent force of character' (*ASIA*, p. 45). It is the lower ranks of non-commissioned officers who actually bear the heaviest burden in the new 'service battalions'; they illustrate 'the conditions of sheer natural leadership' (*ASIA*, p. 46) currently present in Kitchener's Mob. This is particularly true of section leaders, the lance-corporals (or 'lance-jacks') who are put in charge of recruits like themselves with no claim whatsoever to prestige. Hankey discusses their several types: ambitious youngsters, blustering bullies, the plain man who accepts leadership to get things done and because someone must. Lastly, the gentleman—'the most interesting of all from our point of view'. He is a bad disciplinarian but is fair and disinterested. His strangeness to the average private soldier gives the gentleman a certain prestige. 'He does not care a scrap

184

for his rank. He is impervious to the fear of losing it' (*ASIA*, p. 49). Only his sense of duty accounts for his position of responsibility; his unorthodox - manner and methods are 'highly prejudicial to the cause of discipline as a whole' (*ASIA*, pp. 49–50). This gentleman lance-jack is a version of Hankey himself before he accepted a commission. But Donald leaves that resemblance undisclosed, his only point about the gentleman corporal being that 'his authority was purely personal' (*ASIA*, p. 53) and thus not transferable to others in dealing with the men. So Hankey ends this essay by acknowledging the surpassing value of 'perfect discipline', such as would remain in force regardless of the personal qualities of any individual leader (*ASIA*, p. 54). Left at this point, Hankey's critique of discipline and leadership seems contradictory: a principle of leadership based on personal character has superseded an impersonal system of discipline; but perfect discipline, because it fosters trust that prompts men to stand by even indifferent leaders, is a higher good than such individual leadership. In his book's next essay, 'The Beloved Captain', Hankey suggests a resolution that raises the subject into a realm beyond its immediate context.

Based on his admiration for Edmund Hardy, who became for Hankey the model for his own style and conduct as an officer, 'The Beloved Captain' is a personal tribute rather than a disquisition on military leadership, but it nevertheless expands that theme. Hardy was not a professional soldier but the product of an officers' training corps at his college, and Hankey makes clear that before he could lead his men he had as much to learn about soldiering as they did. As an officer he necessarily belonged to what Hankey calls the 'super-class', which distanced him from the actual democratic experiment of the volunteer army. But neither was he a typical example of the system of discipline

embodied in the officer class. The source of his authority—
the unique influence he exercised upon his men—was
surely his personal character. But Hankey seems to be
claiming that this produced leadership so different in
degree as to be of another kind from that Hankey finds
among the non-commissioned officers.

Hardy's, then, was not the sort of leadership that
emerges from within the 'other ranks' as a manifestation of
one or another mark of natural distinction. 'He was not
democratic,' Hankey notes, which perhaps describes his
predilections but even more the source of his peculiar
power. 'He was rather the justification for aristocracy.'

> We all knew instinctively that he was our superior—a
> man of finer temper than ourselves, a 'toff' in his own
> right. I suppose that was why he could be so humble
> without loss of dignity.
>
> (*ASIA*, p. 62)

Hankey's characterization of Hardy is sketchy because the
qualities of such a man defy analysis. 'It was not what he
said. ... It was just how he looked. ... He was good to
look on.' Indifferent with words, Hardy commands as a
presence, and the response he draws from those he leads is
something Hankey can only call love. 'And there isn't
anything stronger than love, when all's said and done'
(*ASIA*, p. 61).

It would be vastly wide of the mark to suppose that
Donald Hankey is claiming the basis of military authority to
be the power of love. Nonetheless, such a conclusion—or
something like it—probably lay behind the sudden and
enormous popularity of this particular essay. 'We loved
him.' 'We were his men. ... he took a paternal interest in
us.' These were assertions that gave Hankey's readers—the
susceptible civilians at least—an image that eased some of

186

their anxieties about the war, an image that might hold its own against reason and common sense. Hankey was registering his admiration for an actual officer, no doubt an extraordinary one; but he writes in a way that placed Captain Hardy in the hagiography of hero-worship, making him the embodiment of loving (and lovable) leadership to which the essay gave emotional credibility. Amid the harsh separations, the cruel impersonality, and the grave anxieties of the war, civilian readers accepted Hankey's portrait of the Beloved Captain as an enticing source of comfort.

From his letters to Hardy's mother and sister it is clear that Donald Hankey's attachment to this man was at once intense and undeclared, sensitive to the barrier fixed between an officer and his men. Accordingly, *reverence* is the tone his essay effects, an almost surreal combination of intimacy and awe:

He came in the early days, when we were still at recruit drills under the hot September sun. Tall, erect, smiling: so we first saw him, and so he remained to the end.

(*ASIA*, p. 57)

The verbal cadences of Oxford-after-Pater—the stylistic legacy of 'Aestheticism'—are manifest in this essay, the most self-conscious of the Student's offerings. That quality illuminates Captain Hardy with an aura that lends more mystery than clarity. As Hardy's coming is vague, so his presence is premonitory of departure. 'We knew we should lose him'—and not only by merited promotion: 'Also we knew that he would be killed' (*ASIA*, p. 64). The parallel to Jesus becomes increasingly (some would now think uncomfortably) evident. To Hankey's initial readers, suffering the strains of war and awash as they were in an emotional atmosphere of mystical signs and portents, that would not have seemed unwarranted or far-fetched. Hardy's aristocratic humility is illustrated by the routine inspection of the men's feet after long marches. 'But with him it was no mere routine.' Hardy is pictured solicitous and full of care, kneeling down before a suffering soldier, tending to him in this lowly way. 'There was no affectation about this, no striving after effect' (*ASIA,* p. 63); but in the eyes of Hardy's men his care for their feet, so Hankey asserts, was 'something almost religious'.

> It seemed to have a touch of the Christ about it, and we loved him the more.
>
> (*ASIA,* p. 64)

This parallel between Christ and his Beloved Captain came naturally enough to the author of *The Lord of All Good Life.* Jesus is Master and Prime Exemplar. His is the secret to true leadership of every kind and degree. 'Somehow he lives', Hankey declares of his dead captain as he imagines him sharing in the life everlasting. He is in close company of 'that gracious pierced Figure', though only, like others, one who has lived true to His example. The citizen army, therefore, may provide wide scope for 'perfect leadership', but its true nature and the source of its power over men, Hankey is saying, transcends all such secular contrivings.

'The Indignity of Labour' attempts no great subtlety or complexity in considering whether anything can be learned from the example of officers and men in the volunteer army that might benefit future relations between employers and workers in a peaceful future. Hankey concedes that he knows much less about industrial life than about the army, but he ventures the opinion that it is the conditions under which men work rather than the work itself that makes labour a curse. The atmosphere of mutual suspicion and mistrust, which seems to prevail between the employer and his workmen, is 'quite adequate to account for the workman's hatred of labour and his denial of its inherent dignity' (*ASIA*, p. 77). Life in the army, on the other hand (which Hankey reminds his reader he has seen both as an enlisted man and an officer), though no less hard and monotonous than the lot of most workmen, is marked by a much more positive spirit. Grumbling, much a part of army life as it may be, is free of bitterness. 'The men trust their officers and the officers trust their men, to an extent which I fancy has no parallel in civil life' (*ASIA*, p. 78).

The question Hankey ponders is whether 'when the war is over and officers become employers, and privates employed, these good relations between them will be reproduced in industrial life' (*ASIA*, p. 82). His answer is mixed. Regrettably, the ruthless pressure of competition will press as heavily on both employers and employed as it ever did before the war. 'Labour will still have to combine against capital for self-defence' (*ASIA*, p. 83). Yet Hankey concludes this essay in the hope that the *ésprit de corps,* a sense of the common weal, learned through war by all the ranks, might 'here and there' produce 'good relations between master and men'. This hope even leads him to speak of 'a better day', of 'partners, jointly responsible', and of the possibility of 'comradeship between man and man' (*ASIA*, p. 84).

In the essay Hankey titled 'The Religion of the Inarticulate' he makes, almost casually, the point that resonates throughout *A Student in Arms*: 'In this case,' Hankey advises his reader, 'the soldier means the workingman' (*ASIA,* p. 108). It was this perception of the common soldier as the English working class in arms, drawn from civilian life and mobilized into a huge mass army, his quality revealed and tested by the extremities of war, that made Hankey's experience in arms the unforeseen goal of his personal pilgrimage. Sociologically speaking, this was of course an oversimplification, certainly an idealization. All classes were represented in the ranks, and Hankey's perspective on his fellow enlistees had—as he realized—a patronizing aspect. But much of his confidence as a writer rested on the belief that as an enlisted man he had merged at last with the labouring classes.

Hankey begins this essay by referring to the fact that the war was being widely regarded as 'the Church's opportunity' to reassert itself in the nation's life. But it appears that the church shows little sign of understanding this opportunity, much less of knowing how to seize it. The ostensible point of Hankey's essay is to assure his fellow Christians that the ordinary soldier/workingman is a kind of Christian unawares, who is as mistaken about true Christianity as the church is about him. Chaplains and others who speak for the church observe the inarticulate common soldier and assume he is without any religious sensibility. On the other hand, what the workingman/soldier has seen of Christianity has left him suspecting it 'consists in believing the Bible and setting up to be better than your neighbours' (*ASIA*, p. 108). In the religion of Jesus, however, the soldier's essential belief in goodness finds its grounding in the teaching and example of a loving Master, a Master, moreover, whose whole life was an attempt to destroy the same 'formalism and smug self-righteousness' that had turned the soldier against what he supposed was Christianity (*ASIA*, p. 109). When the soldier understands that Christ is on his side and when the chaplains are encouraged to make the most of this discovery, that will be time enough to speak of the church's opportunity.

This essay presents its author with his own opportunity: the chance to tell his readers how it is that he presumes to

190

speak for the inarticulate and to attack the ways of the church. Hankey makes his telling crisp and candid, even humorous; it is a spare yet revealing account of what he makes bold to call his 'Quest' (*ASIA*, p. 99). His use of first person plural may be a journalistic mannerism, but it also suggests that Donald identifies himself here with all the young privileged idealists of his generation:

> It was the Romance of the Unknown that enticed us, just as it enticed necromancers and alchemists and explorers in former days. Only our Unknown was quite close to our hand. ... As we stood on the Embankment it frowned at us from across the river, from that black mass of factories and tenements and narrow, dismal streets that crowns the Thames' southern bank. ... It was simply humanity that was our Unknown—the part of humanity which earns its daily bread hardly, which knows what it is to be cold and hungry and ill, and to have to go on working in spite of it.
>
> (*ASIA*, p. 99)

Hankey plays down the altruism of his sojourn amongst Bermondsey's poor and emphasizes his hope to learn from them:

> To cut a long story short, we went and lived in a mean street, opened clubs where we could meet the working man or boy, enticed him to our rooms and regaled him with buns and Egyptian cigarettes, and did our level best to understand his point of view.
>
> (*ASIA*, p. 100)

Hankey represents himself here as an amateur but earnest explorer-anthropologist. Thus one gains a particu-

191

larly useful sense of what he meant by his *nom de plume*. History decreed that his quest for the unknown would lead the Student to pursue his studies among men at war. The attempt to mingle with the urban poor, virtually to lose himself among them, though 'stimulating' left Donald with 'an uncomfortable feeling that we only knew a very small part of the lives and characters of the men whom we were studying.' Managing a boys' club could not adequately bridge the gulf of class difference, and besides that another more shadowy and puzzling element seems to have thwarted his quest:

> They came to our clubs and played games with us, until suddenly the more vital matter of sex took them elsewhere and they were lost to us. ... I think we mystified them a little, and ultimately bored them.
>
> *(ASIA, p. 101)*

But then the war, which seemed at the time to require the Student to abandon his quest, in fact provided him with his true opportunity. 'The war was not the end,' Hankey writes, 'but the beginning.'

> We had failed because we had not gone deep enough. ... We had only touched the surface. To understand the workingman one must know him through and through–live, work, drink, sleep with him.
>
> *(ASIA, p. 102)*

Acknowledging that 'we could never become workingmen', the Student realizes that enlistment offers an alternate route to the same goal:

> ... enlisting meant living on terms of absolute equality with the very men whom we wanted to understand.
>
> *(ASIA, p. 102)*

192

Hankey's sense of the adventure, then, puts him in a category rather different from the Rupert Brookes and the Julian Grenfells. The romance he identifies is not the purifying excitement of a patriotic plunge or a sporting rendezvous with death; it is rather an explorer's chance to live on intimate terms with otherness. Indeed—as if he were Richard Burton or Lawrence of Arabia—to assume its very identity.

But such intimacy brought with it the disappointing reality of boredom and routine: 'Life was dull and prosaic.... No one ever said anything interesting. We never got a chance to sit down and think things out' (*ASIA*, p. 103). In time, however, this disappointment gives way to the valuable realization that the conditions of such a life—'narrow and rather sordid, like the life of all working-men' (*ASIA*, p. 105)—render one inarticulate.

In another context this abandonment of the idealized notion of the labouring man as philosopher in disguise or at least a source of simple wisdom, and an accompanying recognition that what is admirable about such men lies in another direction, might have led Hankey to reassess his own glamorization of menial work and his own relationship to that life. As it is, he settles in this essay for a conclusion that reminds chaplains along with other 'educated Christians' that they are no less inarticulate in their own way than those whose religious understanding they presume to instruct. The workingman's religion may be inarticulate, but the 'real religion of the educated man is often quite wrongly articulated' (*ASIA*, p. 111).

In the next essay in his book's sequence the focus shifts from those beyond the conventional pale of caste to those whom convention has branded as morally reprehensible. Hankey concedes that the army is full of men who fall outside 'any respectable niche in our social edifice' (*ASIA*, p. 117), but in the ranks they encounter—and often wonderfully fulfil–the chance for redemption. 'Of Some Who Were Lost, and Afterward Were Found' views these strayed sheep not with revulsion but with much of the intense fascination that drew Hankey to the working class. Beneath a conventional impatience with these 'wayward vagabonds' (*ASIA*, p. 120) is Hankey's susceptibility to their 'elusive charm of youth'.

> They were lost; but they were not poisonous. That was the trouble. They were so lovable. ... When they were out of sight we hardened our hearts and said that we had done with them; but all the time we knew that when it came to the point we should forgive them. They were such good fellows, the rascals!
> (*ASIA*, pp. 117-18)

Beyond mere forbearance, then, Hankey's affectionate regard for these rascals approaches something almost celebratory. He more than forgives; he welcomes their challenge to respectability:

> If they did fly in the face of the conventions, well, we sometimes felt that the conventions deserved it.
> (*ASIA*, p. 118)

It seems likely that sexual attraction is at the heart of Hankey's sympathy for these charming and wayward young soldiers who affront prim decency. For all their drunkenness and loose morals, they would not deliberately harm another. 'Even in their amours there was always a touch of romance and never the taint of sheer bestiality,' Hankey asserts, on what evidence he does not say. Their code of conduct, whatever else might be said about it, was neither mercenary nor hypocritical–'a natural set-off to the somewhat sordidly prudent morality of the marriage

194

market' (*ASIA*, pp. 118-19). But such sympathy tempts Hankey into sentimental extravagance in contrasting these lost souls with more 'stolid respectable folk' in the way they encounter 'dearth, danger, and death':

> ... they, who had formerly been our despair, were now our glory. Their spirits effervesced. Their wit sparkled. Hunger and thirst could not depress them. Cold could not chill them. Every hardship became a joke. ... Never was such a triumph of spirit over matter.
>
> (*ASIA*, pp. 123-4)

Even making due allowance for the rejoicing appropriate to the recovery of Lost Sheep, this is self-indulgent and unconvincing. War also kills the respectable, and of course brings sorrow; but Hankey suggests there is virtually nothing for tears in the deaths of his lovable vagabonds:

> What else had they been born for? It was their chance. With a gay heart they gave their greatest gift, and with a smile to think that after all they had anything to give which was of value.
>
> (*ASIA*, p. 124)

A strange benefit to ascribe to war: that it provides the opportunity for rascals to demonstrate the saving grace of dying with flair.

As arranged in book form, Hankey's essays offer various paired opposites: the old army and the new, a beloved officer and the generic Cockney enlisted man, democracy and leadership, war as an opportunity for the unlikely scamp and then as a lesson in philosophy for the average sensual (and university-educated) man. In the essay that follows 'On Some Who Were Lost, and Afterward Were

195

Found', the war which makes heroes out of scapegraces works a different, more subjective transformation. Titled 'An Englishman Philosophizes', this essay undertakes to trace a process whereby an 'Average Englishman', possessed of 'a code of honour and morals, based partly on tradition and partly on his own shrewd observation of ... the lives of his neighbours' (*ASIA*, p. 130), living his rather dull and conventional life in self-centred contentment with hardly a shred of intellectual curiosity, is suddenly thrust into war's maelstrom.

> Naturally the transition was a little bewildering. Outwardly he remained calm; but below the surface strange things were happening—nothing less than a complete readjustment of his mental perspective. ... The vaguely good-natured selfishness which had earned him the title of 'good fellow' in the quiet days of peace did not quite fit in with the new demands made on his personality. Much against his will, he had to try to think things out.
>
> (*ASIA*, p. 132)

Hankey's Englishman—for whose experiences the author borrows some of his own—is sustained to some extent by recalling a phrase above the door of a boys' club in poorer London—'Keep Smiling!'—and the motto on the club button—'Fratres'. Cheerful camaraderie sees him through a trying time as a section commander, but it is not until he looks back on that ordeal and realizes he had carried on without fear or even nervousness that this Average Englishman 'stumble[s] upon the very roots of courage—unselfishness.' Hankey resorts to defensive irony in extolling this as 'an epoch-making philosophical discovery' (*ASIA*, p. 141); but the 'great truth' of selflessness had been there all the while, from many sources, but closest to hand (for this Englishman) in Christian teaching. Its rediscovery is claimed as one of the lessons of war.

The essay concludes rather weakly with the reflection that 'Christian education' seldom teaches anything worth knowing about Christianity. In any event, the philosophizing of the unphilosophical Average Englishman comes down to much the same paradoxical point as does the redeeming heroism of the strayed sheep in the preceding essay: selflessness as the ultimate form of self-fulfilment.

'A Englishman Prays', the ostensible complement of 'An Englishman Philosophizes', attempts to enrich this paradox by distinguishing selflessness from mere nullity. Hankey's own experience near Ypres, lying wounded in No Man's Land, furnishes the basis for this essay's central epiphany. The stricken soldier, weak from his wounds and in and out of consciousness, lapses into a kind of reverie as he waits to die or to be found and cared for. The stars appear overhead and make all else 'seem so small and petty'.

All this bloodshed—what was the good of it? It was all so ephemeral, so trivial, so meaningless in the presence of eternity and infinity. It was just a strife of pygmies.

Small and lonely, 'a pygmy soul, on the sea of immensity', he finds no consolation in the stars, 'no sympathy there but only cold, unseeing tolerance' (*ASIA*, p. 151).

Out of this vastness suddenly comes a contrasting sense of distinctive being. His own sentient existence, insignificant though it is, seems borne up by something transcendent to which it is connected. 'Underneath are the everlasting arms'—repeating those words as a kind of mantra, the soldier waits to be rescued, having learned a new way of prayer.

Hankey subtitled his essay on The Army and the Universities, 'A Study in Educational Values'. Slender and wedded to the obvious, it hardly lives up to that description; nevertheless, its bearing on diverse aspects of the author's own intellectual training gives it a place at least in the study of Donald Hankey. The opposing points of view, or educational experiences, are personified by a subaltern and a 'High Church Socialist curate'—products respectively of a military academy and of one of the ancient universities. Hankey concedes he is indulging in generalizations but, on the strength of having himself been to both Woolwich and Oxford, declares that 'the lack of sympathy between these two individuals' reflects the schooling of which each is a representative product (*ASIA*, p. 156).

What develops is a version of the opposition between a utilitarian and a liberal education—the one producing a man wellsuited to action, 'a man with a good deal of simplicity', practical, and lacking individuality, especially in matters of taste; the other with wider sympathies, a cultivated taste, a well-developed imagination and critical faculty, 'full of vague ideals, unpractical dreams, and ineffective good-will' (*ASIA*, pp. 160; 163). Such are Donald's conclusions about his academy and his university; but other elements in his life underlie this contrast: his father the philosophical recluse who nonetheless favoured military careers for his sons, Donald's childhood as the pet of his sisters yet systematically initiated by his brothers into manly pursuits, his attraction to the simplicity and physical rigour of menial labour at odds with his taste in good clothes and fine wine, his 'cello and his paint brushes.

But it is the formative influences of the opposing cultures of Oxford and Woolwich that the Student is here considering, and it is his point that the officer class in general is strengthened by their mixture. Though acknowledging the essential contribution of the military academies in the way of discipline and efficiency, Hankey leaves little

198

doubt as to his own leanings. The essay even ends with a lingering glance towards those 'other University men' who preferred serving in the ranks. 'Who shall say that they are shirking their responsibilities?' (ASIA, pp. 164–5). Hankey does not quite say so, but he intimates that a university man like himself would have chosen better to remain among the common soldiers, to counsel and comfort them with whatever wisdom that particular educational tradition may have put in his way:

And in the ranks the student will find that his philosophy is becoming practical, that his dreams are being fulfilled, and that he is the interpreter of a wider experience of life than even he ever imagined.

(ASIA, p. 165)

Many of Hankey's essays have about them the prim and comfortably self-limiting manner of a sixth-form set-piece. A subject is briskly presented, often in the form of a generalization to be interrogated or a problem posed. Its claim on our interest is disarmingly advanced, a fruitful opposition or a handy division of the topic may be introduced; illustrative examples, perhaps a pertinent anecdote or two, flesh out the Student's thoughts; the conclusion makes its agreeable and fair-minded appeal with no vexing rough edges or audacious assertions. Assent, not controversy, is the aim of these familiar and almost formulaic procedures. 'A Sense of the Dramatic' shows them to advantage. Here it is the typical Englishman's distrust of the 'theatrical' that initiates the Student's meditations. He wishes to distinguish what he means by a dramatic sense from a 'striving after outward effect'. Indeed, the dramatic is in essential opposition to anything so discreditably self-centred and superficial. In developing his thoughts on this ego-less and yet deeply-rooted yearning for *drama* in life, Hankey begins with the concept of 'romance'. That word has a resonance for Donald as lively and persistent as that which pulses through the novella so titled by Conrad and Hueffer which he particularly admired. In our self-enclosure, Donald asserts, we attribute romance to whatever may be in the lives of others that appeals to our curiosity. But within each buried life, Hankey urges, lies romance aplenty for him who is willing to search it out, to apply this sense of the dramatic to his own experience.

In a paradoxical vein not unlike Keats's insistence on the artist's lack of 'identity', Hankey associates the dramatic with 'the faculty for getting outside yourself and criticizing yourself'. 'The artist must not be an egoist,' he further contends, sounding still more Keatsian; a sense of the dramatic is moreover closely akin to a sense of humour, an eye for the ridiculous, not least in oneself. 'The greatest of all,' he concludes (*un*like Keats), '. . . is the man who prays, and tries to see the story as the Author designed it' (*ASIA*, pp. 173–4).

The quality Hankey here celebrates is one that had long interested him. He had identified it and cultivated it as a corrective of the two failings he charged against himself: self-centredness and an inability to feel things deeply. Its relevance to the lot of men in arms and to the religious issues in which Hankey is absorbed is rather fully argued. Regarding one's life as if it were a romance to be played out with all the gusto and talent one can muster may help a soldier meet discomfort and peril. Accepting the part that God has given a man to play, whatever its limitations, is a Christian duty. But one feels that Hankey's sense of the dramatic has a still more inclusive place in his general psychological and philosophical outlook. 'It is a faculty,' he contends, 'which gives zest to life: putting boredom and oppression to flight; stimulating humour, humility, and idealism' (*ASIA*, p. 178). If viewing oneself as a character, however minor, in life's drama could do all that, perhaps it justifies, as well as explains, Hankey's air of detachment, the impression he so often gave of being something of a chance wayfarer rather than a native inhabitant of the here and now.

To make the war seem bearable Hankey tried to imagine as fully as he could the better future that must follow it. Other essays consider lessons learned in war about relationships between England's social classes. 'A Book of Wisdom' frames some aphorisms of Hankey's own within the proposition that 'the present crisis may evolve teachers of a new kind in the ranks of the clergy and the professors' (*ASIA*, p. 183). These war-tempered truth-tellers will provide better guidance than what the church seems presently able to offer. What they have seen of life and death will help them bridge the gap between the hard facts crowding the lives of ordinary men and the official voice of the clergy. Hankey foresees a new pastoral breed looking at its task with fresh urgency and insight:

Perhaps we shall see again something analogous to the old books of wisdom: shrewd commentaries on life couched in short, pithy sentences. If so, they will be refreshing reading after the turgid inconclusiveness of most modern theology.

(*ASIA*, p. 184)

Disguising them as jottings from the notebook of an anonymous fellow-soldier, Hankey presents 'what may prove the first fruits of the crisis'. Much of the content of 'A Book of Wisdom' we have encountered before, in Donald's letters and in *The Lord of All Good Life*. The fundamental wisdom it proposes is to regard religion as the obvious alternative to the hopelessness of a 'world centred in self', an alternative that finds its justification in the kind of life it makes possible. 'Contrasting religion with theology, to the disadvantage of the latter' (*ASIA* I, p. 186), Hankey consistently stresses the power of Christianity to change people for the better, to make differences that count, to make life's burden easier to bear.

> Christianity is a way, and not an explanation of life: it implies Power, and not dogma.
>
> (*ASIA*, p. 190)

How much of traditional Christianity this undogmatic religion must necessarily discard Hankey does not attempt to say. He seems rather less interested in challenging or modernizing belief than in making the church a stronger force for social betterment, a clearer more practical help in moral choices.

Hankey's long-standing quarrel with the church continues in other essays that address its problems and opportunities in wartime and its prospects afterwards. 'A Mobilization of the Church' proposes that younger clergy and all ordinands be 'set free' for active military service. A footnote concedes that, in fact, large numbers from both categories had by that time enlisted or received commissions, some with combat units; but the note goes on to explain the essay has been retained in the collection because 'the present crisis is, for the Church of England, an unprecedented opportunity for either making a fresh start or committing suicide' (*ASIA*, p. 195).

The men who have fought the war, Hankey is arguing, will either accept the church as a comrade in arms or reject it as having remained aloof when its help and comfort were most needed. Without a meaningful sharing in the actual ordeal of war, the church and its representatives will make no credible appeal. The work of the clergy on the home front, he intimates, has not been actual work at all, but at best only distracting make-work, at worst frivolous and unworthy play.

There is a personal side to this, of course. Hankey's hostility and frustration appears to have had much to do with the way the life of the clergy, often reduced to hardly more than listening to gossipy women and keeping children amused, gives them 'no time or opportunity for free intercourse with the adult male inhabitants of their parishes' (*ASIA*, p. 199). Certainly the social emasculation of its clergy is in itself a complaint to which the church is vulnerable; but beneath that lies Donald's sense that a vocation within the Church as presently constituted would thwart his own longings for some form of brotherhood envisioned if not fully achieved in his service with the 'Fratres' of the Bermondsey Mission and more nearly realized among the common soldiers of the Rifle Brigade.

Mobilizing the church means two things in Hankey's essay: encouraging a younger segment of the clergy to 'share in the nation's struggle' by full participation in 'the common life of [military] service' (*ASIA*, p. 200) and also reorganizing the parochial work at home so that the loss of civilian clergy would not be overly disruptive. That some church activities would be suspended seems to the Student a reasonable sacrifice that might in fact result in a renewal of parochial energy and a greater sense of purpose.

'A Student, His Comrades, and His Church' is described by its author as 'horribly egotistical, but frankly a record of personal experiences and resultant personal beliefs' (*ASIA*, p. 209). It is hardly more than an enumeration of those men the author has known as his comrades in arms who comprise, for him, a communion of spirit—indeed, a true church in the sense Donald and his fellow Oxonians liked to speak of Dr Stansfeld's mission in Bermondsey as a church in its own right.[7] They are all fellow-rankers, who seem to be at his side as Hankey—now an officer temporarily on home assignment—kneels to receive the consecrated bread and wine at a Sunday service. Each of these different men has exemplified essential characteristics of a Christian life. They are an imperfect assortment of ordinary soldiers, and in one or two cases Hankey's affection seems connected more with physical grace, personal charm, or endearing failings than with particular moral qualities. Each is remembered by name (though probably these are inventions); however, the collection of Jims, Tommies, and Freds underscores their unremarkable status. Then, having summoned to mind this company, Donald abruptly mentions one who, unlike the rest, is given no name and is identified only by an initial:

> There was D____, the boon-companion, generous friend, and faithful lover.
>
> (ASIA, p. 215)

That is all we learn of D; the author hurries on to 'Albert' and then to 'Jack'. The inclusion of D has served no purpose other than whatever satisfaction Hankey may have gained in yielding to so curious an urge towards semi-disclosure, which both coyly conceals and draws attention to the fact of concealment.

The last two essays in the Student's book, 'The Making of a Man' and 'Heroes and Heroics', close out the collection by considering, first, what army experience has done to or for the individual member of Kitchener's Mob, and second, how the public ought to regard these men who were

---

[7]See Barron, B. (1920) 'The Builders of Barnaby'. *Oxford and Bermondsey Mission Reports*, pp. 3–16.

gathered up as mere boys to fight a horrific war. 'The Making of a Man' treats rather conventionally the subject of how military training transforms slack youth into firm manhood. Hankey focuses on the interplay of freedom and discipline in the process of maturation. Army life, he concludes unsurprisingly, exhibits the paradox that discipline, by incorporating the individual in a larger more purposeful body, is not the enemy of freedom it appears to be but actually the means of 'his fullest self-expression', 'the highest form of liberty' (*ASIA*, p. 271). Even before he witnessed the slaughter on the Somme, Hankey's view of military service could be equivocal, sometimes penetrating; but here it is almost as if his typical recruit has merely put himself in the hands of a south London mission and undergoes the character-forming regimen of a boys' club.

'Heroes and Heroics', the book's concluding essay, sees things from a broader and yet more personal angle. It contains some uncharacteristically harsh recollections of how wounded soldiers are stupidly kept from seeing their families during convalescence. Hankey is scornful of 'Lady Snooks or the Duchess of Downshire'—aristocratic women who, as licensed visitors of the hospital, have easier access to the patients than do their wives and mothers:

> The wounded soldier begins to long to be less petted, less lionized, and instead to be treated as a rational being who is entitled to a certain elementary respect.
>
> (*ASIA*, pp. 284–5)

In some ways this is among the freshest and most striking essays in *A Student in Arms*. Here the author's double role as student-soldier comes most pointedly into play. Being *in arms* is never merely the author-as-student's present circumstance, it is always also his subject of study. And in this essay Hankey speaks not only as a writer regarding his subject, but also as the subject himself regarding someone (such as himself) who would write about him. By what sort of writing would the soldiers Hankey speaks for and writes about most wish—and deserve—to be remembered? What can any such writer remember that would do the fullest justice to these soldiers?

The previous essay endorsed the commonplace claim that military experience makes men out of mere boys; 'Heroes and Heroics' demands of journalists and others who write about the war that they respect these soldiers' common manhood. Given the situation he assumes as a student in arms, it is not easy for Hankey to evade conventional patriotism; but here he succeeds, not by the ironies born of disillusionment—he had not yet come to that point—but by assuming a more modest and direct yet more difficult attitude towards the catastrophe of his time. Hankey explores a middle ground between sentimental affirmation and wilful denial as a way of writing about this tragedy that might be worthy of its sufferers.

Including himself among wartime journalists, Hankey concedes how readily the writing of heroics comes to hand. As public clamour for such writing grows, the journalists then begin to treat their subject with less and less urgency and originality; unconvincing and spurious 'journalese' is the inevitable result. It is offensive to deep-seated English reticence and lacks a decently understated reverence for a fine action. Accordingly, some writers take refuge in satire—the readiest example for Hankey at the time being the work of the popular cartoonist for the *Bystander*, Bruce Bairnsfather. Though Hankey respects Bairnsfather's portraits of 'intensely prosaic Tommies of the British workman type' (*ASIA*, p. 279), he finds these caricatures 'represent the extreme reaction from the heroic'. They bring home important truths about war, its 'ingloriousness', its 'preposterous absurdity', its 'futility as a means of settling the affairs of nations' (*ASIA*, p. 280). Without challenging this satiric–and static–portrayal, Hankey refuses to capitulate to it. There remains for him the possibility that in young men even terrible experiences can produce growth: 'there is hardly a man who will not return from the war bigger than when he left home'. Even if that may be doubted, the sacrifice itself has dignity irrespective of its consequences:

> We who have served in the ranks of 'the first hundred thousand' will want to remember something more than the ingloriousness of war.
>
> (*ASIA*, p. 281)

Whatever else, Hankey would have the writing that comes out of war reflect the legitimacy, the justice, of that desire.

These feelings lead to the Student's concluding emphasis on the simple manhood of soldiers in arms. His experience convalescing in hospital has increased his doubts about what these men may expect at war's end. Romance and satire are merely opposite sides of a single wilful misperception; Hankey foresees a time 'when the war is over, and the craze for petting and lionizing has died down'. Then, so he fears,

> ... all that will survive of the present mixed attitude towards the soldier will be the attitude of authority, which regards him as an irresponsible animal.
>
> (*ASIA*, pp. 288–9)

The Student in Arms makes no claim to final wisdom, but his studies have brought him to the conclusion that the men under arms–that is to say the volunteers in the New Army–are fundamentally neither more nor less than the

British working class that has proven its mettle and earned respect through the ordeal of war. What Hankey refers to as 'the attitude of authority' he then equates with a conception of the working class, 'which before the war poisoned the whole administration of charity, and the whole direction of philanthropy.' Formerly, when the workers had said, ' "We don't want charity, we want the right to live a wholesome life", ' the reply of the privileged classes was to denounce or dismiss this plea as 'the "ingratitude" of the poor'. 'The cry we hear now,' Hankey puts into the words: ' "We are not pets or lions, but men" '; it is but a new form of that older cry: 'the cry of the working classes for a sane respect' (*ASIA*, p. 289).

By implication, then, the ultimate victory would not be one against the foreign enemy but a victory of the working class over the prejudice that has denied it true manhood. It was Donald Hankey's feeling that this victory has been already earned though not yet actually won. Already the 'Mob' had acquitted itself as an army; and Hankey sees in this demonstration the chance for a better society. But he is not confident that this opportunity to 'redeem the error of the past' will be fulfilled by any political reality. The last words in his book speak ominously of the probability of 'intensifying our error' and of 'endless difficulties in the days that are to come' (*ASIA*, pp. 289–90).

9

Repeating the Experiment (May–July, 1916)

By mid-May Hankey's regiment was ready to embark for
France. Writing from Folkestone to his friend Will Clift,
chief officer of the Decima Club (Donald's boys' club in
Bermondsey), he describes himself as 'singularly at ease'.

> The day has come! Just twelve months ago I left Folke-
> stone for the front, and tomorrow I repeat the experi-
> ment.
>
> (*Letters*, p. 420)

The strangeness Donald must have felt in reliving exactly a
year later his earlier journey to war could only have
thrown into relief all that had changed. As he indicates,
there was less anxiety—he had seen the elephant—but this
time he was crossing over as an officer attached to a
different regiment. His repeated remarks that accepting a
commission had been a mistake reflect his sense that he
was better suited for whatever lay ahead as a member of
the rank and file than as a second lieutenant. He would
willingly have endured the greater discomforts of a
common soldier if he could honourably have relinquished
the responsibilities of a subaltern that continued to seem
unnatural to him. And he never changed his mind. Hankey
was now in his thirty-second year and, by the chances and
mischances of war, his cohort of subalterns was becoming
ever younger. Later that summer, after he had been back in

action, Donald compared himself unfavourably to these buoyant younger officers: 'I am too heavy for a sub.,' he concluded (*Letters*, pp. 428-9).

But if becoming an officer had been a wrong step, the other major change that a year's time had brought was highly satisfying: his essays in the *Spectator* had made him a writer of at least momentary consequence, and the book in which they were collected was selling wonderfully. His success as 'A Student in Arms' resulted in a request, earlier that spring, that he contribute to a volume of essays titled *Faith or Fear? An Appeal to the Church of England.* In this book—which addresses 'the really tragic failure of the Church to meet the needs of the nation in this crisis'— Hankey joined four other ardent and reform-minded churchmen, including the editor, Charles H. S. Matthews, in urging the Establishment to make Christianity a truly meaningful part of modern English life. As a mark of his current popularity, Hankey stands first among the contributors listed on the title page.

When *Faith or Fear?* appeared in June (published by Macmillan and Company) Donald did not think very highly of the book and disparaged his own part in it: 'I have missed something rather important somewhere; but I am not quite sure where it is, or what it is.' This dissatisfaction is in sharp contrast to the authorial pride he had taken in *The Lord of All Good Life* during the first year of his enlistment. His perspective has become that of a writer who, having gained a following, has a growing reputation to consider: 'The unfortunate thing is that for everyone who reads *The Lord of All Good Life*, two or three will read *Faith or Fear?*' (*Letters*, p. 437). The earlier work was more positive and heartfelt, less sharply critical of the institution he still supposed he would ultimately serve. Now, in the light of his war experience, Hankey could not go much beyond his certainty that the Church needed 'an awful lot of altering. ... It's great fault is irrelevance' (*Letters*, p. 438).

Donald begins his part of *Faith or Fear?* with a section called 'A Personal Explanation'. By way of introducing himself so that readers may decide how much weight to attach to his ideas, Hankey outlines the evolution of his religious experience and beliefs. Rather deftly he gives his life the shape of a conversion narrative: the luminous piety of childhood shocked to witness the petty immoralities of youth then threatened in 'a distant tropical colony' by exposure to corrosive scepticism. A revelatory experience checks him 'on the brink of materialistic determinism' and reawakens his sense of man's worth and of divine transcendence; at length, after much physical and spiritual wandering, Jesus's example and transforming power—along with various instances of human goodness in unlikely places—brings him to 'a sane idealism' and a resolve to strive for 'the vitality and efficiency of Christ's body the Church' (*Faith or Fear?*, p. 16). Though offered as a kind of personal aside, this preface anticipates the two themes that dominate the rest of Hankey's contribution to *Faith or Fear?*: his dismayed sense of his church's tendency to confuse respectability with true spirituality, and his call to the church to make more of a real difference in the lives of the poor.

As an assessment of the Church of England's shortcomings his chapters in *Faith or Fear?* do not add much to what he had written on the subject in *The Lord of all Good Life*: the church as an institution does not transcend but merely reflects the British class system. 'Class distinctions as we honour them and as the Church recognizes them are a form of slavery'; the enslaved are not only the 'lower' classes but all those, whatever their place on the social ladder, who are prevented by the pressures of class distinctions from openly dealing with individuals in all

211

conditions of life in a spirit of true brotherhood. (Especially, Hankey makes a point of insisting, as such pressures assert themselves in the state of marriage.) 'When one comes to think of it our national life is simply made up of individual pride and mutual contempt' (*Faith or Fear?*, p. 50).

Nevertheless, the present emergency and the raising of a volunteer army—Hankey remains naively idealistic enough to imagine—has created a situation that could serve as a model for a better way to live:

> I have written elsewhere of the men who at this time of national danger have sunk their differences, swallowed their pride, overcome their prejudices, and enlisted in the citizen army to fight with those whom formerly they despised and disliked, for a common ideal. In the army, men are learning what poor things their pride and prejudices were. They are learning the value of the virtues which are common to all classes. ... They are learning to love and honour men with whom in civil life they would have had no dealings. When the war is over it must be the care of the Church to show these men how in the fellowship of Christ's Body they may still use their diversities of gifts, in the same spirit of mutual respect and loyalty, and for the furtherance of a common ideal of life.
>
> (*Faith or Fear?*, pp. 52–3)

It is the army chaplains who stand the best chance to capitalize on this opportunity, to make the church the articulate voice of the social lesson the necessity of war is teaching. But as a body the chaplains remain too remote from the risks and privations and sheer boredom of the trenches to speak convincingly either to or for the common soldier (*Faith or Fear?*, p. 52).

Hankey had been frank enough about traditional military ways for it to be clear that the army *per se* was hardly his idea of a perfect society. But it was *in* the army—in the circumstances that flooded its ranks with volunteers and caused the resulting social microcosm to substitute respect for contempt—that an example of how people of different degrees can live and work together was being formed. No doubt such a view required Hankey to overlook many aspects of the New Army that he must have known perfectly well. Indeed, some of them had received the attention of the Student in Arms. On the other hand, his experience of that army had confirmed two things that civilian society—more particularly the church—should take to heart: the power of worthy leadership and, even more importantly, a better understanding of *work*.

> We must get it out of our heads that manual labour, dirty labour, labour involving obedience to orders are degrading. All honest, necessary, useful labour is honourable.
>
> *(Faith or Fear?*, p. 49)

This is a demand Hankey had long directed at the more fastidious side of his own nature and might have liked to preach to the more staid and conventional members of his family. Earlier that year, writing to his working-class friend John Barker, Donald went so far as to say he had never been happier than when doing rough work in the Australian bush, 'unless it was when digging trenches in Kitchener's Army' (*Letters*, p. 410). A subaltern's easier life makes him long for 'a job worthy of a man's strength'.

> You've no idea [he further explains to this man he addressed as 'Prester John'] what a curse it is to have fond relations whose one wish is to see one clean and respectable!
>
> *(Letters*, p. 411)

Looking into a future that fate did not grant him, Donald tells Barker, 'I want to work with my hands, and mix up with ordinary rough sort of men' (*Letters*, p. 418). Thus to his claim of enjoying the work itself is added the satisfactions of mingling with raw, unassuming masculinity:

> I do like a MAN, whether he wears collars or not, and such lots of them don't! I should like to end up in my old age as a 'labour representative' with a free hand to 'down' all windbags!
>
> (*Letters*, p. 419)

But Hankey's own complicated relationship to hard, manual labour—his long-standing desire to lose himself in it, yet his failure, for both personal and social reasons, to make his attempts altogether successful—was not the same thing as a full repudiation of class difference. He deplored such differences on many grounds, and one of his most basic criticisms of the established church was its virtual identification with the more 'respectable' classes; but he did not clearly envision, much less advocate, radical change in the social structure. When Hankey wrote that 'we have got to face this question of the Church and social distinction' (*Faith or Fear?*, p. 47), he was simply urging a more truly comprehensive identification of the church with all classes of the existing order. He leaves the fact of such distinctions fundamentally unchallenged and rejects the idea of a militant role for the Church in systemic social reform: 'It is not the business of the Church to identify itself with definite political movements' (*Faith or Fear?*, p. 48). But such political neutrality would seem to condemn the church to the very irrelevance with which Hankey is charging it.

In fact it is tempting to conclude that just here can be found the key to why Donald felt he 'had missed something rather important somewhere' in the pages he

214

wrote for *Faith or Fear?* and to his more general suspicion that none of the book's other contributors 'are on the right track in our suggestions of the alterations required' (*Letters*, p. 438). Hankey may sound firm and insistent in saying, 'We have got to settle this question of human values' (*Faith or Fear?* p. 47), but how can such a far-reaching question be resolved with little other impetus or guide besides an exhortation to be better Christians? Hankey could not supply the missing particulars for freeing the church from its domination by the privileged classes, because for all his sympathy for the workingman he believed class distinctions to be inevitable; and though the church should itself (but how?) be classless, it should not meddle in social reform but must 'deal with the social structure that has been evolved by the nation, and . . . make the best of it' (*Faith or Fear?*, p. 48). The best the church could make of that social structure, in Hankey's view, was to be more forthright about privilege in the secular world and the difficulties this made for the church in trying to embody Christ's example and live out His teaching. There-fore, his message in *Faith or Fear?* was, though not absolutely contradictory, a mixture of egalitarian idealism and social conservatism whose flabbiness was at least vaguely apparent to Donald Hankey himself.

*

Donald's published correspondence includes nothing between his May embarkation for France and 8 July, when he posted a letter to his niece from the 4th Army School at Auxi-le-Château. He had obviously been assigned there almost immediately after the horrific first day of the battle of the Somme. During that interval of more than a month there is no personal record of his part in the preparations for the all-out attack. However, the War Diary for the First

Battalion of the Royal Warwickshire Regiment confirms that even the build-up preceding the 'Big Push' involved it in some punishing periods under fire. Those in the Battalion killed and wounded between 22nd June and the beginning of the assault on 1st July total 8 officers and about 250 from the other ranks, mostly victims of shell fire and gas (WO 95/1484). A history of the Royal Warwickshire Regiment adds to this record in the War Diary the information that from 19 to 26 June its First Battalion held the entire stretch of trenches assigned to their division. Twice during that period the battalion resorted to the use of poison gas, but on each occasion a change of wind direction caused the gas to enter the British trenches, resulting (as the War Diary intimates) in a considerable proportion of the total casualties.[1]

How much Hankey's particular unit was involved in these costly preliminaries—increasingly marked by German efforts to weaken the blow about to be delivered against them—cannot be known. Like every other soldier in the huge accumulation of British forces moving by train and then by horses and mules and on foot into the sector of the attack in front of Albert, Lt Hankey would have been fully conscious that something momentous, something of unprecedented power and savagery, was in the offing. Having been in the Ypres salient the previous summer, Donald already knew something of this war's desperate and indiscriminate ferocity, but no one had seen anything on the scale of the Somme offensive. A soldier of his experience would have recognized the evidence of extremely complex and detailed planning. As those signs began more and more to take the shape of an inexorable tide of men

---

[1]Lithbridge Kingsford, C. (1921) 'The Story of the Royal Warwickshire Regiment (Formerly the Sixth Foot)'. In the *Country Life Series of Military Histories*, (p. 149). London.

and materiel flowing across Picardy, would he have found them heartening or ominous? Approaching the battle lines with his company, he would have seen the canvas tenting of clearing stations being made ready for a massive influx of wounded. Probably he would also have encountered a still more unsettling sight: work details nearby digging burial trenches to accommodate numbers of those now marching past who were sure to die in the initial attack.[2]

On the day of that attack—which cost 60,000 British dead and wounded and left a mark on modern consciousness comparable in some ways to 6 August 1945 over Hiroshima—Hankey's company was in support of the First Battalion's main thrust. Describing his own role on 1 July, Donald later wrote that he had been 'in it' for about half an hour, the likely presumption being that he was responsible for getting ammunition and supplies to the forward positions. That would have given him a strong taste of how bad it was. In the same letter (to Strachey) Donald says that having seen his battalion 'wiped out last summer in a fruit-less charge [and] being in it and wounded in it, I was not too depressed. This time it was a good deal worse' (*Letters*, p. 426). Worse because, unlike the time when his wound took him out of the combat, now he was present at the appalling aftermath: 'Although I have once before seen a battle, I have never before seen the day after a battle' (*Letters*, p. 422). That scene included blasted stretches of no-man's land heaped with corpses, a stench that many confirmed to be unforgettably sickening, the hardly human cries of the wounded begging for rescue or for merciful death.

From that day on most of Lt Hankey's writing about the war reflects a new degree of revulsion towards it. The

---

[2]Macdonald, L. (1983) *Somme*, (p. 41). New York.

combination of his nature and his particular perspective upon that terrible 1 July seems to have produced a reaction that focused less upon the victims of war's brutality than upon those who have 'experienced the blood lust' that such extremity appears both to inspire and to nourish:

> I can imagine nothing more horrible than suddenly to feel the primitive passion for slaughter let loose in one, and to know that one was more than at liberty to give it full reign.
>
> (Letters, pp. 422–3)

It is as if that unspeakable half-hour and its sequel left Donald Hankey wondering whether death in such a carnage might almost be preferable to surviving it—'to have killed for one's country and gloried in it' (*Letters*, p. 423). Such 'primitive passion'—surely one of the darkest truths that war reveals—is not commonly explored by even the more clear-sighted writers of The Great War. Few of them had Hankey's peculiar detachment, his 'sense of the dramatic'; few were inclined to reflect, as did he, on the abomination of what war sometimes brought out in those who lived through it 'unharmed'.

By 8 July, with his momentous glimpse of the battle of the Somme behind him, Donald was already writing from the 'No. 2 Mess' of the 4th Army School of Instruction at Auxi-le-Château. Those sent there for special courses of training worked hard and were subject to rigorous discipline, but the seventy miles or so between 'Auxi' and the front separated wholly different worlds. Everything at the training school was orderly and precise. While on duty, dress and the observance of every military form were held to the most punctilious parade standards. Underlying all that, of course, were blessed safety and comfort for the time being. And leisure, which so far from the trenches need not mean utter boredom. Virtually all the pleasures of peace-time were available in the town, and every variety of British sport was pursued in the fields around the school, even including golf (Macdonald, pp. 21–25). Donald now had time to write, but his official purpose, as he told his niece, was to learn 'all there is to know about killing Huns without getting killed ourselves, and this is very important because a lot of people were killed the other day' (*Letters*, p. 421).

That remark—indeed the entire letter of 8 July to young Eileen Spelman—has an uncharacteristic harshness that must be evidence of his recent ordeal. The familiar manner of a playful relative who signs himself 'Your affectionate uncle and godpapa' persists; but Donald's wish to amuse his niece does not conceal something of the stark reality of his experience:

> Well, I am sitting in a great big garden, with a great big house just near, and yesterday I went to a funny old French town to get my hair cut and buy some trousers, because when I came here I was covered with mud, and all my clothes had holes in them. And I had lost my walking stick, but now I am as neat as a new pin.

The avuncular reminder that since the soldiers 'died doing their duty, God took care of them, and took them home with Him' seems to contain an ironic dissonance. In his description of his dug-out at the front as 'a horrid dark place without any windows, which was full of rats', the effort to entertain had taken a morbid turn.

> The rats used to eat my breakfast and my candle, and even my clean socks!
>
> (*Letters*, pp. 421-2)

If this letter to young Miss Spelman contains symptoms of battle shock, Hankey's subsequent correspondence

219

during the interval at the Army School indicates more explicitly how 1 July on the Somme had begun to darken his entire outlook. For one thing, there is a sharper edge to his regret at having been elevated from a non-commissioned officer to a second lieutenant. 'What an idiot I was to take a commission!' he now writes to Dorothy at the end of July (*Letters*, p. 429). Apparently he has been brooding on this misstep. He tells his cousin Valerie that 'really I was much more suitable as a sergeant' (*Letters*, p. 428). In the letter to Dorothy he charges himself with being too 'wretchedly egotistical' to 'climb into' an officer's proper point of view, even though he knows what it should be: 'I am the worst person for an officer' (*Letters*, p. 430). Perhaps the Army School was somehow contributing to this sense of unfitness, though he has little to say about the school itself. He knew he had sufficient actual courage, but one's responsibility to one's men was so overwhelming as to require an officer 'to be a very objective person. . . . The gift of analysis, etc., which is useful to the writer, is worse than useless to the officer, who has got to *do* things' (*Letters*, p. 430). Among those things was ordering young men to face the kind of slaughter he had seen on 1 July.

Donald's way of dealing with the inadequacy he found in himself—with that lack of 'objectivity' which he now branded as 'egotism'—was to concentrate as best he could upon the simple welfare of his men. If he could not protect them, at least there were ways he could care for them. Back in the line in mid-August, he writes to Will Clift, at the Oxford and Bermondsey Mission, asking him to send over 'any sort of fairly serviceable rubber balls,' possibly even 'four stout footballs'. For all its pathetic futility, this gift to his men might be a way, so Hankey explains, 'to keep fellows straight' by occupying them in innocent amusements. Otherwise, 'they do nothing but sleep, grumble, and talk smut, I'm afraid.' This is the familiar stance of a former club-manager, but in his next sentence Donald exposes his deeper feelings:

> Will, Bermondsey has taught me absolutely the love of the boy. The boys here are such topping fellows. You should see the way they smile even when they are fagged out and soaked through and lousy and quaking.
>
> (*Letters*, pp. 432–3)

As the war came to seem more all-encompassing and never-ending, a junior officer's loyalty to his men not infrequently became the one form of duty that made tangible sense, that pointed in a purposeful direction.[3]

These burdens and preoccupations seem to have made it possible for Donald to acknowledge more frankly than before, and to think more freely about, 'the extraordinary affection of officers for their men' (*ASIA, II*, p. 93). That is what he calls it in an essay on that subject, titled 'Romance', which he must have written about this time (see pp. 239–44). In September he refers to the pleasant sound of birds 'twittering in the garden of the farm where I am now billeted'. Then, confessing that he lacks the

---

[3]Lieutenant Hankey's feelings at this time resemble those of a couple of better-known soldier-writers from World War I, whose feelings about their men have been extensively studied: Siegfried Sassoon and Wilfred Owen. One commentator has particularly noted how both these officers represented themselves not as warriors but as solicitous guardians. 'I am only here *to look after some men,*' Sassoon recorded in his diary the summer before the war ended. 'I came out in order to help these boys–directly by leading them as well as an officer can; indirectly, by watching their sufferings that I may speak of them as well as a pleader can,' Owen told his mother in a letter written a month before he was killed. In citing these passages, Samuel Hynes makes the cogent point that whatever they may or may not suggest regarding the sexual impulses of the writers in question, they reflect a drastic revision in the idea of an officer's responsibility to the soldiers he leads that is more broadly significant. Sexuality is too simple a concept to account adequately for all that happens and for the way people react in these extremes. See Samuel Hynes, *A War Imagined: The First World War and English Culture* (Bodley Head, 1990), p. 186.

poet's eye or ear for the things of nature, Donald discloses where his love of beauty has come more truly to be lodged:

> My world is peopled almost entirely with human beings and abstract ideas. I have even lost to a great extent a once passionate love of flowers, and at present the only form of beauty which thrills me at all is the beauty of strong limbs and the beauty of human expression. I am even so limited as not to care for female beauty, but only for the male! A graceful boy with the wonderful smile of youth, or a strong man with a look of resolution and compassion fill me with pleasure. Almost anything else leaves me cold. ...
>
> (*Letters*, pp. 433-4)

Even now, his sense of his own feelings contained a degree of wry humour, which is often his response to self-recognition. Donald's cousin Valerie Bakewell had sent him a watercolour she had painted of a ballet dancer resting her foot upon a chair while she ties her slipper. He acknowledged this evidently Degas-like image, promising to keep 'the exquisite little lady in pink' in his safekeeping 'as long as ever she will stay'. But this amiable reply betrays some reservations: '... I have little experience of such charms. ... She is far too artistic and ingenue to 'raise the temperature of my dug-out!' '' (*Letters*, pp. 427-8). Later (17 August), Donald writes again to Valerie to report the loss of 'the young woman in pink'. He couches this comically in the form of a complaint that 'she eloped with a dashing young temporary Captain'. He adds in mock melancholy that 'I know I am neither young nor dashing ... nor a Captain'. By this time, however, he knows rather more than that—enough to make this small incident into a fanciful masquerade that speaks by conscious contrast to the actual tendency of his affections.

222

Meanwhile, Donald's more general feelings about the war had become broadly negative. 'I am not and never shall be a good soldier. ... I never before felt such a distaste for the whole business' (*Letters* [to Hilda, 12 July 1916], p. 423). Surprisingly soon after that first day of the Big Push, but probably not until he found himself amid the orderly routine of the Army School, Hankey sent Hilda a batch of his writing to be forwarded to Mr Strachey at the *Spectator*. These included 'A Month's Reflections' and 'Imaginary Conversations', both of which appear in the posthumous *Second Series* of *A Student in Arms*. To his sister Donald speaks of the first as ' "A Diary" in four parts' and describes it as 'very much founded on fact'. Then he goes on, as if to warn her: 'You will probably be surprised at a certain change in tone; but remember that my previous articles were written in England, while this was written on the spot' (*Letters*, p. 422). Later he tells Hilda that '["Imaginary Conversations"] represents in its totality what I believe the ordinary soldier feels' (*Letters*, p. 425).

The change in tone that Donald acknowledges was obvious to St. Loe Strachey, who rejected both pieces. This was not unexpected by their author (*Letters* [to Hilda, 23 July], p. 425); he sends Strachey more pieces he thinks might suit him better, taking the opportunity to explain that the 'Diary' [i.e., 'A Month's Reflections'] was not his own, 'but a literary composition designed to accentuate somewhat' the happenings it recounts (*Letters*, p. 426). As for 'Imaginary Conversations', Hankey tells his editor, 'I quite understand your unwillingness to use the piece at this juncture' (*Letters*, p. 427); but he defends it unapologetically, saying it—like the other—was an attempt 'to bring out the intrinsic evil of war'. In current speeches and writings—and Donald does not exempt his own efforts—that evil has been 'too much slurred over' (*Letters*, p. 426).

In this letter Donald puts the *Spectator's* editor politely on notice that he looks forward to including this rejected work in a second volume of *A Student in Arms*. He indicates that a balanced view of the war was his aim; he does not regard his recent work as representing an absolute about-face, but it is clear he now feels more urgently, especially for the sake of those fighting it, the need 'to bring home what an abominable thing war is' (*Letters*, p. 423).

10

A Change in Tone (A Student in Arms, Second Series)

The second collection of Donald Hankey's works, published as *A Student in Arms, Second Series*, did not appear until 1917. He had contemplated a second volume of essays, but there is no record of any detailed plans for it. The 'Second Series' is a bringing together of several 'Student in Arms' essays that were published in the *Spectator* after the first collection appeared, accompanied by a number of previously unpublished writings. This miscellaneous gathering includes a two-part autobiographical fragment given the title 'My Home and School', a short play or masque titled 'The Potentate', and another brief dramatic piece that had been privately printed in the winter of 1915–16 with illustrations by Valerie Bakewell under the title *A Passing in June, 1915*. In addition, extracts from Hankey's letters to Hilda appear as an Author's Foreword; Hilda herself provides by way of introduction a substantial 'Something about "A Student in Arms"' and some personal reminiscences in the form of 'notes' to her brother's autobiographical pieces. The resulting book approaches the length of its similarly titled predecessor. Some of what has obviously been included to flesh it out is of considerable value, but it makes this second series a much less cohesive work than the first.

If four American printings from June to September 1917

is any indication, this second volume shared, though it hardly equalled, the public success of the initial one. Because it contains so much that bears upon the life of its late author—his own and his sister's recollections—the second series contributed rather more at that time to Hankey's reputation as a heroic figure than to his stature as an interpreter of Britain's war experience. 'His life was a romance of the most noble and beautiful kind,' are the words Hilda Hankey chose to begin her Introduction. In some ways it is unfortunate that the second series has so much the look of a posthumous tribute to the man who had stirred the public with his earlier essays. The fact is, the later work has some harder truths to tell, truths which bear out the author's own sense of a change in tone and reveal more starkly than did the first volume 'how loathsome war is'.

Since Hankey's sketches of 'My Home and School' really belong to the celebratory paraphernalia that surrounds the actual war writing found in the book, there remain fourteen pieces to be considered as constituting the 'second series'. Even these, as has been noted, comprise a variety—and an uneven variety—of writings. The first and last (as they appear in the volume) are both written in dialogue, a form that perhaps came to interest Donald as a result of his involvement in theatrical productions of the Oxford and Bermondsey Mission. Aside from that—and their common concern with the war—they are vastly different from one another. 'The Potentate' may, as Hilda says, have been intended for inclusion in the first volume of essays, but there it would have been even more incongruous. It is a brief scene, histrionic and with no pretence at realism, in the camp of the enemy. The Potentate (a kind of Punch-and-Judy stand-in for the Kaiser), gives audience to sundry minions: the Court Chaplain, a General, a Sage. Imperial Germany's moral righteousness and military invincibility are vaunted, only to be—unsurprisingly—confounded by magically revealed events and by a visionary intimation that this potentate will go the way of others of his ilk who have claimed to be God's chosen favourite.

The piece is interesting only by its coincidental resemblance to Sir James Barrie's play, *Der Tag*,[1] and by the way it captures the flavour of national anxiety implicit in its exaggerated portrayal of German self-confidence. Hankey's humourless squib regards the enemy as neither cabbage-headed oafs nor baby-eating savages, but as a race of swaggerers whose claims of superiority apparently have come troublingly close to seeming almost justified.

The elegiac mood of 'A Passing in June, 1915' is more suited to Hankey's bent as a writer; but dating from before the full shock of war had penetrated his writing, it too dilutes the overall effect of the second series of *A Student in Arms*. Hilda notes that a 'rough sketch' for this abbreviated drama had been written in France in 1915 and finished later that year while Donald was back in England recovering in hospital. Possibly he began it in the trenches near Ypres in early June, under fire for the first time and with the memory still vivid of what he recorded in his letters as 'a splendid time' marching up to the front:

> Anything in more complete contrast to the sordid business of war than the manner of our life for the past ten days it is difficult to imagine. It was more like a holiday camp than anything.
>
> (*Letters* [2 June, 1915], p. 363)

---

[1] A note to 'The Potentate' explains that it was written before Donald had any knowledge of *Der Tag*. Barrie's play—which Virginia Woolf saw performed and dismissed (in her diary of 16 January 1915) as 'sheer balderdash of the thinnest kind'—opened in London as a curtain raiser in December of 1914.

227

In a prologue and four short acts 'A Passing' depicts the day on which a soldier called Cecil meets his end. Danger, thirst, the loss of comrades, and the Shadow of Death itself all belie the beauty and glory of living nature and lead Cecil to curse the war and the fools who started it. ('Why did I ever come out here? What a way to spend a morning in June!' [*ASIA, II*, p. 186]). In a letter that sounds as if it were written at the time when Donald conceived this play (to Mrs L, 4 June 1915, *Letters*, p. 365) he mentions 'bullets pattering round' and comments on the rashness of anyone at the front talking of 'after the war', then mentions his father having once told him 'that he would rather "rot in a trench than rust in a furrow".' So in 'A Passing' he makes Cecil's father an example of manly courage. But if the brave words derive from the elder Hankey, it was actually Donald's oldest brother Hugh, killed fighting the Boers at Paardeberg, who was his true model for bravery and sacrifice.

Bravery–the overcoming of physical fear, a resolute readiness to meet death if need be–naturally figures in many places in *A Student in Arms, Second Series*, and it is the commanding issue in at least one of the essays. 'The Fear of Death in War' is the work of a writer much more taken up with the psychology of men in extreme peril, much less interested in portraying courage as moral grandeur, than he had been in 'A Passing'. That little play was an idealization of how Hankey wished to meet the dangers ahead; this essay, on the other hand, draws conclusions from what he had seen of others and experienced in himself. 'I am not a psychologist,' Donald declares at the outset, but writes here as one who now knows too much about war to regard it simply as a test of courage. He writes as an observer–indeed, a student–of behaviour, not a judge of conduct. His tone is not celebratory but almost clinical.

Given the strong likelihood of a violent death, fear would

228

hardly be a surprising emotion. 'And yet in the present war,' Hankey contends, 'hundreds of thousands of men have gone to meet practically certain destruction without giving a sign of terror' (*ASIA, II*, pp. 115–16). Though lacking a scientist's technical grasp and terminology, his effort to treat this subject in a new way, a way free of pious cant, is nonetheless impressive. His aim is not to proclaim these 'hundreds of thousands of men' as national heroes; they are rather a representative group of more or less ordinary chaps who have shared an experience as striking as it is now common:

> The fact is that at the moment of a charge men are in an absolutely abnormal condition. I do not know how to describe their condition in scientific terms; but there is a sensation of tense excitement combined with a sort of uncanny calm.
>
> (*ASIA, II*, p. 116)

As Hankey further characterizes such calm, two things stand out: his own detached grasp of this mental state and his insistence that what he must consider 'abnormal' is nonetheless *natural*. 'Nature has an anaesthetic ready for the emergency,' are his telling words. It is the emotions that are mercifully numbed, not the mind itself or the senses. There is a kind of mental clarity and extreme sensory alertness. So concentrated is the attention of men in this state that the smallest details of both sense and thought may be unaccountably vivid, but the dire implications of the immediate situation are entirely repressed:

> ... with the issue before them, with victory or death or the prospect of eternity, their minds blankly refuse to come to grips.
>
> (*ASIA, II*, p. 117)

229

During the tense period before an attack the situation is far different. Its typical features also interest Hankey. He traces the mind's various manoeuvres for holding fear in check as the moment of maximum danger approaches. Particularly hard on the nerves is having to cower helplessly in a trench during a bombardment, or the peculiar dread of an anticipated gas attack. Yet Hankey argues that such experiences do not truly involve 'the fear of death'. '[They belong] wholly to the physical organism' and as such, so he contends, 'can be, and nearly always [are], controlled by the mind.' There is thus possible 'an act of physical dissociation from the behaviour of one's flesh.'

Your teeth may chatter and your knees quake, but as long as the real *you* disapproves and derides this absurdity of the flesh, the composite you can carry on.

This is his basis for the nevertheless surprising assertion that 'very few men indeed fear death' (*ASIA, II*, pp. 120–1). Hankey's account of how men function under the extremities of combat thus incorporates both mindless bravery and conscious mental strength. In the frenzy of 'jumping the bags' and charging against a wall of bullets, the soldier acts in a kind of trance; he endures extended and passive periods of nerve-wracking danger by holding his mind deliberately aloof from what is merely 'a physical and instinctive shrinking from hurt' (*ASIA, II*, p. 122). By risking a degree of self-contradiction, this essay achieves a view of the ordeal of war that substitutes for the conventional praise of individual heroism a sober respect for how quite ordinary and otherwise unremarkable men manage in vast numbers to endure all they are required to suffer.

As has been mentioned, some of the contents of the Second Series of *A Student in Arms* do not fit the pattern of Hankey's *Spectator* essays. 'A Month's Reflections' reads like a slightly modified version of the author's journal; 'The Wisdom of "A Student in Arms"' is a brief culling—probably by his sister Hilda—from Donald's other writings; 'Letter to an Army Chaplain' is dated 'April 17, 1916' and had been provided to the *Spectator* by the anonymous chaplain himself and published there in its 2 December 1916 issue. Besides this wider variety of writing occasions represented in the later series, one notes the author's clearer sense of a divided audience: the readers at home, with their various anxieties about the citizens' army, and also the Student's companions-in-arms at whatever stage in their own military service they might be.

The two essays, 'The Bad Side of Military Service' and 'The Good Side of Militarism', are doubtless for home consumption. Donald wrote them for the *Spectator* after Strachey rejected the unsettling pieces The Student offered him in the wake of the bloodletting of 1 July. In discussing the 'bad side' in the first of this pair Donald concentrates on the sexual profligacy that has been a part of military life for as long as there have been armies. 'Let us be frank about this,' he exclaims at one point (*ASIA, II*, p. 59), and the essay strives earnestly to do just that.

Hankey is conscious of the common civilian presumption about the sordid behaviour of rankers in the regular army. In a general way he concedes that, owing to obvious causes, life in the New Army—especially across the Channel and close to the front—does lead many men to 'go wrong'. But at the outset he strongly contradicts what he believes to be the common notion that private soldiers, 'being naturally coarser and more animal than the "upper classes",' are more inclined towards lusts of the flesh than officers:

Officers and men necessarily develop different qualities, different forms of expression, different mental

231

attitudes. But I am confident that I speak the truth when I say that essentially, and in the eyes of God there is nothing to choose between them.

(*ASIA, II*, p. 52)

Hankey's view of the subject, then, includes 'fighting men of every class and rank' (*ASIA, II*, p. 53). Few are saints, none lack temptation; but there is something about men who have tasted battle that Hankey imagines his civilian readers are unlikely to have considered:

You who sit at home and read of glorious bayonet charges do not realize what it means to the man behind the bayonet.

(*ASIA, II.* p. 57)

A familiar enough point about the brutalizing effect of combat, and one Hankey discusses elsewhere; but its particular relevance to the issue of sex gives that point here an added and suggestive dimension. 'You don't realize the repugnance for the first thrust,' Donald informs his uninitiated readers, '–a repugnance which has got to be overcome.' The cost of victory over this reluctance is high: 'You don't realize the change that comes over a man when his bayonet is wet with the blood of his first enemy' (*ASIA, II*, p. 57). The Student in Arms pursues the parallel between this yielding to 'blood lust' and its consequences in sexual aggression. Maddened by primitive urges that 'the laws and principles of peaceful society' have held in check, the soldier whose weapon is thus blooded is overcome 'with the desire to kill, kill, kill!'

And that letting loose of a primitive lust is not going to be without its effect on a man's character.

(*ASIA, II*, p. 58)

In this mixture of prim and melodramatic language Hankey is not merely saying that a soldier's bloody-mindedness in battle may thereafter leave him more inclined to acts of violence. The specific character change he foresees transforms a tractable young man into a sexual predator. This portrayal of male sexuality as the acting out of primitive blood-lust discloses Hankey's personal sexual aversions as something more than typical late-Victorian prudery. While he urges that understanding of the young soldiers who 'go wrong' is more to the point than moral condemnation, Donald here betrays an antipathy approaching revulsion from ordinary male sexuality. The essay's preoccupation with 'what a doctor might call "appetites" and a padre the "lusts" of the body' (*ASIA, II*, p. 59) imposes obvious meanings on this virtual reduction of war's desperate violence to bloody thrusting into another human body whose radical otherness (in this case as the estranged 'enemy') incites aggressive desire.[2] Hankey's feelings about war and about sex interact, harking back to what he has revealed elsewhere of his youthful mortification at the goings-on of fellow cadets in Woolwich Academy and of his anguish for those appealing but wayward scamps serving under him.

Fortunately, there are countervailing influences in a soldier's life, and support for these more wholesome elements, Hankey claims, can foster strong idealism able to 'prevail against the flesh' (*ASIA, II*, p. 61). He cites four such 'powers' acting to preserve the soldier from degradation: absorption in duty, the strength of religion, 'the love of a noble man which is hero worship', and 'the love of a

---

[2]Chapter VIII of Paul Fussell's *The Great War and Modern Memory* ('Soldier Boys', pp. 270–309) contains a sensitive and wide-ranging discussion of the relationship between Mars and Eros—the literal and figurative, public and secret, linking of war and sexuality.

true woman' (*ASIA, II*, p. 59). Censoring the mail of his enlisted men as an official duty provided him with favourable evidence: 'The letters of my platoon are largely love letters—often the love letters of married men to their wives' (*ASIA, II*, p. 58).

'The Good Side of Militarism' addresses itself to army life as a system of indoctrination rather than, as in the previous essay, an encounter with one's darker nature. Despite Hankey's claim to have changed from hating militarism to apprehending its ethical, indeed its spiritual meaning, the actual case he makes is in some ways less appealing than his perspective on the 'bad side' of military service. As he often does in his essays, Hankey presents his argument as a rejoinder, in this instance to 'an Oxford friend' who has declared a loathing for militarism in all its forms. This is the pretext for the author's reflections on his own feelings before the war.

> I suppose that in those days the great feature of those of us who tried to be 'in the forefront of modern thought' was their riotous egotism, their anarchical insistence on the claims of the individual at the expense even of law, order, society, and convention. 'Self-realization' we considered to be the primary duty of every man and woman.
>
> (*ASIA, II*, p. 65)

It is hard to associate Donald Hankey with the prewar generation of rampant individualists he thus describes, or to credit what he goes on to say about his own contempt for soldiers and his 'bitter mirth' at watching the Guards drilling in Wellington Barracks as if 'they were not men but manikins' (*ASIA, II*, p. 68). This rings false from a man who had always revered his military brother Hugh and who as a child fought battles with his toy soldiers as if they were living men. Nor did the negative aspects of his personal military experience, at 'The Shop' and on Mauritius, ever move him to a comprehensive condemnation of army life. No doubt part of his nature was at odds with his family's traditions regarding military service, but here Donald surely exaggerates his former feelings as a way of giving his current opinions the dramatic colouring of a drastic change of heart.

Hankey, writing after the disastrous opening of the Somme offensive, is attempting something uncharacteristically bold. He is reflecting on that disaster—virtually reliving it, in fact—and claiming for it a positive value even in the face of its hideous cost:

> For though the part of the 'great push' that it fell to my lot to see was not a successful part, it was none the less a triumph—a spiritual triumph.
>
> *(ASIA, II*, p. 69)

Surely such a claim asks for an explanation, and Hankey struggles to provide one. The point he is making—his justification for daring to regard the slaughter he has seen, and does not blink at seeing, as a splendid victory of the spirit—is that those involved were able by and large to subordinate their ordinary selves and rise to what the moment at hand required of them.

Hankey's boldness is disguised by his modesty and earnestness. It emerges in the contrast he draws between the picture of British soldiers provided to the public in the accounts of war correspondents and his own deeper and more intimate knowledge. The journalist 'only sees the outside, and can only describe the outside of things' (*ASIA, II*, p. 69).

He gives us a picture of men without nerves, without sensitiveness, without imagination, schooled to face death as they would face rain or any trivial incident of everyday life. The 'Tommy' of the war correspondent is not a human being, but a lay figure with a gift for repartee.

(*ASIA, II*, p. 70)

Like Donald Hankey's own professed prewar impressions of soldiers on parade, the journalistic accounts in their different ways reduce these men to manikins. As a seasoned member of Kitchener's Mob, he now challenges these impressions:

We, who are in the Army, who know the men as individuals, who have talked with them, joked with them, censored their letters, worked with them, lived with them we see below the surface. ... We know that each of these men is an individual, many of them full of tender affections, many of them writing tender letters home every week, each one longing with all his soul for the end of this hateful business of war which divides him from all he loves best in his life.

(*ASIA, II*, p. 69-71)

This is the aspect of the soldier Hankey instinctively values most, that thoroughly human aspect to which he opens his heart. Nor can he logically deny that the basis of what is human and the grounds of his affection is the soldier's individuality. But in this essay it is 'militarism' Hankey has chosen to defend, the system and training and discipline he credits with the 'spiritual triumph' of transcendent selflessness he has witnessed on the Somme.

Over and above the individuality of each man, his personal desires and fears and hopes, there is the corporate personality of the soldier which knows no fear

236

and only one ambition—to defeat the enemy, and so to further the righteous cause for which he is fighting.

(*ASIA, II*, pp. 71-2)

Conscious as he was of his own inner divisions, it is perhaps only natural that Hankey seizes upon the idea of the soldier's 'dual personality' as a way of accommodating his mixed feelings about what the army was doing to these young men. Yet one wonders how he could have been satisfied with his emphasis on—his acceptance of—this 'corporate personality' that militarism seeks to produce.

In each of those men there is this dual personality: the ordinary human ego that hates danger and shrinks from hurt and death, that longs for home, and would welcome the end of the war on any terms; and also the *stronger* personality of the soldier who can tolerate but one end of this war, cost what that may. . . .

(*ASIA, II*, p. 72)

Surely there are signs here of an uneasy struggle, a manifestation of Hankey's persistent disapproval of his own 'egotism' at odds with his longings to be at ease with his true self, with his regret at having left the ranks to become an officer, with his wish to divest himself of the 'lendings' of status—authority, conventionality—the approved insignia of respectable manliness.

An explanation as to why in this essay the military virtue of self-subordination wins out over the human urge for self-realization lies in Hankey's situation at the time. He had lived through 1 July; he had a duty to his men; getting the war over with had nothing to do with self-realization. 'I make no claim to be a good soldier,' he concedes, 'but I think that perhaps I may be beginning to be one' (*ASIA, II*, p. 76). With that as his present aim and hope, what would have been the point of asking himself why a German version of 'corporate personality' was any less splendid than the British one? It would hardly have entered his mind to wonder whether the 'higher and bigger personality' to which the soldier learns to subordinate himself might lead not to 'the Kingdom of God on Earth', as Hankey puts it, but to something he clearly did not suspect but which future years would see in all too many destructive forms.

Understandably, Donald's thoughts were fixed more on his immediate situation than on any hypothetical future, but he did dare to imagine that the military discipline acquired in war would make those who survived 'better citizens, better workmen, better servants of the State, better Church men' (*ASIA, II*, p. 76). It has become seemingly impossible in our era to read any war writing without in some way considering the issue of *blame*. Surely no one as innocently involved in The Great War as was Hankey can be blamed for hoping some good might come of it. Yet who in these days can read a phrase like 'servants of the State' without the kind of restlessness that comes when sympathies are dampened or ironies aroused? Whether it is the excessive naïveté of the author or the unwarranted cynicism of the reader, something, no doubt, is to blame for this feeling.

The essay ' "Don't Worry" ' is one of those which, if not addressed directly to the Student's fellow-soldiers, aspires to advise those with a special responsibility for their morale. Here Hankey mounts the pulpit and delivers himself of a modest little sermon reminding his readers that 'worrying is about as un-Christian as any thing can be' (*ASIA, II*, p. 166). Christ calls the faithful 'to a life of external turmoil and inner peace' (*ASIA, II*, p. 167). So the Student preaches against 'too much stress on conscience, self-examination and personal salvation' and urges instead 'a kind of spiritual recklessness'. 'The whole teaching of

238

the Gospels is that we have got to find freedom and peace in trusting ourselves implicitly to the care of God' (*ASIA, II*, pp. 169–70).

The dominant impression of Lt Hankey recalled by those who served with him in this last phase of his life is of one who exemplified such peace–sitting in an open trench, calmly occupied with his pipe and his writing materials during a bombardment. Yet for all that, to some extent Donald was surely preaching this sermon against worry to himself. Twice he alludes to the worry commonly borne by officers who feel themselves unsuited to their responsibilities, perhaps having reluctantly moved higher up in rank. It is clear Hankey considered himself one such, and that after what he had seen on 1 July the prospect of again leading men into battle made him anxious. When it came to personal danger, perhaps Donald found it easier to follow his own counsel and leave the issue to God. The more he saw of war, the more stoical he became about his own chances of survival, and he seems confident that his nerves would not fail him. But he knew his shortcomings as an officer and needed to remind himself that his men, ultimately, were also in God's care.

Hankey's concern about those men, his feelings for them, underlies 'Romance', which appeared posthumously in the *Spectator* (4 November 1916) and is one of the most telling of all the Student in Arms essays. Here the aspect of soldiering under consideration is, as he states it, 'the extraordinary affection of officers for their men' (*ASIA, II*, p. 93). It looks at a reality beneath the surface of the official prohibition against officers treating men with 'undue familiarity'. Of course this 'extraordinary affection' has since then been recognized and well explored as an aspect of The Great War, but Hankey's discussion of it in 'Romance'–conventional, discreet, and sentimental though it may be–must be seen as relatively outspoken for its time and further distinguished by its author's dual perspective on the relationship between junior officers and their men.

'Romance' should be juxtaposed with 'The Beloved Captain' of the first series, for each in its way accepts love as an essential concomitant of a hated war. In 'The Beloved Captain' Hankey assumed the collective voice of the rankers who loved Capt. Hardy as a modest and humane officer, the selfless leader whose qualities of character and spirit were embodied in his physical beauty. It is an unabashed and extravagant essay in hero-worship. Romance, the title and crux of the later essay, represents hero-worship's complement: a contrasting sentiment that does not inspire noble resolve but engenders tender nostalgia. Here Hankey writes in his characteristic Student's voice from a junior officer's point of view. The love he acknowledges thrives more particularly at the front, amid the extremities of hardship and violent death, than in soldiering at home. It includes affection for 'the old men' in the ranks ('Any one over twenty-three or so is an "old man"' [*ASIA, II*, p. 98]) and for dashing younger officers; but the primary object of this poignant romantic attachment is 'the boy soldier':

> Gallant souls, those boys, and all the more gallant because they hate war so much.
>
> (*ASIA, II*, p. 97)

In a chapter on homoerotic tenderness between officers and men (titled 'Soldier Boys') in his book *The Great War and Modern Memory*, Paul Fussell contends that at the front very little such love was of 'the active, unsublimated kind'. Much more common and characteristic, 'especially in the attitude of young officers to their men', was something similar to the 'crushes' many of these officers must have experienced at their all-male public schools—

240

idealistic, passionate, but non-physical. 'In war as at school,' Fussell writes, 'such passions were antidotes against loneliness and terror' (Fussell, p. 272). Then he evokes words from *Gravity's Rainbow*, in which Thomas Pynchon contemplates 'the trenches of the First World War' and asserts that

> English men came to love one another decently, without shame or make-believe, under the easy like-lihoods of their sudden deaths. ... While Europe died meanly in its own wastes, men loved.
>
> (Fussell, p. 277; *Gravity's Rainbow*, p. 616)

Donald Hankey's essay on 'Romance' bears out this view of the subject and elaborates its emotional texture:

> When he goes over the top and works away in front of the parapet with the moon shining full and the machine guns busy all along; when he gets back to billets, and throws off his cares and bathes and plays games like any irresponsible school-boy; even when he breaks bounds and is found by the M. P. skylarking in _____, you can't help loving him. Most of all, when he lies still and white with a red stream trickling from where the sniper's bullet had made a hole through his head, there comes a lump in your throat that you can't swallow; and you turn away so that you shan't have to wipe the tears from your eyes.
>
> (*ASIA, II*, pp. 96-7)

Senior officers are also susceptible to romance; some, at least, find themselves admiring the boy soldier, marvelling at his resilience, grateful for the spirit in which he endures his harder lot, even shamed by its drastic inequality:

For you have slept in a much more comfortable place than he has. You had unlimited tobacco and cigarettes. You have had a servant to cook for you. You have fared sumptuously compared with him.

(*ASIA, II*, p. 96)

Hankey cites a major ('with, as I thought, a good deal of regimental stiffness') who choked with emotion when talking about his men, their uncomplaining cheerfulness, and confessing, 'They make you feel that you're not fit to black their boots.' He reports having a letter from a captain in the artillery, in France almost since the beginning, who writes that 'One of my best friends has just been killed.' The friend was not a fellow-cadet from 'the Shop' or someone with whom the captain had played polo in India or hunted in Ireland, but 'a scamp of a telephonist, who had stolen his whisky and owned up; who had risked his life for him. . . .' (*ASIA, II*, pp. 94-5).

'There is indeed a glamour and a pathos about the private soldier'—and the more boyish the more glamorous and pathetic—that his exhaustion, his filth and fear and misery, only intensify. Hankey's 'Romance' goes a long way towards explaining this. His perspective—enriched and complicated by his having been both an enlisted man and a commissioned officer—does considerable justice to the element of distance, of radical separation, that provides this extraordinary affection with its particular poignancy. Detachment is as important to his testimony as his thorough knowledge of the common soldiers' experience and his intimate involvement in whether they fare well or ill. This is a practised stance for Donald Hankey, an attitude he assumed as an Oxonian presiding over, guiding, yet sharing in the lives of scruffy and boisterous waifs in Bermondsey. Far from the hearty or jocular sort, but enigmatic, curiously self-contained, absorbed in thought

242

and pipe smoke except when a smile would suddenly transform him, Lt Hankey's presence often seemed mystifying but never registered with his men as indifference. It is probable, too, that performing the task of censoring those men's letters home—this almost voyeuristic access to their least guarded most confidential moments—drew the Student more strongly to these men while at the same time increasing his sense of separateness from them.

During his experience as an officer the combination of longing for identity with the common soldier and the difficulty of such inclusion made Donald keenly conscious of whatever signs there were that his feelings for his men might be reciprocated. Ironically, as with his Bermondsey boys, any such signs made him feel somehow inadequate, and so he blames himself for coldness and superficiality.

> And then when he thinks how little he deserves all this love and loyalty, the subaltern's heart aches with a feeling that can find no expression in word or deed.
>
> (*ASIA, II*, p. 98)

But Hankey is not so caught up in the ebb and flow of his own complicated emotions that he fails to see beyond that time to the larger issue of whether the excruciating encounter with 'romance' in war will leave any trace worth the price so many are paying for it. He surely accepts that one thing to be learned from this war is to hate it; but revulsion simply by itself is incommensurate to the sacrifice. The 'extraordinary affection' that could flourish in the midst of severe discrepancies of class and rank taught a different lesson. Hankey warns the future of its importance:

> For the time will come when we shall need to remember it, and when it will be easy to forget. Will you

remember it, O ye people, when the boy has become a workman?

(ASIA, II, p. 99)

He does not sound confident that the nation will make itself truly fit for its heroes, that his warning will be heeded. What then will be the legacy of his generation's encounter with 'love and loyalty and fear and pain' if it is not? Hardly more—and yet this is something—than that any survivor can say, even when life is at its dullest and most routine,

> 'I have lived! I have loved, and endured, and trembled, and trembling, dared. I have had my Romance.'

(ASIA, II, p. 105)

Considering all that England lost in The Great War, 'romance' may seem a trivial item to enter on the credit side of the ledger, yet for Hankey's generation it was a word of enormous consequence, not least because it escapes definition. In a famous passage in 'A Room of One's Own' Virginia Woolf can do no more than call it 'some feeling one used to have,' but there is no mistaking how much she misses it. For her, of course, it was the war itself that explained the loss of romance; Hankey, however, lived the war as Virginia Woolf could not and even she herself—as the case of Septimus Smith (in *Mrs Dalloway*) shows—would not have been shocked by Hankey's point that for some the war could harbour romance.

The two pieces Strachey refused for the *Spectator* would have been unsuited to that journal's format even had they sent a more positive report on the war to the home front. 'Imaginary Conversations' appears in *A Student in Arms, Second Series* in four parts. These are not printed consecutively, and indeed each is a distinctly separate dialogue involving different *dramatis personae* in different situations. The first involves three Cockney soldiers bivouacked in Flanders, indulging themselves in the soldiers' commonest pastime of grousing. The only survivors from their original platoon, they air their differing outlooks on the chances of life and death. 'Fred' is fed up and jumpy; 'Bill' is gloomily resigned; 'Jim' resorts to shopworn slogans for making the best of it. 'Imaginary Conversations II', from a distinctly higher rung of the ladder, shows a group of junior officers over tea in a dug-out; then, after an action, the two survivors display their contrasting reactions. The third sketch returns us to the rank and file, a scene in the trenches after bombardment. Here Hankey achieves real variety and liveliness in his character vignettes; the grousing seems less contrived and more pungent, but so brief a scene can hardly make good on its author's claim that 'it represents in its totality what I believe the ordinary soldier feels' (*Letters*, p. 425). In the last conversation a subaltern fresh from the front engages another patron—a French civilian—in a barber's shop. The barber himself interjects a promisingly discordant note by an insinuation about England's performance in the Boer War, but potential drama flickers out when the two principals steer past that bit of potential rough going and agree that France and England are the truest of friends.

'A Month's Reflections'—or as Hankey himself described it, 'the diary'—is a more substantial effort. He was right to feel that it expresses 'the intrinsic evil of war' more explicitly, more successfully than he had managed to do in his earlier work (*Letters*, p. 420). He insisted to Strachey that it was 'a literary composition', not an exact personal account, but it obviously captures a fair amount of its author's experience of the Big Push and clearly speaks his mind.

As it stands, this simulation of a fragmentary diary achieves a modest but effective wholeness. It begins almost idyllically, the diarist and 'Timothy', his twenty-two-year-old captain, billeted with 'M. le Curé' and messing at the home of the village schoolmaster:

Timothy is immense. He is that rarest of birds, a wholly delightful egotist. He is the sun, but we all bask and shine with reflected glory.

(*ASIA, II*, p. 81)

This aura extends to the diarist himself as subaltern and to all the men, who are 'splendid'. But when the company moves into the line this bright scene is suddenly beclouded. First the misery of rain as a foreboding of much worse: rats, sleepless nights, and nameless fears. Then the great bombardment as prelude to the Push. To his disgust, the diarist is left out of the assault and put in charge of carriers ('Damn! . . . I see myself counting ration bags while the battalion is charging with fixed bayonets' [*ASIA, II*, p. 84]). But he does find himself briefly in the thick of it—in fact 'the only officer of my company to set foot in the German lines' (*ASIA, II*, p. 85)—and that experience is well captured in his account. The attack fails, the ground taken at such a bloody cost cannot be held, and the diarist admits his joy at being sent back out of the maelstrom with a report to HQ. The fragment ends with the diarist contemplating the wretched aftermath, recalling a day and night spent bringing in the dead and wounded, and meditating on all the futility and suffering and bravery he has witnessed.

It cannot be said that Hankey's 'diary' stands out in the accumulation of first-hand descriptions of what combat was like in The Great War. In that company it is perhaps neither particularly graphic nor unusually informative, though its conciseness and its narrative shaping make it a nonetheless worthy contribution to the record. As for its

246

value to the body of Donald Hankey's writing, one may speak with more assurance. 'A Month's Reflections', despite whatever fictionalizing Hankey subjected it to, clearly establishes his alert sensitivity to the stark realities of combat. Those things he brought with him to the experience—an ordinary Englishman's confidence in a righteous cause, a seriously religious person's assumption that the ordeal was a test of moral as much as physical strength—did not give a coloration to the war that obscured its full horror. ('I loathe war. It is futile, idiotic. I would gladly be out of the Army tomorrow' [*ASIA, II*, p. 84].) Deliberately, he did not choose to denounce the war; but he saw himself as a student of how a citizens' army responded to an excruciating and complex spiritual trial.[3]

---

[3]Contemporary recognition of this complexity can, even now, seem striking. For example, in an Author's Note which Joseph Conrad added in 1920 to his novel *Victory* the following phrase leaps out. Conrad describes the recent war as 'tragic enough in all conscience but even more cruel than tragic and more inspiring than cruel.' It is the word *inspiring* that, in this context, carries the electric charge and completes a peculiarly affecting circuit.

11

'Resting Quite Long Enough' (July to 12 October 1916)

In the early days following the calamitous beginning of the Somme Offensive, the First Battalion of the Royal Warwickshire Regiment remained in trenches and took stock. Fifty-seven casualties are reported for 1 and 2 July —not an inordinate number considering that the total of British dead, wounded, and missing for the first twenty-four hours of that attack was about 60,000. Nonetheless, the Battalion War Diary for that period assumes a grim formality. On the afternoon of the 6th Brigadier-General Wilding visited the trenches accompanied by the commanding officer and by the company commander of the Royal Dublin Fusiliers to arrange for relief. In 'A Month's Reflections' Donald Hankey records the cheery expectation among the soldiers prior to the Push that this effort would end the war. Subsequently he describes the attack in the immediate sector as 'a failure' (*ASIA, II*, pp. 82, 85). That morale was consequently a concern in the aftermath is suggested by Corps Commander General Hunter-Weston's visit in connection with the battalion's move out of the line on 8 July. That general 'addressed the Battalion at 11:30 a.m. and complimented all ranks on the work accomplished' (War Diary, 1st Battalion, Royal Warwickshire Regiment [WO 95/1484]). There was a period of training, and a draft of 83 replacements arrived on the 11th. On the 18th

Commanding Officer Lt. Col. Bannerman—now described as 'Major J. A. M. Bannerman'—left the battalion for reassignment at 'Reserve Army H.Q', presumably with a reduction in rank. On 23 July the First Battalion arrived at 'K camp' on the Poperinghe–Watou Road; by the 27th of July it had occupied trenches on a canal bank in front of Ypres. However, Lt Hankey did not participate in most of that month's regimental vicissitudes. Very shortly after the failed attack he was assigned to the Fourth Army School at Auxi-le-Château, where he remained until he returned to regular duty some time in August.

We have already glimpsed, through his letters, something of Donald's life at that school where he found himself with about two hundred other students. The bulk of his free time while there must have been spent with his writing and in corresponding about it with his sister Hilda and the editor of the *Spectator*, Mr St. Loe Strachey. His mental preoccupations during this interval—his intensified aversion to war, his regrets at having become an officer, his equivocal feelings about discipline, his experience of how men manage to face bloodshed, and his increasingly poignant affection towards the soldiers for whom he was responsible—are reflected in the contents of *A Student in Arms, Second Series* discussed in the previous chapter.

While on his training course Donald reported having 'a very good time'. 'One can't by any stretch of imagination call it "active service",' he told his cousin Dorothy (*Letters*, p. 429). He messed with 'some awfully nice Ulsterites' who led him to revise his previous prejudice against people from the north of Ireland as 'a dour, pig-headed, self-righteous, narrow-minded lot!' Many taking the course had been promoted from the ranks, which for Lt Hankey would have made them kindred spirits, at least to that extent. He was pleased to note that only one in his group was a product of a military academy:

249

He is a Rifle Brigade man, to boot, and I am afraid is rather too conscious of his superiority to the rest of us to be quite happy. But he is very young and will learn better.

(Letters, p. 428)

In general, these associates confirmed Donald's growing sense of 'what a staid elderly old thing I am!' But at nearly thirty-two he could still relish the charm and high spirits of such a company. 'We had a good laugh at your Zepp raid,' he told his cousin Valerie, adopting the *sangfroid* of a soldier at the front who had seen much worse than a few German airships floating above London (*Letters*, p. 428).

In a letter to his Australian cousin, Dorothy Gurner, he singles out one 'really congenial friend' he has met at the training school. He was the son of a wealthy cloth merchant from Derry, 'a most awfully nice clean-minded person', who wrote home to his wife 'every day without ever missing' (*Letters*, p. 429). Donald also records having met the Rev. Neville Talbot at about that time. Talbot, who had a connection with the Oxford and Bermondsey Mission of somewhat earlier date than Hankey's, was a co-founder of Talbot House (named in honour of his brother), the much-celebrated spiritual refuge in Poperinghe for soldiers of all ranks seeking respite from the horrors of Ypres. This meeting (which Donald mentions in a letter dated 13 August) may, in fact, have taken place in 'Pop', in which case Hankey's battalion must still have been in the Ypres sector when Donald rejoined it from his training course. In any event this acquaintance with Neville Talbot obviously meant a good deal to Hankey. 'He is the very best sort of parson, and the son of the Bishop of Winchester,' he explains to Hilda. He further tells her that Rev. Talbot 'afterwards wrote me a very nice letter about *A Student in Arms*', and then he adds a bit of choice serviceman's gossip (on what authority who can say?):

He is a tremendously manly parson and his last exploit
was to turn the 'Loathed Captain' [this is Hankey's designation for Capt. Hardy's successor and the officer
whose command Donald gave up his sergeant's stripes
to escape] out of the club at _____ 'Vi et armis' (by the
strength of his arms) for using obscene language and
refusing to desist from doing so.

(*Letters*, p. 431)

Whatever the exact place and date of Hankey's return to
it, his battalion did not leave Flanders until mid-September
and did not return to the trenches on the Somme until the
early days of October. Donald's letters scrupulously avoid
sending through the post any mention of his or his battalion's exact whereabouts. On 19 August he writes the
letter to his friend Will Clift of the OBM asking him to
send 'some balls for my bhoys [*sic*] to play with' (*Letters*,
p. 432); on 10 September he mentions 'birds twittering in
the garden of the farm where I am now billeted' (*Letters*,
pp. 433-4). A letter to his 'other sister' Gertrude of 18
September implies that he is again in the neighbourhood
of the Somme trenches and expecting 'another show
soon' (*Letters*, p. 435). In the meantime a copy of *Faith
or Fear?* has finally reached him, and he discusses its
contents and related religious matters with some of his
correspondents.

Donald's spirits must have been at least somewhat lifted
to receive, enclosed in a letter from Mr Strachey dated 19
September, an unusually acute commentary on *A Student
in Arms* published in the 16 September number of the
Spectator (pp. 308-9). The article appeared as a communication which the *Spectator* titled ' "A Student in Arms"–
How It Strikes a Transatlantic "Tommy",' subscribed with
the initials 'J. N. H.' Hankey replied promptly to Strachey
on the 19th:

Thank you very much for your letter and for the American's article on *A Student in Arms*. I know of no appreciation that I value so much as that of a fellow-soldier, and of a fellow-Yankee.

(Letters, p. 438)

The reference to a *fellow*-Yankee is puzzling unless it means something like 'a kindred democrat-at-heart'. In any event, Donald would have valued his appreciation even more had he known anything about this 'Transatlantic Tommy'. He was James Norman Hall, an Iowan who had enlisted as a private in the British Army on almost the same day, and in the same place, as Hankey himself. Back in Iowa, after having fought in the Battle of Loos as a machine gunner with the Royal Fusiliers, Hall wrote a series of articles for the *Atlantic Monthly* which had been published in book form in the spring of 1916 under the title *Kitchener's Mob: The Adventures of an American in the British Army*. Jimmy Hall's 'adventures' are less concerned with his personal exploits than with his self-effacing observations of that army of inexperienced volunteers he became a part of. It is a fine piece of writing, honest, humorous, and affectionate. Donald Hankey would surely have felt some affinity between his own experience as a 'gentleman ranker' and Hall's as a quiet and dreamy young man from America's heartland thrown in with a crowd of Cockneys. But Hall's modesty was such that his *Spectator* article makes no mention of his own book, which appeared in England about the same time as *A Student in Arms*.

This 'Transatlantic Tommy' begins by noting the spate of personal narratives produced by the war and acknowledging their value; but 'any normally observant soldier with a gift for facile expression', he contends, 'can write such a tale, and be certain of finding an audience.' It is another kind of book, however, that Hall has 'chanced upon': one that has 'little to say of the actual experiences of war, but much of men's reactions in the face of them.'

It [speaks] for hundreds and thousands of the inarticulate. It [reveals] to these men their own souls, and show[s] them how they were fashioned anew during the stress of battle, or during the long comfortless days and nights, when they stood on sentry, vainly trying to think things out for themselves. Such books will be as rare as the others are common. ... The first one has appeared, and it is called *A Student in Arms*.

Hall refers to the fact that he too, like the author of this book, had been a student in arms, 'but there the analogy ends'. He includes himself among 'that great body of silent soldiers whom the English student calls "The Inarticulate".' His own efforts at 'self-analysis in the light of new experience' failed, so he says. He could himself give no adequate account of the 'profound changes [that] were taking place, both in his comrades and in himself.' Then, reading Donald Hankey's book at one sitting 'with a feeling of admiration nearly akin to awe', Hall discovers

... the written record of a philosopher-soldier, a man who could think as well as fight, and whose reasoning powers were not atrophied by an overwhelming sense of the futility of mental effort in the face of unspeakable experiences.

Hall finds that The Student's conclusions square with his own 'inarticulate' ones. He is relieved that 'a scholar and a gentleman' should speak his very thoughts, both positive and negative, about the officer class, 'the army of aristocracy' whose dogmas and ritual of military discipline control the citizen 'army of democracy'. The Englishman and the

American seem to have shared the discovery that 'however dogmatic the dogmas, and however rigid the ritual, they have not concealed from men the fact they are brothers under the skin.' Hall responds to Hankey's feelings on this score with his own generous testimony:

The American [as he refers to himself], professed democrat though he was before he joined the British Army, first learned the meaning of true comradeship in the trenches on the Western Front. That is why he has a feeling of kinship with his English comrades, even deeper than with his own countrymen. . . . It is only by living together through experiences of this kind that men learn to say, in deep sincerity: 'Brother, I salute you!'

Obviously conscious of the Student's religious leanings, Hall supports at some length his 'luminous criticism' of Church of England army chaplains' inability to minister meaningfully to men in arms; but the part of his critique that must have had a particular impact upon Donald Hankey had to do with what Hall refers to as 'the ultimate effect of this new sense of comradeship on the life of the nation.' He confesses himself 'not so sanguine, not so hopeful, as the Englishman.'

Men are not created 'free and equal,' regardless of the generous declaration to that effect of the American Constitution. . . . With the coming of peace and the return to the normal pursuits of life, the old free-masonry of the trenches will become a radiant, wistful memory.

The letter Donald wrote to Hilda on 23 September reveals clearly that he has taken these words of the 'Transatlantic

Tommy' to heart. He shares with his sister 'a depressing thought' concerning a hypothetical future:

> I should not be surprised if, when we are old, we see a repetition of this war. I have little doubt that it will take most of our lifetime (if we survive the war) for the belligerent nations to recover their strength. But I have little doubt that if, as seems likely, we best the Hun pretty badly, he will start the moment peace is signed to prepare for his revenge.

In this darkly prophetic vein Donald goes on to predict that the British themselves will not long remember as they should the terrible cost of this war:

> The rising generation won't know what we know, and we shall forget much that is bad.

Such an unwonted outburst of pessimism puts him in mind of what the young American had written, or he may even have been led to it in the first place by Hall's calmly bleak view of human nature and of the future. Quoting J. N. H's very words, Donald concludes wryly:

> When a soldier can write that the brotherhood of the trench will be 'a wistful radiant memory' now, what shall we be writing twenty years hence!
>
> (*Letters*, p. 440)

Strachey of the *Spectator* wrote to Hall and told him Hankey 'was very sympathetic about your article'. Donald's feelings towards the part of Hall's piece he quotes to Hilda seem 'sympathetic' but complicated. Both men value 'the freemasonry of the trenches', even as a memory; but Hankey, who substitutes 'brotherhood' for Hall's somewhat anticlerically-tinged term, is clearly more pained than the American by the thought that such camaraderie within the ranks may, when peace does come, fade without inspiring the social transformation he had allowed himself to hope for England.

'You must try and meet,' Mr Strachey told Hall, who had returned to France and would soon join the Lafayette Escadrille, 'but of course I know that only chance can do that' (Strachey, J. St Loe. Letter to James Norman Hall, 4 October 1916. Ellery Sedgwick Papers, MHS.) Chance was unaccommodating and capricious. Donald Hankey had only a few more days to live; James Norman Hall learned to fly as one of that adventurous company of American volunteers in the French flying corps, was shot down and interned, but survived to know fame, in due time, as co-author of *Mutiny on the Bounty*.

*

As September wore on, Donald continued to expect and even hope for some more decisive action. 'When one is really fighting the spirit rises to the occasion,' he writes, 'but I think that the combined discomfort and dreary monotony of more or less danger in the ordinary trench warfare, especially in bad weather, make far greater demands on the character. One has no "sense of the dramatic" to help one!' (*Letters*, p. 435). The letter to Hilda of 23 September includes the report that 'We are still at peace; though I am hoping that we may get a scrap before winter' (*Letters*, p. 440). Hateful as war is, feelings of uselessness and impatience to press on with it at all costs are beginning to dominate. Three different letters refer to a possible 'slide into winter' without an attack on the enemy, a prospect described as uncomfortable and squalid. At the beginning of October Donald's company was quartered at Daours (according to the Battalion War Diary); he was finding 'this life ... far too monotonous and irritating for words unless one has just had a spell of something worse to enable one to appreciate it.' The persistent rain was 'simply loathsome'.

Inaction had put a more than usual strain upon discipline. Donald mentions to his sister that a couple of men in his platoon 'have got into serious trouble' and blames himself, saying that 'if I hadn't been so essentially a bad disciplinarian it wouldn't have happened, and a good man or two might have been saved from going to the dogs.' Perhaps the likelihood of serious fighting in the offing made Lt Hankey all the more self-critical. His experience and training, as well as his maturity, left him little excuse: 'I know what an officer ought to be like and I am not a bit like it!' (*Letters*, p. 440). Would he be able, in the face of the fearful action he presumed was coming, to provide his men the leadership, the example, they would surely need?

On 6 October Donald wrote again to Hilda. He tells her that two of his articles will soon be appearing in Mr Strachey's *Spectator*. In the light of subsequent events these subjects seem peculiarly apt and must have seemed so at the time to Donald himself: 'Not Worrying' (the essay is actually titled 'Don't Worry') and 'The Fear of Death in War'. For he was sure now that something serious lay immediately ahead. 'We shall probably be fighting before you get this,' he writes, then adds to ease Hilda's anxiety, 'but one has a far better chance of getting through now than in July.' To someone like Lt Hankey who had been at the front on that fateful 1 July, that was a desperate way to summon comfort. In any event, he once again assures her that he will be glad of a scrap: 'we have been resting quite long enough' (*Letters*, p. 441).

Next day the battalion left Daours and, according to the War Diary, had a bad march ending in bad billets on a wet night. On the 8th the troops reached Mansell Camp near Mametz. They were close to the front, and the following day found them in position trenches east of Lesboeufs. Their accumulating presence must have warned the enemy that an assault was coming, and in the morning the German artillery was very active. On their side the British guns began their preliminary bombardment. This continued throughout the next day; strong enemy retaliation caused twelve casualties in Hankey's battalion and considerable damage to its position. The weather had turned for the better and conditions looked favourable for the attack on the German trenches the next afternoon, Thursday, 12 October.

Special orders, written in longhand and signed by Lt. Col. Forster, laid out the plan of operations. The Battalion War Diary's account of the action is detailed and orderly, but it hardly conceals the confusion and uncertainty that seems to have been the actual state of affairs during much of the assault. A fine morning dawned; the artillery opened fire at 7:00 and continued until 2:30 that afternoon. At 2:05 the 'creeping barrage' began. The battalion, having extended, was ordered to move out of its trenches on the double in four waves. By 2:40, with the Irish Fusiliers on one flank and a French formation on the other, all companies were reported 'going well'.

But at some point the plan of attack broke down. Enemy machine gun and rifle fire became fierce, men were falling in numbers and the rest, unable to advance, were told to lie down. When the order came to push on, the German firing grew even more deadly, and again the attack halted. On the right the French forces began to retire. Seeing this, the Irish on the Warwicks' left flank also fell back. The men furthest forward wavered but their officers urged them on. Having lost touch with the rear, and the situation having become desperate, they were ordered to dig in and 'hang on for all they were worth' (Battalion War Diary, Appendix I, 'Diary of Operations for 12.10.16'). Pinned down by enemy machine guns, the men responded as trained and began to make holes for themselves and then dig towards each other to make a rude trench. Lt Hankey had been seen waving his men forward and they obeyed. Gradually the remnants of 'C' and 'D' companies collected themselves. The sheltering trench was enlarged and some of the wounded were brought in and attended to. Lt Glyka, badly wounded, died before a stretcher could carry him to the rear. Captains Harrison and Somers also lay dead. Then Private Woods appeared out of the chaos of battle to report that his officer, Lt D. Hankey, had been killed.[1]

*

At the end of Donald Hankey's letter of 6 October he assured Hilda that he had sufficient pipe tobacco ('lots of baccy—1 1/2 lb. to be accurate') and described having enjoyed a pleasant afternoon in 'a jolly little town' nearby—a hot bath, tea with a friend, and some necessary shopping. The tone of his letter is cheerful, but it is obvious Donald was aware that this letter could well be the last he would live to write. He warned Hilda that soon he will be risking his life. 'Of course one always has to face possibilities on such occasions,' he told his favourite sister, 'but we have faced them in advance, haven't we?' Occupied as he naturally was with such 'possibilities', Donald also turned his thoughts to the men with whom he would share the chances just ahead.

I have a top-hole platoon—nearly all young, and nearly all have been out here 18 months—thoroughly good sporting fellows.

---

[1]Details of the fighting taken from Pte Crudgington's letter in Budd, pp. 140–46.

I have also some of the best NCOs in the battalion,
so if I don't do well it will be my own fault

Along with as much cheer as he can give her, he wanted
Hilda to be certain he was in the best of company—that for
what he then faced he could not choose better.

And as zero hour approached in the trenches less than a
week later, if one credits the recollection of Private
Crudgington, Donald Hankey's mind was very much with
the men around him. Crudgington remembers receiving Lt
Hankey's thanks for the miserable tea he had made for
some of the officers; he remembers Lt Hankey speaking to
his men words that became the dramatic climax of an
heroic legend, a moving affirmation of literal faith: 'If you
are wounded, "Blighty"; if killed, the Resurrection.'
However, these words, if Donald did utter them, were no
grandiose bid to make himself memorable. In fact they
reflect his characteristic trust in the pragmatic value of
belief as a source of worthy action, a practical way of
regarding the alternatives of faith or fear.

His chosen authorial identity was that of 'Student', which
implies a degree at least of psychological distance from the
object of study; it is anything but the identity of one who
celebrates his own deeds or even puts himself at the centre
of a story. One must rely on the likes of Private
Crudgington for any vivid glimpse of Lt Hankey—the man
amidst a troop of men as they marched along some muddy
road into a very uncertain future.

'... you would see him with his pack and rifle slung on
his shoulders the same as his men. He would give you
anything if you wanted it—notepaper, fags and tobacco.
... His men did not love him for his position in life, as

260

they did not know who he was, but they knew that he was a chum, besides an officer.'

Whether Private Crudgington, writing twelve years later from Queen Mary's Hospital for mutilated ex-soldiers in Roehampton Lane, was saying what he personally and precisely did recall, or whether he was putting down as best he could what he felt was expected of him, these words would have pleased Donald Hankey infinitely more than any idealized picture of himself leading his men in a charge.

Lt Hankey's name may be found—along with others more famous and many thousands entirely obscure—inscribed on the towering Memorial at Thiepval dedicated to the 70,000 missing and unidentified dead British soldiers who fought on the Somme. As his body was never recovered, and no grave was ever found, he is officially remembered as one among that staggering number. But Donald Hankey's actual burial, as described by Pte Crudgington, suits better the kind of man he was and what he wrote about soldiering: a shallow pit somewhere near Le Transloy, shared with three fellow officers, dug by a couple of scared and exhausted but sorrowing common soldiers who laid him into it.

Afterword

Four days after Lt Hankey's battlefield burial on the Somme his brother Maurice, Secretary to the Committee of Imperial Defence, was in his office in Whitehall Gardens dictating memoranda to his private stenographer Mr F. W. Owen. The telephone rang and, according to Lawrence Burgis his private secretary, Col. Hankey answered it himself. He listened impassively to the voice at the other end; then, as he replaced the receiver, he merely remarked, 'Donald's gone.' After only a brief pause Maurice Hankey turned again to his stenographer. 'Where was I, Owen?' were his only words.

In his biography of Donald Hankey's distinguished brother, Stephen Roskill tells us that 'this seemingly heartless reaction shocked those who heard it.' The biographer himself chooses to interpret otherwise this vivid glimpse of how Maurice Hankey received the ill-tidings. Burgis's recollection 'certainly accords with Hankey's character and upbringing,' Roskill acknowledges; but evidence of the 'deep bonds of affection' between the two brothers is, so he claims, 'abundant and convincing'.[1] Must we take it, then, not as a chillingly un-fraternal instance of emotional paralysis but simply as a classic display of the stiff upper lip? Perhaps a veritable model, in that time of darkening

---

[1]Roskill, S. (1970–71) *Hankey, Man of Secrets*, (Vol. I, p. 308). London: Collins.

national crisis, of how an Englishman's natural feelings should be mastered for the sake of the job at hand. After she learned of her brother's death, Hilda Hankey wrote repeatedly to the War Office. On 23 October she asked to know where 'on the Somme' her brother had been killed and received a courteous letter referring her to the 'Officer Commanding' of the First Royal Warwickshire Regiment. She was much concerned about the disposition of Donald's effects and continued to inquire into the following year and even later than that. In particular, a plaque and scroll of some kind belonging to Lt Hankey should, she believed, have come to her, since her brother had left his manuscripts in her keeping and she felt 'certain the rest of the family would wish' those items to be hers.

Regimental accounting of Lt Hankey's finances at the time of his death shows a credit in the amount of seventy-two pounds, sixteen shillings. Evidently Donald had received his pay for October, because seven pounds, two shillings and six pence of the above sum is then subtracted from the amount owed to his estate as representing payment for service during a portion of that month (13-31 October) to which Lt Hankey, having in fact died on the 12th, was not entitled.

The details of his will are difficult to make out from Donald Hankey's War Record. The 'informal will' contained on page 28 of the Officer's Small Book is described as having been 'struck through diagonally with a pen and … not signed at the foot and may be disregarded' (WO 339/5889). However, there is reference to a will having been probated which left all of the deceased's estate to his brother Clement (the executor being the Rev. Arthur Patrick Spelman [the husband of Donald's sister Gertrude]). The gross value of Lt Hankey's estate is given (in a letter of 11 July 1919 from J. E. Bush, 22 Ship Street, Brighton, Solicitor and Borough Coroner) to be five thousand seven hundred seventy-six pounds, nine shillings and seven pence. The most likely explanation for Donald's decision to leave all of it to his eldest surviving brother Capt. Clement Hankey (then serving in Palestine while his family remained in London) probably lies in the presumption that Clement, having been 'hammered' on the Stock Exchange in the early days of the war (Roskill, p. 114), was in the least comfortable circumstances among Donald's surviving siblings. Hilda, unmarried and with her portion of the family money, was reasonably well provided for. Gertrude Spelman, his other sister, would depend upon her husband's resources, whatever they may have been. Both the surviving brothers had families of their own; but Maurice, who then held the rank of Lieutenant Colonel, was well along in his notable government career and must have been considerably better off than Clement.

The death of the Student in Arms rather quickly produced public comment. In its 21 October 1916 number *The Challenge*, that liberal Church of England periodical in which Donald had published several items in the summer of 1914, solemnly informed its readers that Lt Hankey had been killed in action. That notice praises 'his beautifully fresh and sincere grasp of many sides of the Christian faith' and describes Donald as 'a man who had had the advantage of a singularly varied experience, and in all of it had come into intimate relations with the people among whom he was thrown.' His essays in the *Spectator* and *Faith or Fear?* are cited, along with his articles in *The Challenge*, as reflecting 'the very spirit of Christianity'. The essay 'Don't Worry' ('which it is beautiful to think of as being among his last published utterances') is then reprinted in its entirety by permission of the *Spectator*.

The Challenge for 10 November included a poem 'by the late Second Lieutenant Donald Hankey'. Using the same title as his book, that poem 'The Lord of All Good Life' is conventionally pious but displays a well-managed refrain and a verse pattern of some ingenuity. Then the next week's *Challenge* featured ' "A Proper Gent" ', by the late Donald Hankey.' Typical of his sympathies, it is a slight thing, making the point that 'proper gentlemen' in the army as elsewhere come from all ranks and conditions; but clearly Hankey's name on the journal's contents page at just that time had value as an attraction for readers.

In its much more widely circulated pages the *Spectator* also paid extended tribute to its Student in Arms. The 21 October number carried Strachey's editorial salute along with 'Don't Worry'. Other Student essays Donald had written during that late summer and autumn appeared in subsequent issues: 'The Fear of Death in War' on 28 October, and 'Romance' on 4 November. The 25 November *Spectator* included a gathering of aphorisms from Donald's earlier essays comprising 'The Wisdom of "A Student in Arms" '; the 2 December number printed the letter 'An Army Chaplain' had received from Donald the preceding April; on 9 December appeared 'The "Student in Arms" in Elstead', Mrs Coppin's cherished recollections of the then Sergeant Donald Hankey while he was billeted in her home during the winter of 1914–15. Apparently readers of the *Spectator* had a virtually unlimited appetite for anything that journal could offer them by or about the lately mourned Student.

Strachey's announcement, printed only nine days after Donald fell in battle, surely fed this appetite. An extended eulogy, it goes far beyond an editor's memorial to a highly valued contributor in elaborating a sense of personal loss and presuming access to Donald's state of mind at the end. One might suspect that the enormity of Britain's accumulated sufferings at that point in the war had overstimulated Mr Strachey's literary powers and impaired his editorial judgement.

I do not believe the readers of the *Spectator* will think me a pedant, or misunderstand me, or wonder when I say that one of the things I should like most to do, and shall do if I live, is to put up in some place near my home, on some spot facing a wide horizon of English country, a memorial stone telling, with the emblems of art and with a suitable inscription, his name, his mission, and his death ... , linking the memory of a great-hearted soldier with the waving branches of the oak and ash, the blue distances of the hills, and the sweet airs of Heaven.

(The *Spectator*, 21 October 1916, p. 467)

Much of Strachey's characterization of Hankey the man simply rings false: phrases like 'gallant warrior', 'God's soldier', 'the "Happy Warrior" if ever there was one', and 'soldier saint', assume an element of the warlike in Donald's nature which is contradicted by all the evidence.[2] Yet even so, the *Spectator*'s remembrance does make a cogent, if overstated, point or two about its subject. It is not altogether fatuous to speak of Hankey as 'an inspired interpreter of the private soldier. ... worthy to be named *liaison* officer between the nation and the Army.' As to Hankey's personal qualities, Mr Strachey seems to have been in some respects a credible, even perceptive witness:

In spite of a certain fierceness of soul, and a disposition to an occasional outbreak of something one might almost call waywardness of judgment, he was at heart

---

[2] A review of *A Student in Arms: Second Series* in the 26 May 1917 issue of the *Spectator*, while persisting in the view that Hankey's writings 'assume the warrior's attitude', offers a contrary impression of the man himself: 'Though one would not expect this from his writings, Donald Hankey was by nature the least combative of men. None could fight with greater gallantry than he did, but his natural instincts led him away from strife' (p. 589).

one of the most reasonable men I have ever known. ... he was never happy but in making other people happy. ... no man sought to parade an easy optimism less than he did. The notion of trying to write 'an encouraging book' was, I know, never in his mind.

However, when Strachey ventures the opinion that 'there was something natural, almost inevitable, in the end when it came', and concludes that 'He was not only ready to go, but was hastening to be gone', he takes a vast liberty with Donald's distaste for inaction, his expressed readiness to return to the trenches. On the other hand, however, he is so far right in noting that Hankey conveys a detached calmness at the prospect of death that suggests something close to indifference. From one of his last letters 'the waft of death seemed to come out to me', Mr Strachey puts it melodramatically.

The Oxford and Bermondsey Mission Annual Report for 1916 contained a more simple eulogy: 'It is difficult to write about Donald,' it begins.

Many people have already done so with truth, with love, and in better language than we can. To his great gifts, to his genius as a writer, to his integrity as a man and his gallantry as a soldier the editor of the 'Spectator' has paid a fitting tribute. To us of the O.B.M. he was more than all this. ... He gave us more than he received from us. ... And to us who remain behind there is left the vision of his purity of heart, his sincerity, his love for his fellows, his utter unselfishness, for which we may be content to give thanks throughout our lives.

(O.B.M. Annual Report, 1916, p. 11)

In the conventional and obligatory words of these earnest and idealistic young Oxonian missionaries there is a convincing note of uncommon and unfeigned admiration.

After the author's death demand for the two *Student in Arms* volumes—especially the first—continued to grow. A British review dated 1 March 1917 gives a summary account of the first series of essays' commercial success to date. Four printings had been sold out in the four months following the appearance of *A Student in Arms* in May of 1916, and each subsequent printing was larger than the one before. Fourteen reprintings were required before the middle of the following year. Canadian and American editions were published and orders for Hankey's book poured in from virtually all parts of the British Empire. 'Purely from the point of view of a commercial success, *A Student In Arms* is probably the most notable literary event since the war broke out,' the reviewer asserted.[3] As the United States drew closer to entering the war, the Student's essays became more relevant. 'For Americans,' the *New York Tribune* stated, 'the book will increase our conviction and resolve that our army must be a citizen army, based on universal service, and that the natural democracy of such a mingling must be fostered by every means in our power.'

The religious emphasis in Hankey's essays is commonly praised in these reviews, and it is obvious that readers found a more conventionally patriotic tone—and of course approved it—than more dispassionate examination actually reveals. Mr Northman, cited above, is transported by 'the thrilling spectacle of a national army of two million men to whom the sublimest heroism is not only possible, but is the opportunity that each longs for.' Praise of this sort advanced the popularity of The Student's books, but it skewed Hankey's reputation in a misleading direction. Although his sensitive regard for the common soldier could hardly be ignored, to

---

[3] Alan Northman, *London Christian Outlook*, 1 March 1917. Quoted in *ASIA, I*, American Edition, New York, E. P. Dutton & Co. 1917.

reviewers—and no doubt to vast numbers of contemporary readers growing weary and dispirited in the later years of the war—the most affecting message heard in Donald Hankey's work was a call to high purpose and self-sacrifice:

> Every parent [Northman wrote] who has a boy at the Front would like to believe that in the face of death he had the sustaining vision that the 'Student' describes.

Whatever their appeal to wartime susceptibilities, Hankey's essays clearly stood apart from the ruck of shopworn patriotism and journalistic propaganda. Charles Seymour, in a survey of war literature for the *Yale Review* of April 1918, placed *A Student in Arms* among the 'two or three most notable books produced by the war. There is no other that gives so admirably the social sense of the new British army.' This suggests, more accurately than most of the attention Hankey's work was receiving, the real nature of its distinction. It is, indeed, his *social sense* of the new citizens' army that defines Donald Hankey's particular place among British war writers.[4] The public

---

[4]In *Mr Britling Sees It Through* (1916) H. G. Wells's conscientiously British protagonist reflects upon the outbreak of total war and is struck by 'how apart the [pre-war] army lived from the ordinary life of the community.' It had traditionally been 'a thing aloof, for a special end,' that end being to engage in wars inherently remote from 'the broad mass of English life.' Its 'necessary psychology' was that of 'a small army under a clique government.' But since the present enemy is a thoroughly militarized Germany, England cannot fight this war as if it were 'an incidental adventure'; it must involve the entire nation. So Britling finds the phrase *this is* our *war* 'more and more essential to his thoughts' (*Mr Britling Sees It Through*, Book II, Chapter ii, section 3[New York, The Macmillan Company, 1916] pp. 240-45). These considerations (to the extent that they were as Wells represents them) underscore the timeliness of Hankey's 'Student' essays. The hoards that emptied factories and shops and football clubs to enlist had, by so doing, created for the general public an immense cognitive vacuum concerning the life to which all those who answered Lord Kitchener's appeal were committing themselves. Hankey's work, marked by its author's varied experience with the small pre-war army's cliquish psychology and with the motley ranks of a largely citizen army, must be valued as an effort toward filling that vacuum.

were anxious for authentic report of this military force that had been formed from the sons and husbands and neighbours who had marched away. How would such a 'rag-time army' fare? What trials of the spirit and physical ordeals would they be subjected to? Could such amateur soldiers be expected to do themselves and their country credit against German militarism? Donald Hankey's readers found in him a knowledgeable writer who took such men seriously. He posed convincingly as an earnest student of their circumstances and spoke from the army's midst, not from some safe and exalted point of vantage. His consuming interest in religion was apparent but neither doctrinaire nor holier-than-thou. There were truths about the war that would have to be learned from other, mostly younger, writers who witnessed and suffered it with more bitterness and less equanimity than did Donald Hankey; but his readers valued him as someone who regarded his fellow-soldiers with confidence and love, who admired the Tommies for their irrepressible humanity even more than for their occasional heroism.

When *A Student in Arms, Second Series* was posthumously published in the spring of 1917, the reviewer for the *Times Literary Supplement* declared that Donald Hankey's 'fame as a writer has survived him' (*TLS*, 236: 1917 [17 May]). The volume's biographical and autobiographical inclusions captured much of the reviewer's attention. 'Here, if anywhere,' he writes, 'was a man to whom fate offers a cushioned chair at tea parties for all his days .... But if Hankey's mind and body shrank from the coarseness of life, his spirit overcame them and made them serve his needs.' The review further contends that 'the whole book is an autobiography,' and explains this surprising characterization by noting that the point of view from which other people are described enables the author to dramatize, through them, 'his own emotions and questionings'. 'In any case he himself is the most interesting person in his book.' Nor does the *TLS* review fail to note Hankey's particular sensitivity in representing the 'emotions and questionings' of other soldiers besides himself. 'His weary "Tommies",' the reviewer writes, no doubt contrasting his work with that of such popular sources as journalist-cartoonist Bruce Bairnsfather, 'are not in the least like the epigrammatic comedians of the picturesque writers.' Hankey, this review concludes, discovered among his men what he was ever looking for: simple human goodness.

There are ironies connected with Hankey's achievement that must be conceded in any summing up of his life and work. On the whole, The Student's main field of study was the essentially unheroic nature and circumstances of the common soldier. Yet his most celebrated essay, 'The Beloved Captain', is an exercise in unmitigated hero-worship. Indeed, when it was reprinted in 1956 as the title essay in a belated selection from *A Student in Arms*, the editor praised this particular item as 'one of the greatest pictures of leadership ever written'.[5] Moreover, that editor (R. S. Wright) finds 'the argument that runs through all this book' [i.e., his selection of eleven of 'The Student's' essays] is 'that what matters most is the right sort of leader' (p. 21).

Such an emphasis takes far too narrow a view of all Hankey had to say about the citizen army that fought the war, nor does it even adequately suggest the kind of anguished and ambivalent attention he actually gave to the particular issue of leadership. In a sense Hankey's conception of Jesus in *The Lord of All Good Life* addresses that

---

[5] *The Beloved Captain*: based on selected essays by Donald Hankey (a Student in Arms), edited with notes by Ronald Selby Wright, foreword by Lt. Gen. Sir James Cassels, Director General of Military Training [London, Geoffrey Blas, 1956], p. 31.

issue but, far from resolving it, leaves it instead a continuing problem in balancing the claims of authority and obedience, responsible privilege and humility. His 'Beloved Captain' embodies Hankey's ideal of leadership, but he reacted to it personally as something of a curse. Private Crudgington saw something essential in the man when he described Lt Hankey as a comrade, as much a chum as an officer, and remembered him 'with his rifle slung on his shoulders the same as his men' (Budd, p. 144).

However much he was drawn to and identified with the unheroic, Hankey himself came to be regarded, in the period following his death and before 'anti-war' literature in the later 1920s had cast its pall over the very concept of heroism, as more a hero than a writer. The flavour of his reputation in those years may be sampled in the chapter devoted to 'The Student in Arms, Donald Hankey' in E. B. Osborn's *The New Elizabethans*, published by John Lane in 1919. Osborn (who, as a jingoistic journalist on the *Morning Post*, had been the target of H. G. Wells's scathing abuse in his novel *Boon* [1914]) put together a florid memorial to some twenty-five young men, all possessed of unusual promise (and all of them officers!), who died in the war. As a whole the volume is a chauvinistic, sentimental, and at times quite absurd tribute to a ghostly world of might-have-been. Had they lived, so Osborn intimates, these men would have summoned in a new age to rival that of Shakespeare and Sidney and Ralegh. Hankey's part in the book, contributed by a 'Lieutenant Power', is considerably less overblown than other chapters, or 'characters', devoted to such figures as 'The Absolute Poet' (Charles Sorley), 'An Oxford Cavalier' (Robert William Sterling), 'The Happy Athlete' (Ronald Poulton), 'The Man About Town' (Thomas Vade-Walpole), 'Castor and Pollux' (Julian and Billy Grenfell). The presiding tone of adulation, however, attaches firmly to the Student

272

in Arms, whose last words to his men, 'If wounded, Blighty—if killed, the Resurrection', had, as Lieutenant Power puts it, 'now become historic' (p. 185).

In 1921 the publisher of both volumes of the Student in Arms essays, Andrew Melrose, Ltd., brought out an edition of Hankey's letters (edited by Edward Miller). Though far from complete, this collection of letters made a volume of well over 400 pages. It includes photographs and reproduces many of the pen and ink sketches with which Donald liked to amuse some of his correspondents. *The Story of Donald Hankey, A Student In Arms*, by K. G. Budd, appeared in 1931. Clearly, Donald Hankey was not entirely forgotten, even though for some years younger more urgent voices had made disillusionment, bitterness, anger, and irony the more or less accepted modes for writing about most things pertaining to The Great War. Budd's earnest and reverent biography reflects a confident assurance that the story it tells will inspire its readers. On the jacket flap of the book Hankey is described as 'one of the revelations of the war. ... a man of heroic and prophetic mold, a voice in the wilderness, a writer with spiritual vision and the power to record it in telling prose.'

By that time, however, The Great War and those who suffered in it had taken on for many a much different aspect, an aspect influenced by growing distrust of such notions as heroism and spiritual vision. Disillusionment neither burst suddenly upon England's national consciousness nor ever came entirely to dominate it. Illusions about the war had been challenged from its beginning; on the other hand, some of them died hard. But by the late 1920s, even in the midst of general indifference, strongly negative voices were the ones making most noise. Hankey's work was not so much discredited as increasingly overlooked, then mainly forgotten. Recent studies dealing in one way or another with the literature of the Great War seldom mention Donald Hankey, and if they do so give him only the most cursory notice. In one such book he is misidentified as the son of Sir Maurice Hankey; in another it is suggested that his essays appear to reinforce a class system.

His moment of high acclaim was relatively brief, its brevity the consequence, in part, of an untimely death which had contributed to his momentary glamour. With the–admittedly important!–exception of poets such as Wilfred Owen and Isaac Rosenberg, who, like Hankey, died in action, the war writers who made the most memorable and enduring mark were those who lived to remember it. They survived the accumulating horrors and felt the numbing and coarsening effects of the war's last two years, then experienced the dashed hopes and comfortless hindsight that came with a trouble-filled peace. Necessarily, it is their memories which have dominated our understanding. And memory, as the psychoanalyst Adam Phillips makes bold to suggest, 'must always be complicit with what it remembers' (*London Review of Books*, 19 July 2001, p. 25).

Phillips deliberately challenges our conventional pieties when he speaks of 'the gloating present in every dirge'. It is that self-congratulatory element in the 'survivor literature' of World War I–even (or especially) that produced by writers most deeply embittered and appalled–which led to the disregard or marginalization of work by the likes of Donald Hankey, who did not live to share fully, and thus benefit from, the disillusionment of so many survivors. Without in any way discounting the value of what those survivors witnessed, remembered, and transmitted about the war in memoirs and novels and other forms of writing, we should recognize how hard they have made it for us, who continue to read and admire their great dirges, to judge a different sort of writer. Hankey also detested the war but died in it before its horror had entirely overwhelmed him or deprived him of hope.

'I would not like to finish my life feeling disappointed and cynical,' he had written before his first taste of battle in 1915 (*Letters*, p. 362). Had he survived the war, there is no telling whether or how Donald Hankey would have continued to write about it. Had he done so, however, it is likely that there are some illusions–religious ones, mostly–that he would have clung to. Others, embodying his hope (already beginning to waver) that the war would lead the privileged classes to make good their debt to the Other Ranks when those men returned to their working lives, he would have discarded. Such a loss might have embittered or perhaps radicalized him. Private Crudgington was sure Lieutenant D. Hankey would have become a leading pacifist. How his brother Maurice's important career might have figured in Donald's own future invites interesting guesses. Would the elder brother's work as cabinet secretary throughout the inter-war years–especially his considerable role in the Versailles treaty negotiations–have affected Donald's writings and other activities, or indeed been influenced by them?

But speculations of that sort are idle. As for what he did write, among its most notable qualities is the absence of any note of self-congratulation. He believed he was fortunate, but he felt no call to gloat. This is a form of innocence, and perhaps it accounts for his particular failings, for the tendency in his writing to 'softness' and sentimentality. But his freedom from smugness is fundamental to Hankey's appeal. In the article I have cited, Adam Phillips ponders the question 'how one writes about cruelty without being cruel'. Or, it might further be asked, how can one witness savagery and suffering and remain free of any retributive and savage urge to cause pain? Donald Hankey would not have presumed to know the answer, but he possessed that gift. Somehow he was able to discover in war–or at least glimpse intermittently and deeply value amid all he despised—a 'freemasonry of the trenches'. Under heart-rending circumstances, but on an astoundingly broad scale even so, it was a living out of the promise of a camaraderie beyond class, such as was implied in the Bermondsey Mission motto *Fratres*. That, so he believed, was the aim of all good life. He recognized— even insisted—that, much as he hated it, war brought him something he had always sought, put him in a dreadful place which also held what he had long wished for, believed in, and dared to imagine.

Index

278